Destined to be change-agents

'Ordinary' people serving significantly

Fanie Richter & Laetitia Bull

CLF Publishers

CHRISTIAN LITERATURE FUND
CHRISTELIKE LEKTUURFONDS

© Fanie Richter & Laetitia Bull
Christian Literature Fund
19 Oude Pont Street
Wellington Business Park
Wellington
South Africa
www.clf.co.za

Design and layout by:
MRD Designs 083 440 4548

Printed and bound: Print on Demand (Pty) Ltd

First edition: 2020

ISBN: 978-1-86804-486-3

Recommendations

What an inspirational book! It is probably so inspiring because it's a story of how the Spirit of God moved men and women to make a huge difference in the lives of people. These are people who allowed the Spirit to take control of their lives in order to use them to do what the Spirit of God intended. And what is more, the range of these ministries is just amazing. These people serve in all areas of life... like the Lord of the Church did in person. I would like all my brothers and sisters to read this book!

Dons Kritzinger, Professor Emeritus of Missiology, University of Pretoria

A book giving a concise glimpse on the unique stories of men and women from different walks of life who were touched by the spiritual, material and social needs of people in communities who are suffering in one way or the other – children, people with AIDS, poverty, the disabled, people living on the street, the unemployed. It tells the stories of men and women who were willing to forfeit the luxuries of life and were driven by a vision and a calling from God to bring hope to those who have to cope with the brokenness of day-to-day realities. They make a difference by bringing into practice the love of Jesus Christ for those in need. A call to the reader to get involved!

Kobus Kellerman, Emeritus Professor, Faculty of Theology, University of the Free State, Bloemfontein

Reading this book, I felt as though I was scanning a contemporary adaptation of Hebrews 11. Every chapter told the story of men and women whose faith and actions would qualify them for the 'Hall of Faith.' Their stories encouraged and inspired me to know that as we live a life of obedience, we can discover our destiny, achieve our life's purpose and then leave a legacy for the Kingdom.

Graham Power, Founder: Global Day of Prayer and Unashamedly Ethical

It always inspires me to listen to other people's stories. It is even more inspiring if 'ordinary people' tell their stories of how God called them to be an agent of change in His Kingdom. The stories in this book will inspire and transform you to live a life of significance. Do not miss the opportunity to read it.

Tommy O'Kennedy, Managing Director of Halftime SA

The testimonies brought together in this book form a rich and harmonious chorus declaring that Jesus calls us to follow Him into places of need and opportunities to make a difference. They claim to be ordinary people, but that it is God who actually does the extraordinarry things they are involved in. Amid the diversity of the stories presented here, there is this one golden thread – a persistent call from God to an adventurous yet often costly and scary journey of following Jesus into unknown areas and types of ministry. I have the privilege to know the main characters in this book and can therefore confirm that what you are about to read is true and worth hearing. May God richly bless the message of this book and use it for the expansion of his kingdom.

Johannes Malherbe, Head of Academics, South African Theological Seminary (SATS)

i

Your people will rebuild the ancient ruins
and will raise up the age-old foundations;
you will be called Repairer of Broken Walls,
Restorer of Streets with Dwellings.
(Isaiah 58:12)

Contents

Introduction

As I drove away, thinking of the interview and the management meeting I attended, I again had a rush of excitement thinking about the strategy they shared with me – it made so much sense! Is this the place where the Lord would use me in future as a catalyst to further his kingdom?

But I also sensed an underlying fear and uncertainty and asked myself, 'What on earth am I getting into? How will I survive if I leave my paid job? Is this You speaking, Lord?'

You may also experience the urge to be more relevant in bringing transformation, there where God has placed you or wants to lead you to. Then we believe that God's Spirit has awakened yours to use your Kingdom potential. And then this book is for *you*.

The idea to write this book was birthed late one afternoon on the lounge balcony of my colleague, Laetitia. Around a cup of coffee, we discussed the significance of some 'ordinary' but remarkable friends, who are making a significant difference in communities, countries and even internationally by extending God's kingdom, being a blessing to so many people. As I was on the brink of sharing what I believe the Lord has laid upon my heart, she affirmed it in words – "We should write a book about those we know, to help others with examples and guidelines to take a step of faith and trust God in using them to bring his kingdom here on earth."

In one's formation as Christian, you may at some point wonder if going to heaven one day should be the *only* (maybe even selfish) reason for your conversion and being made new? You might have become aware of a latent consciousness that life's significance goes beyond satisfaction with the ordinary – that the rest of your life as Christian should be more meaningful and lasting, yearning to serve a purpose. You may also experience it as a calling from God – and struggle to find clarity.

Furthermore, it might seem so 'impossible' to accomplish if you do not have the means to support yourself.

Reflecting on our past, both of us found ourselves on that road and felt called to a specific fulltime ministry. And yes, we also went through the kind of experiences of which you will learn about in the following chapters.

For us, that was the beginning of a new chapter and journey in life for which we had to leap in faith. However, through this, we discovered the blessings and outcomes, beyond expectation, of being willing and available to the King. And we were amazed at how God had set it up.

So we left the balcony with a list of the people we were talking about, inspired to conduct interviews with them – and discovered much more than we thought we would.

These friends are from different occupational and cultural backgrounds, countries and regions of the world, serving in various ministries. They represent numerous others who currently live their God-given passions and serve with enthusiasm, making significant contributions and difference for the blessed transformation of immeasurable numbers of people in many countries.

Their stories will help you see how the kingdom of God is coming on earth – and how *you* can contribute too.

Our wish and prayer is that you will find answers and direction through their stories and that the lessons, values and principles of their significant lives will bring light, insight and inspiration upon the pursuit of your life's purpose and role on the way forward.

May you discover your God-given adventure to reach much more than success and status in life – if you are willing and available.

Be richly blessed under His guidance!

Fanie & Laetitia
August 2020

Chapter 1

Who are you, and where are you going?

*There have been many defining moments in the lives
of human beings that changed their lives for ever.
These defining moments often set the course
for the balance of their lives... The secret of a great life
is often a man's ability to discern the defining moment.*

- Os Hillman

*Nobody devotes years of service to a company
with the idea that what she has done is insignificant.
Nobody wants to think that at his funeral,
the eulogy will declare that his life didn't matter.*

- John Ortberg

You *are* destined to be relevant – to make a difference in society, leaving behind a significant legacy – no matter who you are.

Looking for direction on your way forward to fulfil a meaningful purpose – what should be next? You may ask, "Is there a calling from God on my life – requiring vital decisions, and maybe risks? Should I remain where I am? Can *I*?"

There's a beautiful story of a rich businessman who one day took a walk in a forest where he was found by a forester, asking him, "Who are you, and where are you going?" This question struck him as a decisive moment for deeper contemplation, clarity and focus on his own life. He then decided to appoint the forester in his business, with one of his tasks to come daily to his office and ask him, "Who are you, and where are you going?"

Dan Pink wrote about what *purpose* is, saying it comes down to, "Am I doing something in service of a cause larger than myself,

1

or, at the very least, am I making a contribution in my own world?"[1]

The kingdom of God and I

Who are *we*, and where are *we* going?

While the kingdom of God is the central theme of the Bible, somehow, unfortunately, there is a misunderstanding and reduction of the Gospel by many – that Jesus (only) died for forgiveness of our sins so that one day we can go to heaven, and that one becomes a Christian so 'that your case is in order'.

In saying this, we don't want to downplay the God-given salvation from sins through the atoning love of God in Christ on Calvary. *That* is just indescribably precious!

But if I have accepted Christ as my *Lord* – what about now, and until then? Why am I a Christian (and what does it mean) – now and here where I am?

Therefore, we have to understand the purpose of God's kingdom. It is not only about a kingdom in heaven where we hope to go. We miss the essence of our lives if we miss the purpose of God's kingdom *coming on earth* as in heaven (Matthew 6:10).

The essence of our lives is not to be found in being saved and experiencing self-centred delight in welfare and the joy of good relationships, and about going to heaven and having the assurance of eternal life. Heaven and eternal life is God's priceless *bonus of grace*. When we were forgiven our sins, atoned and reconciled with God, we not only received salvation but received second chances with renewed life purpose and potential. Sadly, many Christians choose to live as if life is meant as a mere consumer's item. And if the main emphasis of our focus is on Jesus as Saviour, we must be careful that we don't reduce Jesus to only be the 'assistant' for our desire to *go to heaven*.

Therefore, the rest of this chapter, before we get to stories about friends who follow and serve God in creating God's kingdom on earth – while providing us with much insight in what they've learned under his providence – is not meant to be a complete exposition of the Kingdom. It is rather a concise glimpse of what it is meant to be for us living in it.

---

[1] Dan Pink, *Drive: The Surprising Truth About What Motivates Us*, Canongate Books, Main Edition 2010, quoted by Eric Barker, *Barking Up The Wrong Tree* weekly update for May 14th, 2017.

God created us to rule over his *good* creation (Genesis 1:26-31; Psalm 115:16), but in due course, we've made a mess. On the contrary, when Isaiah announced that the future King (Jesus the Messiah) was on his way, he said that the people in darkness will see a great light, and then described its positive effects they will enjoy. There will be a deeper God-given dimension of reality, and what it's meant to be, than what people see and experience around them (Isaiah 9:1-7).

The apostle Paul says the mystery of God's will, which He purposed in Christ, is "to bring unity to all things in heaven and on earth under Christ" (Ephesians 1:9-10), so everything can be restored to be very good again. For this reason, God brought his kingdom into this world through the redemptive and miraculous works and teachings of Jesus, under Jesus' rule as the anointed King above all kings (Revelation 17:14; 19:16) – to be here "among us" (Luke 11:20; 17:21)! "In him was life, and that life was the light of men" (John 1:4).

Destined with a royal mandate

Jesus said that He was sent to proclaim the good news of the kingdom of God (Luke 4:43; 8:1; Mark 1:14-15). It was also the main theme of his conversations and instructions with the apostles before his ascension (Acts 1:3), as well as the message that the apostles preached in the early church (Acts 8:12; 19:8 and 28:23, 31) – the gospel of Jesus about the kingdom of God.

So, here *among us*, God showed the church through his kingship in Christ how He is King *on earth* as in heaven – how God wants the world to become his kingdom, as in heaven. From his Father-heart, God intends blessings for his people. We have learned it already from the first chapter of Genesis, and after the fall of humankind we've heard it again as God called Abram (Genesis 12:1-3).

God's kingdom has everything to do with our lives and how it affects us and society – how He wants us to live and serve in society – to become as God meant it to be, to make the change from *hell on earth* to *heaven on earth*. For this reason, Christ's kingship is focused here among us, in the *marketplace* and in the community, where we spend most of our time.

Living in God's kingdom implies that we are redeemed and adopted as part of his *royal family* (John 1:12; Ephesians 1:5, 11), under his mercy and counsel. But to be part of this family doesn't mean that once saved and reconciled, we can now conveniently retreat from the world to our *holy huddle*.

Authority – to serve

In this regard, Jesus set an example and taught that *lordship* and *authority* was granted by God the Father to Him – *to serve*. And as King above all kings, Jesus gave new meaning and value to service. He raised service to the most esteemed lifestyle and activity – "But I am among you as the one who serves (Luke 22:26-27), just as the Son of Man did not come to be served, but to serve, and to give his life as a ransom for many" (Matthew 20:28).

His words, "As you sent me into the world, I have sent them into the world" (John 17:18), should be heard in the same breath when Jesus said, "As the Father has sent me, I am sending you" (John 20:21) – thus, to serve, hís way. And through Jesus' servant leadership, he influenced the hearts and minds and will of the people – to help establish the kingdom of God on earth.

And as with the creation, and ever since, God chose to work through *people*. In this relationship and plan Jesus has *appointed* us *all* who follow Him – with a mandate under his authority above all – *to serve* one another, fulfilling our God-ordained purpose and relevance (Genesis 1:26-30; Matthew 28:18-20). We must be salt and light – in his Name – to affect and reorder our workplace and society, and bring transformation through the powerful love of God in Christ, for his glory and blessing of all, including ourselves.

So, we remain in the world, and in the workplace, with a royal assignment and responsibility for his purpose, there where Jesus wants to use us. As Jesus was the Father's representative on earth, we, the church, are now his sent representatives (John 20:21), commissioned with his authority and affairs in our hands.

> God works through his church (people) in the marketplace and community.

Paul mentioned to the Corinthians: "We are therefore Christ's ambassadors, as though God were making his appeal through us" (2 Corinthians 5:20; read from verse 17).

As God's sent people, He wants to use us as his voice and hands in a world that does not know about reconciliation with Him and do not share in the blessings of his kingdom plan. As change-agents, we have a responsibility to bring God's kingdom into the world.

Therefore, we need to have a biblical worldview – seeing the world in perspective to God's Word and plan, and how it currently compares – and learn from Him how we should get involved in the situations and opportunities – to make it new.

Jesus says in John 13:20, "Whoever accepts anyone I send accepts me; and whoever accepts me accepts the one who sent me." Paul says, "We implore you on Christ's behalf." This is the authority with which Jesus' representative is equipped. *This* is our authority! And with this authority, we ought to win back the territory where Christ is not yet accepted as King.

God works in us to will and to act according to God's good purpose (Philippians 2:13). God calls and enables. God is the guarantee! It is the Lord working *through* us. So, it is therefore not true to say we cannot; we will not succeed. We can step out and go in boldness, for the Lord is with us (Matthew 28:20b; Philippians 4:9).

From this, it is so clear that we are saved, not only for heaven, but to live and serve hand in hand with God in the blessings of his redemptive and restorative purposes, here and now – to help build according to God's plan, as He meant it to be for us. This is what the Gospel – the good news – is about.

> "For we are God's workmanship, created in Christ Jesus to do good works, which God prepared in advance for us to do."
>
> Ephesians 2:10

This is the essence of our lives. When God wants things done in his kingdom (to bless his people), He works through people! He wants men, women and children to take up their tasks and fulfil it.

God purposed *you* for a specific task in his kingdom, even before creation. This is because in God's masterplan, there is something specific that needs to be done in the Kingdom, and the Lord created *you* to fulfil that task.

And yes, God's call upon individuals may also become a call and responsibility on a congregation. The Holy Spirit said to the church in Antioch, "Set apart for me Barnabas and Saul for the work to which I have called them" (Acts 13:2). Later, Paul wrote to the church in Philippi, thanking them for their partnership (Philippians 1:3-11; 4:10-19).

Calling and vision – determine your source

If this speaks to you and you struggle with thoughts about your life's purpose and future, we have to deal carefully with the words *calling* and *vision*.

Could it be that I feel an impulsive wave of enthusiasm, an urge coming from within? Or that I am concerned about something for my comfort or even my standing in the community? Or am I concerned about something that requires me to sacrifice my precious leisure activities? Maybe that I will have to live and work where I'll have to adapt my pleasant lifestyle, leaving behind family, friends and some niceties?

George Barna helps with perspective, saying, "The best response to any self-doubt is to *determine the source of the vision for your ministry*. Was it a vision you developed with the gifts and talents God gave you, or was it a vision that you sought, prayed and waited for and then received from Him?"[2]

Serving in the kingdom of God is according to *his masterplan*. As God works in you to will and to act to fulfil his good purpose, you shouldn't try to define *your* calling according to your dreams, goals and preferences, even though it seems to be so inviting and fascinating.

Further doubt and questions

And even when you are convinced and believe that God has laid it on your heart and you want to obey, you may still wonder, "But who am *I* actually? What can *I* do? Will *I* be able to accomplish it?"

When discussing your considerations with family and friends, you might perhaps find yourself (as many others before you) in a situation, such as David with his brothers at the battlefield (1 Samuel 17:28), when someone close to you asks, quite irritated and annoyed, "What on earth is going on with you? Why are you doing this? And your responsibilities?"

This might even intensify some challenges and fears going hand in hand, especially if you have to give up your security – your current career, environment and accommodation: "How will I cope? How and where will I find financial and material support?"

---

[2] George Barna, *The Power of Vision*. Regal, Ventura, California, Third Edition, 2009, 23.

Such experiences are normal. We also went through it, as well as the people you will read about in the following chapters, and we believe their stories will shed light upon your challenges and encourage you.

Also, don't look away from yourself as if it should have been for someone else, someone better qualified or more gifted. David was the unlikely one when Samuel had to anoint one of Jesse's sons to be the new king, but God looked at the heart. In God's eyes, the smallest and humbly obedient person becomes relevant – and the Lord lets his Spirit become powerful in him or her (1 Samuel 16:6-13).

Maybe you should ask yourself, *"Am I perhaps underestimating God's ability and power with my life?"*

Don't make the mistake to think about yourself in terms of other people's giftedness and successes. God knows your potential *with Him* and creates opportunities according to his purpose and plan with *your* life, trusting you for your specific life purpose and task – as God did with Abram who had to obey and trust God with his future, to be blessed and to be a blessing (Genesis 12:1-5). And don't mind your age!

Blackaby & King wrote about God guiding us out of our self-centeredness, saying, "Do not try to understand what God is like from the middle of your circumstances. Go to God and ask Him to help you see his perspective on your situation... Adjust your life to God and what you see Him doing in your circumstances...[3] Whenever God involves you in his activity, the assignment will have God-like dimensions to it...[4] Then God says something like: '...I will lead you to places where I am working, and I'll include you. You will be an instrument in my hand so I can touch a world. When I do that through you, you will really experience my blessings.'"[5]

When Abram started out from Haran, as the Lord had told him, he entered a future only possible based on God's promise and presence. God looks past your human *disqualifications*. He looks at a heart, including your faith and willingness, and the Lord perceives you in his plan. So, your weaknesses and dependency could be the point of departure on spiritual growth.

---

[3] Henry T. Blackaby & Claude V. King, *Experiencing God: Knowing and Doing the Will of God* (text for course CG-0119, Lay Institute For Equipping / LIFE). LifeWay Press, Nashville, Tennessee, 1990, 98.

[4] Ibid., 116

[5] Ibid., 186

Paul said his work was a demonstration of the Spirit's power, so that the fruit "might not rest on men's wisdom, but on God's power" (1 Corinthians 2:4-5). This is a firm foundation when your self-confidence is challenged and you don't know what the way forward will look like. Think about the (poor) characters in the Bible whom God included in his process of redemption and blessings to the nations!

It's not about your inadequacy – what matters, is your decision. What would have been the consequences for Israel's future if Abram didn't go as the Lord had told him, or if David yielded to his brother's reproach and decided not to take on Goliath?

As with Abram, God expects trust in his wisdom, promise and presence on your road ahead. Therefore, one should commit your way to the Lord and ask the Holy Spirit to implant his will and desires into your heart. Ask in anticipation for peace, discernment and confirmation that it comes from God and that self-made or egoistic thoughts and desires (perhaps even by the deception of Satan), will disappear. It's about listening to the Lord concerning every aspect of your life within the perspective of his plan and assignments *entrusted to you.*

> *"God, send me anywhere, only go with me. Lay any burden on me, only sustain me. And sever any tie in my heart except the tie that binds my heart to Yours."*
>
> David Livingstone

So, if you want clarity on an inner quest for relevance and future life purpose that will glorify God in serving his kingdom, you need to spend time with God so that He may speak to your heart and mind. John Piper says:

> ... if you want to be most fully satisfied with God as He triumphs in the history of redemption, you can't go on with business as usual – doing your work, making your money, giving your tithe, eating, sleeping, playing, and going to church. Instead, you need to stop and go away for a few days with a Bible and notepad; and pray and think about how your particular time and place in life fits into the great purpose of God to make the nations glad in Him.[6]

When you take delight in God and his desires become yours, to will and to work for, God will give to you accordingly and help you realise the vision He gave you (Psalm 37:4). Then you will have the

---

[6] John Piper, *Don't Waste Your Life* (Group Study Edition), Crossway, Wheaton, Illinois, Text updated 2009, 177.

honour and joy to help bring about the Kingdom's relevance and blessings to a world in need. It's a commission from God's heart, similar to the following, "...before you were born I set you apart; I appointed you..." (Jeremiah 1:5); "You are my servant ...in whom I will display my splendour" (Isaiah 49:3).

> *"As Moses obeyed God, God accomplished through Moses what Moses could not do."*
>
> Henry Blackaby & Claude King

It is so liberating that in obedience to God we need not doubt in ourselves and the results, for example as Moses did, to whom the Lord said, *"Who gave man his mouth? Who makes him deaf or mute? Who gives him sight or makes him blind? Is it not I, the Lord? Now go; I will help you speak and will teach you what to say"* (Exodus 4:10-12).

Coming down from the mountaintop

But this might mean *leaving your comfort zone.*

When Peter, James and John were with Jesus on the mountaintop where Jesus was transfigured and Elijah and Moses appeared to them (Mark 9:2-8), it was so nice for Peter that he wanted to stay there. *But as a disciple of Christ, you have to come down the mountain to the harsh reality in which we are called to serve* (Mark 9:14-20).

In this regard, William Barclay stated

> ...that in religion there must be *solitude*, but not solitariness. The solitude is necessary, for a man must keep his contact with God; but if a man, in his search for the essential solitude, shuts himself off from his fellow-men, shuts his ears to their appeal for help, shuts his heart to the cry of their tears, that is not religion. *The solitude is not meant to make us solitary. It is meant to make us better able to meet and cope with the demands of everyday life.*[7]

John Ortberg gives the following perspective:

> The reality of this world is that I was born into Someone Else's kingdom. My life came to me as a gift I did not choose... Surrender to God is not passivity or abdication... *Surrender means I accept reality.*[8]

---

[7] William Barclay, *The Daily Study Bible – The Gospel Of Mark*, Revised Edition. The Saint Andrew Press, Edinburgh, 1975, 214-215. (Italics added)
[8] John Ortberg, *When the Game Is Over, It All Goes Back in the Box.* Zondervan, Grand Rapids, 2007, 63. (Italics added)

God's calling upon your life is also being *supported* by his sovereign purpose, plan, power and authority based on his kingdom principles. It is a purposeful call with urgency for far-reaching decisions that surpasses all human and earthly concern. And the challenge of God's transforming work calls you to an act of selfless obedient faith, *down the mountain*, casting yourself into God's grace and help, begging, "Lord, I believe; help Thou mine unbelief" (Mark 9:24)[9].

But God himself as the source, infallible power and authority who moves to fruition what He has set in motion, serves as comfort and inspiration to us who may think that we are so insignificant and unable to achieve much. God's kingdom is like a very tiny mustard seed that becomes the largest of garden plants where birds can come and find shelter, or like yeast that will raise all the dough, *guaranteed by his power and authority* (Matthew 13:31-33).

Serve according to Kingdom principles

The core motive for our zeal and service in the Kingdom through the church and its mission should be God's *kingdom purposes, passion* and *sovereign rule* in all the earth.

God shows his passion for this world, birthed in his Father-heart even though people walk astray, to reform us, as the potter the clay (Jeremiah 18:1-6). God demonstrated it in serving us through his utmost self-offering of Jesus Christ on the cross (John 3:16a; Colossians 1:19-20). And Christ's love and reason to enhance his kingdom and reign on earth – in which He calls us to participate – is frequently explained in his teachings.

So, as God extends his hand to the world through us as his ambassadors, we should learn from God about his kingdom purposes as well as the rules of protocol and style of the King. The desired working style and results in his kingdom will not be obtained without the right focus. It is not based on human concern or ambitions and cannot be achieved our way and on *our* terms – just look at our messy results! It requires the renewing of one's mind and a completely new way of thinking and living according to kingdom principles and purposes.

> God uses *Kingdom* principles to accomplish *Kingdom* purposes. God reveals his ways to us because they are the only way to accomplish his purposes... You cannot continue

[9] Mark 9:24, King James Version and Revised Standard Version

doing things your way and accomplish God's purposes in his ways.[10]

A Kingdom lifestyle under the reign of Christ must determine and transform every aspect of our lives and activities through learning from Him and acting accordingly. It's a safeguard for us who tend to live by common sense and trust in ourselves or circumstances.

Jesus called those He wanted to send out, "that they might be with him" (Mark 3:13-14). Before one can serve Christ as an ambassador, you need to be a disciple and get acquainted with his character, purposes and style to be sent out, represent and serve Him among others and be a blessing to them.

And the style of Christ the King and his message is the style of *love* and *humbleness*. Christ was showing his disciples what it meant to live by the principle of love. He didn't come to earth to show his grandeur, but the gospel of his love for a sinner and person in need – where no one is too low or miserable. And for that, Jesus accepted the stature of a servant.

This is the style of God which He taught the disciples through Christ. This was the style in which God wanted to extend his hand through them to others. And to this end, we too must be prepared to be servants in humbleness and love to people in need of his grace and upliftment into the restoring goodness of his kingdom. In the style of Christ, we must also seek them and reach out to them (Mark 2:17).

This love is powerful. Christ's holiness in love and humbleness is a holiness that draws people to Him.

Paul understood it. He experienced that the love of Christ urged him to reach everyone as and where they were – to be able to speak into their situation (1 Corinthians 9: 19-22). And where an ambassador of Christ speaks, God by his Spirit persuades and awakens faith and attraction in people's hearts (2 Corinthians 10:4-5; Cf. Ephesians 1:19-22).

This is the style of examples and principles that Jesus brought to us to renew our lifestyle, work ethics and focus, suitable for his kingdom purposes.

Then, before his last Passover feast with the disciples, Jesus promised them a "Counsellor" – the "Spirit of truth" – who will guide them in everything (John 14:16-17, 26; 16:8, 12-15), including his

---

[10] Henry T. Blackaby & Claude V. King, *Experiencing God*, 81, 133.

values and principles on which our activities should be based. We need to "listen" and "hear" what it means to be a builder in the Kingdom or a sower expecting a harvest (Matthew 7:21-27).

Paul says, "The Spirit searches all things, even the deep things of God" (1 Corinthians 2:10). So, the Spirit will explain and implant God's love, kingdom agenda and principles in us. This causes us to "have the mind of Christ" (1 Corinthians 2:16), "entrusted with the mysteries God has revealed" (1 Corinthians 4:1) "in accordance to his good pleasure and will, which he purposed in Christ" (Ephesians 1:5, 9).

Consequently, his presence, values, principles and glory should be our driving force.

Kingdom living and its expansion exists when and where we allow God through Jesus Christ as King of our lives – to live, equip and control in and through us, according to his kingdom purposes – to bring light and life-change in society, where there are darkened minds with futility of thinking, separated from the life of God (Ephesians 4:12-13; 17-18).

Our service in his kingdom must therefore be an act of worship, to search, understand and demonstrate the Kingdom – causing his glory among the nations – that his salvation and restoration may reach the ends of the earth (Isaiah 49:6), who are waiting in hope for his rule (Isaiah 51:4,5; 64:4).

So when we walk, listen, learn and serve under his guidance, we need to "demonstrate the Spirit's power" (1 Corinthians 2:4). What we need to do, is to know, understand and practise the love of God. It is living out the basics of his kingdom plan which Jesus taught and demonstrated about living and serving in the Kingdom on earth. He wants us not only to hear and believe but also to demonstrate and practise these basics and principles – that people who don't have and don't read the Bible, must be able to read it from our lives – that the kingdom can be seen, experienced and understood in and through our everyday living. The light that shines from us may be the only *Bible* that some people will ever read. Hopefully, it will be the initial *Bible* that brings light to them, which will lead to the reform and transformation of their lives and communities (see 1 Peter 2:12).

And when we do it, we will be stewards according to his plan, principles and style. Then the Lord's glory, power and authority over everything, everywhere, and his fullness in everyone and everything in every way is the guarantee for the fruition of our obedience in serving as church in society and missions – and the kingdom of God will grow (Matthew 28:18,20; Ephesians 1:22-23).

It's about your availability

So, it comes down to your availability and willingness to adjust some areas in your life. As we have tried to indicate, God works through *ordinary people* to fulfil *Kingdom purposes*. But there's another point of view on Matthew 13 verses 31 to 33 – if we are not prepared proverbially to be planted as even the least of all seeds, or used as leaven, there will be no shelter or bread.

God creates the potential and opportunities for your calling. The Lord supports it, trusts you and entrusts his authority to you. The following three stories serve as examples:

When Dwight L. Moody, one of the world's greatest evangelists in the history of Britain and America, felt God's calling to preach the gospel, he was a poorly educated shoe salesman. His friend, Henry Varley, a British revivalist, mentioned something to him that made quite an impression on Moody – *"The world has yet to see what God can do with and for and through and in a man who is fully and wholly consecrated to Him."*

It struck Moody that Varley didn't say it must be a highly educated, nor a highly gifted man. He realised that the emphasis was on *"a man who is fully consecrated to God!"* And *that* convinced Moody that God can speak through him also, with the result that thousands and thousands came to Christ.[11]

John Eliot was 27 years old when he crossed the Atlantic to America in 1631. A year later he became the pastor of a new church in Roxbury, Massachusetts, where there were twenty tribes of Indians in the vicinity. But something in his faith let him become much more than an ordinary pastor.

Eliot believed in the practical implications of his theology: if the infallible Scriptures promise that all nations will one day bow down to Christ, and if Christ is sovereign and able by his Spirit through prayer to subdue all opposition to his promised reign, then there is good hope that a person who goes as an ambassador of Christ to one of these nations will be the chosen instrument of God to open

---

[11]   J. Gilchrist Lawson, *D.L. Moody*, www.wholesomewords.org/biography/bio-moody4.html,
R.A. Torrey, *Why God Used D.L. Moody*, www.eaec.org/faithhallfame/dlmoody.htm

the eyes of the blind and set up an outpost of the kingdom of Christ.

When he was slightly over 40 years old Eliot set himself to study Algonquin, the language of one of that indigenous North American people groups. Eventually, he translated the entire Bible as well as books that he valued. By the time Eliot was 84 years old, there were numerous Indian churches, some with their own Indian pastors. This is the amazing story of a man who once said, "Prayers and pains through faith in Christ Jesus will do anything!"[12]

And there's another true story of a 'has-been' multi-millionaire civil engineer and his wife, Gerry and Mary Schoonbee, who spent their millions on the kingdom of God, so much so that they ended up being ordinary pensioners, having just enough to live from.

Was this a waste? No! Their steps and changes in life laid the foundation which made it possible for several ministries to serve, fulfilling their roles in equipping people for ministry and to equip yet others. This already resulted in thousands that were trained, and thousands more being trained by them – and the numbers are still multiplying.

Indeed, it was a very strategic investment already causing hundreds of thousands of people's lives to bear the fruit of the Spirit – even more so, taking the steps that make the difference – people who serve significantly, creating more than success – bringing heaven on earth.

Building blocks for your assignment

All the things that God has done in your life, every act, were building blocks to prepare you for his divine purpose and plan for which *you* were created.

In considering transition to a future role, and pondering on what the way forward may ask of you, it helps to take your life in retrospect. You may be pleasantly surprised to understand now the meaning and sense of earlier things that equipped you for your future role and responsibilities. It might be experiences or things you've overcome through suffering or even the unplanned little 'fun-tasks' you have fulfilled during your student years or any task elsewhere in society.

---

[12] John Piper, *Let the Nations Be Glad! The Supremacy of God in Missions,* Baker Books, Grand Rapids, Michigan, Copyright 1993, Seventh printing, 1996, 50,51, according to Cotton Mather, *The Great Works of Christ in America,* Vol. 1, Edinburgh: The Banner of Truth Trust, 1979, originally 1702, 562.

You become empowered to what you are called for by firstly submitting to God, and trust God for wisdom and equipping you for the opportunities and challenges entrusted to you. The Lord knows exactly what his plan involves and is already there ahead of you. You are no longer limited by your own thoughts and insight, and nothing should prevent you from achieving his dream for you. Then let God guide you in applying and further developing the skills gained through previous experiences and your gifts to serve Him.

In *that*, we find the true essence and joy of life. This can fill you with so much enthusiasm when you realise that God has so much faith in you – that God trusts *you* for tasks and responsibilities bigger than your thoughts.

Blackaby & King explain,

> When God invites you to join Him in his work, He has a God-sized assignment for you... How you respond at this turning point will determine whether you go on to be involved with God in something God-sized that only He can do, or whether you will continue to go your own way and miss what God has purposed for your life... If God works through you to do what only He can do, you and those around you will come to know Him... in a way that will bring rejoicing to your life.[13]

God has so much faith in you that He trusts you for tasks and responsibilities bigger than your thoughts. His kingdom perspective enlightens insight and peace beyond ordinary reasoning – that God trusts and calls *you* to be relevant, fulfilling your life purpose within his kingdom purpose!

The greatest encouragement and sense of awe, when using our gifts and skills to the best under his authority and power, remains the wonderful awareness that over and above all we have done (the little, in proportion), are written the words of Ephesians 3:20-21 – "Now to him who is able to do immeasurably more than all we ask or imagine, according to his power that is at work within us, to him be glory in the church and in Christ Jesus throughout all generations, for ever and ever! Amen!"

God-inspired tasks will be blessed if obediently implemented. On the contrary, can we imagine the loss when people ignore God's calling to his purpose with their lives?

---

[13] Henry T. Blackaby & Claude V. King, *Experiencing God*, 109, 153, 155.

Therefore, it is God-given mercy to recognise the voice of the Holy Spirit in your life and to be faithfully obedient when He asks you to do something, even when it seems to make no sense to others but for God.

> *Nothing before, nothing behind;*
> *The steps of Faith*
> *Fall on the seeming void, and find*
> *The rock beneath.*[14]

If only every child of God would realise and think about the fact and importance that he or she was created by God for a purpose for such a time as this...

---

[14] John Greanleaf Whittier, from his poem, *My Soul And I.* http://www.poemhunter. com/best-poems/john-greenleaf-whittier/my-soul-and-i-3/

Chapter 2

To become the hands and feet of Christ

The mission of the Church includes both
the proclamation of the Gospel and its demonstration.
We must therefore evangelize,
respond to human need
and press for social transformation.

- Patrick Johnstone

In his own words, Arnau van Wyngaard was not the typical leader or manager – "I did not have any management experience; on the contrary, I was not even a prefect at school and never served on a house committee at university – I'm not that type of person. And to find myself in the role of the CEO of an organisation with 1 400 people to be managed, with great logistical tasks that have to happen within five major focus areas, is not me. And perhaps this is part of SHBC's (Shiselweni Home-Based Care) big success story – it is not me. It really is the Lord."

Arnau van Wyngaard   Remarks that run like a refrain through out our conversation are good advice to anyone searching for God's will for his or her life: "The Lord took me on this journey," and "Again, I see the hand of the Lord in it."

Missions became a passion

What follows, is the remarkable story of an ordinary South African theological student's journey with God to where he now has more than 25 years of experience as full-time missionary-pastor in eSwatini (Swaziland)[1]; being the general secretary of the Swaziland Reformed Church (SRC); has done a PhD on Theology of Mission and is presently specialising in the problem of HIV/AIDS and how the church should approach this pandemic.

This is a story of obedience upon which international awards followed – a *Courageous Leadership Award*, co-sponsored by World Vision and the Willow Creek Association for outstanding work done in the field of HIV and AIDS, as well as a *Best Student Award* (Advanced Health Management Programme in association with the Yale University School of Public Health in 2010-2011). Furthermore, he is also representing the SRC on the Reformed Ecumenical Council and the World Communion of Reformed Churches.

Although his first career thoughts were to become a chartered accountant in forensic auditing, he later became convinced that God called him to become a pastor. During Arnau's early years of theological studies, the friendship and guidance from a senior student led to his exposure and participation in mission outreaches. This, as well as books by Brother Andrew and Richard Wurmbrand, made quite an impression on him and gave birth to a passion for missions. He finished his theological studies with Missiology as major subject and a two years' compulsory service as an army chaplain at a Zulu battalion, before accepting a call to serve as a missionary pastor for the Shiselweni congregation of the SRC in the south of eSwatini.

Discovering horrific trends regarding HIV/AIDS

When we asked Arnau how he became involved in a specialised ministry to people with HIV/AIDS, he replied:

"The Lord took me on this journey. After finishing my studies in 1982, my decision not to touch another theological book only lasted for almost six months, when I decided to do doctoral studies in Missiology at the University of South Africa (UNISA). Today, I can see it as an act of the Lord's providence that the renowned Prof. David Bosch referred me to Prof. Willem Saayman, who, at that stage, had an important influence on many aspects of my life.

---

[1] On 19 April 2018, King Mswati III of formerly known Swaziland announced the renaming of the country from Kingdom of Swaziland to Kingdom of eSwatini during celebrations of the 50th anniversary of independence and his 50th birthday. The name Swaziland is used in this chapter regarding events before the name change.

"Towards the late '80s, he started to discuss with me the occurrence of AIDS in Swaziland and gave me a book of which he was co-author, *AIDS: the Leprosy of Our Time?* At that stage, I was quite ill-informed about the situation, as people did not openly speak about it. Gradually, I became more aware of its reality and towards the end of my doctoral study, I asked Prof. Saayman if he would help us facilitate a conference on AIDS in Swaziland during 1992, to which he very favourably agreed.

"However, the unexpected death of Prof. Bosch prevented Saayman from participating, when everything was already organised for a big interdenominational conference in Mbabane. Thrown in at the deep end, I facilitated it for three days. But again, I saw the hand of the Lord in this, because then I developed an interest in AIDS that I might never have had. By monitoring statistics in Swaziland, I learned that the number of HIV positive people has doubled every 7½ months – a horrific tendency unless something drastic would happen that could bring about a change.

"A request from the secretary of the Reformed Ecumenical Council (REC) for an article on AIDS, published in 2004, led to a further request for workshops on *AIDS and the Church* at the following meeting of the Council in Utrecht, The Netherlands, in 2005. However, the more I prepared, the more I realised that I do not know what the Church can or should do about it. As I sat in my office, I felt the Lord actually telling me, 'It's nice to sit in an office behind a desk and write about the matter, but what are *you* practically going to do to make a difference?' This kept on agonising me – what can our church do to make a difference?"

Turning point at a special lunch

"The Sunday, after facilitating the third workshop, we travelled by bus from Utrecht to attend a worship service of the Scottish Presbyterian Church in Rotterdam. After the worship service, the minister told us how the congregation functions, and it comes down to interest in their people and their neighbours – to be on the lookout where someone is suffering, sick or has passed away, and then visit those affected families. *That* creates a need for people to become part of the church – and unlike other churches that are shrinking, this church is growing. So, the story about their involvement in the community has gripped me – just ordinary things they did, such as getting involved with a neighbour.

"After this session, we moved to the church hall where the congregation offered us lunch – all of the REC church leaders (moderators, general secretaries, etc.) worldwide were gathered there. While I was eating, I noticed a man approaching the door – half-stumbling – realising he is mentally disturbed. I still remember a terrible discomfort in myself – at other places they would probably have helped him out and told him he was not welcome. As I wondered what was going to happen, a woman from the church stood up and asked the man if she could bring him food. At that moment, I snapped inside. I sat at that table crying inwardly, asking God, 'Lord, what can I do to make my church like this church?' This was my second conversion.

"On the way back to Utrecht I said to the Lord, 'I do not fully understand – I only know something happened today.' It felt like a holy moment and for the first time in my life I truly heard the Lord speaking to me, with an audible voice in my mind, telling me, 'I want you to go back to Swaziland, and I want you to become my hands and feet in the community.'

Be on the lookout where someone is suffering, sick or has passed away, and visit those affected families. That creates a need for the people to become part of the church.

"That evening, things started to make sense to me. As I lay in bed and thought about it all, the whole picture came together – I should go back and tell my congregation, 'Forget about the rest of Swaziland. All we have to do is focus on our community, and then we will make a difference. Then it becomes an achievable goal.' As I was lying there, I realised what the Lord told me is: 'Make your tent a little smaller. Do not think big. Think small. *Make it manageable.*' And then I realised the mistake I had made up to that point – asking all the time, 'What can we do to change Swaziland?' The question I should have asked is, 'What can I do to change *the community* where my church is?' In other words, much smaller and more practical.

"Then I got this plan: if I can train the congregation and they get involved in the community, then we can make a difference. However, at that stage I did not know how, but through what I experienced in the church

Make it manageable, much smaller and more practical. Then we will make a difference.

that day in The Netherlands – that every person makes a difference and in the way they welcomed the mentally disturbed man amongst all the leaders (almost like an honorary guest) – those two things, have drastically changed my life."

Back home – a culture change

"Back home, I began to pray and preach and told my congregation that something happened in my life. Every Sunday I was just talking about one theme, and it was that the Lord cares. The Lord cares for sick people. The Lord cares for poor people. The Lord cares for women. The Lord cares for children. The Lord cares for all those on the fringes...

"Luke 5, the story of the leper who came to Jesus and kneeled before him and said, 'Lord, if you are willing, you can make me clean' deeply touched me, because something significant happened: in all the Synoptic Gospels we read that Jesus stretched out his hand, touched him and said, 'I am willing. Be clean!'

"The fact that Jesus touched a leper means that under Jewish law, Jesus made himself unclean. Because of this, I prayed, 'Lord, I undertake to never refuse to touch a person who has AIDS. I will embrace people even though I know they have AIDS' (I knew well enough that you do not contract the virus just by touching a person). But that message removed the stigma for me, and I started to put my arms around people when I greeted them and hugged them. *This* caused a culture change in the congregation, not only making it acceptable for people to hug each other when they greet but also to say, 'No matter who or what you are; whether or not you have AIDS, we are willing to touch you.'

"Then one Sunday, after about three months' sermons, I said to the congregation: 'You have heard what happened to me, what the Lord did to me in The Netherlands. And you have heard what the Lord expects of us; you have heard how the Lord thinks about people. Now I want to ask you today, what did the Lord say to you through this?' They talked a little and then said to me, 'We believe that we as a church should start to take care of people with AIDS.' And for the first time in all the years I have been in Swaziland, no one asked, 'Where are we going to get money to do it?' They did not ask, 'Who's going to pay us salaries as we do such work?' They just said, 'We want to do it.' It was a miracle!"

In this regard, Brand Pretorius, outstanding business leader and retired South African motor industry icon, once remarked:

I learned that it's not sufficient to just engage the minds of employees. You also have to touch their hearts. In fact, before you can ask for a hand you need to touch a heart. And how do you do it? You do it in only one way, by caring for people and even being willing to serve people.[2]

Arnau continued, "Then I asked them, 'How are we now going to handle this?' They then asked me to arrange an AIDS conference – that we should get people talking to us and get ideas on the table. So, I contacted some experienced people. One of them was Corrie Oosthuizen, who was involved in home-based care of people with AIDS. I also invited her to participate in the conference, to discuss the way forward. In the end, the people said, '*Home-based Care* – as Corrie said – that's what we want to do.'

"Another miracle happened. I told them that according to Swazi culture, we cannot just jump in and do this work. We need to obtain permission from the chief of that area. Meanwhile, an old man from another congregation was sitting among us. He got up and said, 'There's no need to go to the chief. I am his representative and I permit you – you may proceed with the work.'

"After we agreed on what we wanted to do, the next question was, 'How are we going to take it further?' The representative of the chief told me that a small group of 16 people was already involved in such work. As they were not part of our church, and not wanting to compete with them, I arranged a meeting with them to see if we could join hands and work together. We found that they were also volunteers, but without any training. When they realised that we want to work on a more formal level, they asked to come under our protection, and we agreed.

"The first training session was arranged for January 2006, in collaboration with Corrie Oosthuizen. I learned about the ways of the Lord in more than one way: we decided on Saturday to start with the training. On Monday there was a cheque in the mail with a letter saying, 'This money (R1 500) is for your AIDS Project.' We then discovered that it was already mailed the previous Wednesday and I realised that the Lord sometimes provides money in supernatural ways.

---

[2] Brand Pretorius, *Does servant leadership still have a place in the harsh business environment?* Message delivered at a dinner evening of the Bible Society of South Africa in aid of Bible Distribution, October 2014.

"A few days before the training, I was in doubt and said to the Lord that if there were 20 people, I would accept this is what God wants from me. When I arrived at the church on Monday morning, there were 21 people! Tuesday morning, there were heavy rains and while I was driving, I again doubted and struggled with the Lord, because the people had to walk to church and they would not show up when it was raining. It was still raining when I arrived. Everything was wet and water was flowing everywhere. As I entered the church, 26 people were present! On Wednesday morning there were 36! And so we were able to start in a structured way to visit the people with AIDS in the community."

It mushroomed

"This group started working in the community of our congregation in Dwaleni. We got together every week to hear how things were going, to sort out problems and encourage them. Initially, I did not consider expanding the work. But at the end of 2006, another congregation in Matsanjeni asked us to train them too. We decided to start early in 2007 and to train them during that year.

"On my way there, I received a call from a person who later became minister of health in Swaziland, asking me whether we could start with a group at Lavumisa. At first, I did not see my way open because of the workload. He accepted my excuse, and I continued on my way.

"Then, at the end of discussions at Matsanjeni, I noticed a girl from Lavumisa in the group, whom I had known since she was at school. At that moment, cold chills went through me. I asked, 'Lord, what is happening here?' When I was done, I walked over to her (Elizabeth) and asked why she was at the meeting. She responded, 'I have heard about your meeting and decided to come and ask you if you could please come and train a group at Lavumisa?' I experienced this as a Macedonian call, and said, 'OK, I believe the Lord wants us to do this. I will come and train you at Lavumisa.'

"After training in Matsanjeni and Lavumisa, more and more groups were emerging from communities who asked for training. In 2007, we trained five more groups. In 2008, we trained another six groups, after which this movement only grew and grew. At the moment we work in 46 communities, with 1 400 caregivers serving ± 5 000 people at their homes regularly."

Principles and structure

We asked Arnau about guidelines, values, principles and structure that work for them. He replied:

"Firstly, our vision – *To become the hands and feet of Christ in this community* – is our great driving force. We want to represent Christ within the community.

"Our mission statement: *In a community devastated by poverty, sickness, broken families and death, we want to bring back true Christian hope, not only through our words but also – following the perfect example of our Lord, Jesus Christ – by reaching out in love to those in need, comforting and supporting them by all means available to us.*

"About the structure: because of the extent of the work we later implemented a business model and therefore work with a board of trustees who oversee the projects.

"But the bottom line is: *the most important people of the entire project of SHBC are the clients.* We are in service of our clients. Therefore, the focus of the 1 400 caregivers in 46 communities is on the clients, and in each of the 46 communities we have a small committee with a coordinator. Once a month we meet to discuss the problems they are experiencing, as well as the good news. Then again my point of departure is: the coordinator's focus is not the caregivers, but the clients. However, for proper functioning, we need to train and support the caregivers, should there be a problem.

"The first focus of the board of trustees, therefore, is the clients. Their second focus is the caregivers. Their third focus is the coordinators. We uphold *a servant leadership model*, serving the clients in the best way we can.

"*Good management*, including good financial management, is also important. Meetings and spending time with the coordinators are important. Reporting is an absolute priority for us, because you cannot do the work if you do not know what you are doing. SHBC – not only in eSwatini but also internationally – is known to have a *unique reporting model*. Even with illiterate people, we have developed a reporting system that is captured and maintained on a database: what we do; who the people are that we reach and what their condition is. At any given time we know how many of the people are HIV positive, how many have tuberculosis or are suffering from high blood pressure, and so on.

"On the one hand we have the *spiritual side* of the ministry, but on the other hand also very *good business principles* as well as a *holistic approach* to the ministry.

"If we are asked what we are doing, we say, 'We do what the Lord lays upon our hearts to do.'

"This resulted in changing the paradigms about AIDS. We are not dealing with the extreme cases of AIDS to the same extent as before. These days, it is maybe to help someone having a bath; or helping someone who had a stroke with physical exercises; to support a person emotionally; sometimes to explain the Gospel or to support a person spiritually. *It depends on the real need of a person at that moment.* To one, Jesus said, 'Take up your bed and walk,' and to another, 'Your sins have been forgiven.'

"Thus, we address the need of the moment, but always realising that we are there as the hands and feet of Christ to bring hope in this particular situation we now face."

Making the difference

"What difference does it make? Does eSwatini look different from what it looked like before?" we asked.

Arnau replied: "In the church itself, a change of mind took place, changing from a very rigid, legalistic way of thinking, often condemning, to where they came to a point to say, 'We do not only accept them, but also embrace people who have contracted AIDS, in spite of the fact that we know that their views might be different from ours.' The whole attitude in the church now is that of embracing and welcoming these people in spite of differences.

"However, it did not make a huge difference in our membership numbers. I hoped it would, but that has not happened on a large scale, probably because people traditionally want to remain members of their churches where they are at home. But what has happened is that the church is being seen as an aid to bring about change in eSwatini.

"Although articles were published and TV programmes were produced about the work, we want to stress that this is not about a selected special group of people. It is about ordinary church members – initially from our church, but later also

> *The whole attitude in the church is of embracing and welcoming people who may even be different, to make a significant difference as Jesus would have acted.*

25

from other churches – who, in spite of their circumstances and their poverty, said 'I want to make a significant difference in other people's lives. I want to act in my community, as Jesus would have acted.'

"That's the message I try to make known every time I write an article or speak on TV or in interviews with newspaper reporters. I really want to say, 'It's not an exceptional group of people; they are ordinary people, saying, 'We want to make a difference.' They are a group of people who stood up and volunteered to become part of a programme to go into the homes of people, even worse off than themselves, to serve them, to do the most basic things, such as fetching water from the river, washing the patients. In many cases, where the people have lost control of their bodily functions, they change their diapers, share food with them and in general doing what we believe Jesus would have done, had he been living as a human person in eSwatini today."

An action that left me dumbfounded

"I want to tell a story about something that left me dumbfounded. I went out to one of the home-based care projects and on arriving, I was told that the volunteers were helping someone to build a room at his house. I assumed it was someone too sick to care for himself.

"At the place where they were building – a small room, perhaps six square meters, made of sticks, stones and mud with a thatch roof – I enquired about the man whose house they were building, assuming that he was lying somewhere and wanted to visit him. To my utmost surprise, they told me that the man, not a member of the congregation, was at the *shebeen* (a bar in local language).

"I thought I had misheard them: 'Do you want to tell me that you are building this man's house for him and he is at the *shebeen*!' 'Yes,' they answered. 'He's a drunkard.'

"I could not believe what I had just heard. This is so stupid, I thought. 'Why do you build his home if he's a drunkard?' I asked. 'Because we want him to see that God loves him!'

"Driving back to my home I could not help saying over and over to myself: I was wrong and they were right! If we are serious in becoming the hands and feet of Christ, then we are going to have to do things which surpass all human understanding!"[3]

---

[3]   https://missionissues.wordpress.com/2007/07/26/when-charity-surpasses-all-human-understanding/ (With permission from Arnau)

Change within the younger generation

We asked Arnau, "Has there been a change among the younger generation regarding the church, AIDS, morality, and so on? Can you see a difference?"

"I definitely think so," he replied. "The AIDS epidemic in eSwatini is much more under control. The mortality rate has decreased dramatically.

"We have good reporting with the data we keep. Each year, it is less – from 35% in 2008 to less than 5% in 2015. Part of the conclusion is that with the care we give they receive emotional support to continue their medication. Now, the death rate of our client group is half the average death rate of the country. Whether it's mainly as a result of the medication or whether people live a lot more morally, is difficult to say with certainty. We also decided not to make surveys about it.

"But I think there was a change among the young people about how they see the church. Where the vision, *To become the hands and feet of Christ in the community*, was the vision of the group, it has now also become the vision of the church.

"So, even those who were not involved in the AIDS project now consider themselves to be here for the community and to represent Jesus in the community. Thus, there has become a broadening in thinking about the role of the church and I experience that they feel it is very important."

A challenge for the future

"You once mentioned to us how you stood on the pulpit in Dwaleni and noticed that there are mostly children in the church, which is also a challenge for the future because many of the parents have died. Please tell us about your focus on orphanages and trauma counselling?"

"In this regard, two things have happened," said Arnau. "Right at the start of the AIDS project, in 2006, the headman came to us and asked for two things – firstly, whether we could help provide food to orphans (while he undertook to get maize meal from the chief's side), and secondly, can we start a nursery school? We started with an informal playgroup (not kindergarten), where the children at least could be safe in the daytime, instead of being at home where one does not always know what is happening. In addition, we also started a food programme for them.

"Then, in 2008, when I received the Courageous Leadership Award, with US$40 000 prize money, we decided to build a decent kitchen at Dwaleni. But we still could not feed many children because we did not have enough money for food yet, while at the same time we also saw the need at Matsanjeni. Through personal contact, we received a visit from someone involved in the Taiwan Fund for Children and Families. Having seen the need, he asked for a proposal upon which they decided to start funding for a kitchen and to feed the children.

"Currently, we have feeding programmes in eight different places, providing food every day for approximately 750 children at the church. However, the contributions are being reduced each month. As far as the crèches are concerned, a business foundation in eSwatini has become involved and is now funding it."

On a personal note

Coming back on a personal note, we asked Arnau, "Thinking of your vision of becoming the hands and feet of Christ to the people of eSwatini – how do you experience it?"

Tongue-in-cheek he replied, "I say to many people, 'You know, my life could have been awful; I could have been a minister, somewhere in the wealthy east of Pretoria.'"

We laughed a bit, and Arnau continued, "First of all, if I could have my life over again, I would have chosen the same place, eSwatini again, but I would probably have started earlier with what I'm doing now and would have done the same. I have five years left before I retire and I think I can look back and say that I've bequeathed something – by God's grace I've made a difference in people's lives, on a much larger scale.

"I know myself; I am an introvert, very rational in my thinking, wanting to do things step by step. I am not a person who takes risks, daring to see what will happen. And I feel, as far as SHBC is concerned, the Lord was with me from being an ordinary missionary who preached on Sundays and tried to do something here and there, to where I can now look back on my ministry and know that the Lord used me to make a difference.

"Together with this, I believe the Lord has released me from being a person who wants to regulate and keep my finger on everything, knowing things go right all the time. Therefore, I am now much more willing to delegate and to invest in people to eventually take over. Also, the legacy will be much bigger when I leave eSwatini one day, and the work will continue. It is of greater importance to me that the work can continue, than for me being there.

"So, when I'm lying down at night, thinking, I have often wondered who the Lord actually wanted for this job, because I am not the typical leader or manager of these types of projects. And maybe *that's* part of SHBC's big success story – it's not me. It really is the Lord.

"And of course, also the opportunities I've been blessed with – the *Advanced Medical Health Programme* I did – was an intervention of the Lord to help me learn principles of management, proposal writing and a lot of other things I did not understand. I surely realised that the Lord opened a door for me because I would never have done an MBA in my life, but can see now how it serves the organisation. And I'm exceedingly grateful that the Lord made these things happen in my life."

"What makes you excited? What dreams do you still have?" we asked.

He answered, "Currently, things are pretty good, but what worries me at this stage is feeding the children because they do not have other sources. If the current organisation is going to withdraw, we have a problem. As for now, we already buy food on a very strict budget.

"However, I am excited that the work is growing. At first, the emphasis was mainly on AIDS; today, approximately 50% of our clients are HIV positive. But we are facing a major problem of people who have high blood pressure, have strokes or diabetes, which is a major problem in eSwatini. This is becoming a great concern – how can we help people develop a healthier lifestyle in order not to suffer from it? It may be a part of our future ministry to concentrate on this type of wellbeing – that we begin to act preventatively, now that AIDS is a bit more under control, especially with medication."

"Are there negative things you experience – some obstacles?" we asked.

Arnau continued, "I still believe that the idea I had – that the caregivers all work as volunteers – came from the Lord. They do not receive salaries, as we do not have the money. But we said if we receive donations, we would give them food as it is the biggest need in eSwatini. I have initiated a project, *Adopt a Caregiver*, which allows individuals to donate a small amount monthly, but it just does not deliver the desired results, even after eight years of trying. So, my biggest disappointment is that there are fellow believers who have no idea of the conditions in which other fellow believers are living."

We asked Arnau a last question – "Through all the years, what kept you going and what does the future hold?"

He replied, "The fact that people adopted the dream of SHBC, *To be the hands and feet of Christ*, and that there are people who support me. Also, that I have the conviction this is what the Lord wants of me and I can see it working.

"The initial dream I had in 2005 in Utrecht's hotel room in The Netherlands, has happened and hasn't stopped yet. It continues and still grows. Also, this group of people whom the Lord has given me – an incredible team of councillors who support me, as well as the people in the project themselves – and to see that plans being made actually work, *that* indeed energises me.

"In conclusion, I think it's important to say that in preparation for retirement, much of my energy has to go into training people who can take over both in the congregation and in SHBC so that the work can continue."

We thought about the question that was asked about Jesus Christ, "Could something good be coming from Nazareth?" However, from this small country, the Lord is sending a prominent message to the whole world.

Website: http://www.shbcare.org

Chapter 3

State pensioners feed 2 000 orphans

Faith is deliberate confidence in the character of God
whose ways you may not understand at the time.

- Oswald Chambers

When the concept of this book was born in our thoughts, some of the 'ordinary' people who are making a huge difference and who first

John & Antoinette Robinson

came to our minds were John and Antoinette Robinson. They are an exemplary couple in the broader White River community who are quietly bringing the *bread of life* literally and spiritually to thousands in the surrounding areas – but perhaps not such *ordinary* people in the years before we met them.

When we asked them about their life's road to their current ministry

for the past 12 years, John started to unfold a story from which many life lessons can be learned, especially for those who are struggling through the unexpected and uncertain valleys of life.

"I come from a business background. I worked for Leyland South Africa for 20 odd years and I ended up as a director on the board of Leyland (operations manager, controlling 22 branches).

"Then, during 1984 with the apartheid era heading towards its end, Leyland decided to shut down and pull out. I wasn't part of what they called a *management buy-out*, so I decided I would take over two of the branches in the country and we continued selling trucks."

Atheist meeting God... and bankruptcy

"But to add perspective to God's journey with us, I have to mention that during my time with Leyland, I was an atheist. I did not know the Lord at all. However, Antoinette was already a Christian, having several good Christian friends visiting us frequently, while she and our daughter Lara were also praying for me.

"Later, in 1992, we won the award for *Truck & Bus Sales of the Year* in the Lowveld. So we went on a two-week holiday to Greece and Turkey as part of our award, but what I will always recall from that time is that I was trying to give up smoking." Antoinette interrupted, "Eighty cigarettes a day!"

John continued with a smile, "Then, one night in Turkey I picked up a Bible in the hotel room and opened it at John 14. After reading a bit, I said to Antoinette, 'Agh, I don't know what it is with you guys, because this is repetitive, it's uninteresting', and I closed it and put it down.

"Anyway, on the plane coming home, we had a set of seats behind us that was open, which I used to lie down. And there, thinking that I'm up here *nearer to God*," John said with a smile, "I had a conversation with the Lord in which I said, 'God, I want to give up smoking; however I don't know much of what You can do in my life.'

"We got home and went back to the business, and about two weeks later we were sitting in our lounge and there was a Bible which I picked up and started to read at Genesis. After those first few verses, I made a commitment to the Lord and accepted Christ into my life. A day later, I stopped smoking and never touched a cigarette or a cup of coffee from that day. I knew that my body was healed – I had no after effects, no withdrawals, and today there's nothing wrong with my lungs. So, that was how I started my walk with the Lord, going to church with Antoinette and got involved.

"But only a few days after I've accepted the Lord Jesus to reign in my life, there was some irregularity from the side of another company who wanted us out and eventually we ended up losing the business."

Antoinette asked to interrupt – "He came to the Lord, and it was only two weeks later that we lost our business – we lost everything we had, *everything*! It was hard. Now, at that stage I was a firm Christian, he for only two weeks, and yet, immediately, he was the strong one, saying to me, 'What does the Bible say? What does the

Lord say in this instance?' – He, after being an atheist, not believing in God!"

John continued: "During those two weeks after my conversion I've told everybody at the business that I've accepted the Lord in my life, and then we lost everything. However, I withdrew from our bank account R44 000 with which we intended to pay the staff. But back home we went to the Word which said: *no compromise!* So, that Tuesday I took the money to the bank manager, who didn't know that the business collapsed, and said to him that I want to give it back."

Antoinette added: "When we lost the business and everything, we had three children at university. And that night we sat in front of the fireplace and John asked, 'What do we do?' and I said, 'We read and we pray.' We continued where we stopped the previous night, and the next part was where Jesus went into the desert and was tempted (Matthew 4:1-11). And we realised this message is from God. The Lord will take us through. And the commentary on that part really helped us, saying, you never compromise. That's the reason why John took back that R44 000, and that's what we've done ever since – we don't compromise."

John continued: "And from that day on the Lord has helped us. We had our ups and downs, but God provides. Today we don't have much, but we have enough and we are satisfied.

"After the collapse of our business we started doing various things and eventually moved to White River and helped to set up *Lowveld Fruit & Veg*. But we never reached the heights of what we did when we were much younger. We helped the children and lived our lives more comfortably than before."

A step in faith

"John and Antoinette, you were successful business people; now you're feeding children," we noted. "How did the change come about that you started the feeding schemes?"

John replied, "From 1992 onwards, a change took place in my life. I became less driven by performance – pursuing success, money and so on. While still helping our children and getting Lara through university, it was a question of moving forward under different circumstances.

"Then came 2004, and Lowveld Fruit & Veg that we helped to set up, came to an end and we then didn't have work."

John hesitated a second and then continued, "I guess, it's more *humbleness* that one needed to do all of that, because you had to keep on doing things and carry on. When we moved to the farm, I became a craftsman – we had to fix homes and all sorts of things. That's what I had to do. Six years earlier, when I was 57, I had around 850 people working for me! And here I am now; it's just John. And John has a few tools, and he has to repair that door, and so on. So I've learned a lot and we had to *adapt*, and I think we adapted well. Indeed, we had tough times, but it was a change that was needed."

He continued, "As the Lord was teaching us about stewardship, a friend introduced us to Bishop Joseph Motaung, an old man – then already 93 years old – of Bethesda Christian Church in a nearby black township called Masoyi. We decided to pray together regularly, got to know each other well, and built up a wonderful friendship and good trust between us, across the racial barrier. It was *there* that the change came – when I saw the situation in that community, with many homeless orphans suffering because of the HIV/AIDS pandemic. This led us to a point when we sensed we ought to do something for the children. And this led to the birth of their ministry, A Step in Faith, to feed these helpless children.

"I believe the strategy was set up by God through our prayers together with Bishop Motaung and his son Michael, also a pastor. I'm a businessman, but God led me into the *what, where* and *how*. So, this businessman and prayer complimented each other. The decision was to feed, but the 'food' must be Jesus Christ to the children, because humanitarian feeding can be done by anybody. The real *food* must be about the Lord – how God works and what God does. That is why we then decided *we only work with churches*, and through prayer and God's guidance, we were led to the churches where we could sense the presence of the Holy Spirit. And over the years, through prayer, God has brought us food, people and much more."

Then Antoinette added. "We lost everything. Previously, we *had* everything. Financially we were strong. We had a beautiful home, cars, boats, everything. But in the losing, John was always the strong one, asking 'What does the Bible say?' I was the rebel, asking 'Why?!' And when he said to me we have to feed the children, I said, 'What!? We can't even feed ourselves! How can you feed other children...?' But when we were at our lowest – in that – God worked with him, and God worked with me. The Scripture we received then was from Matthew 6, and we asked, 'What does it mean to search and expand the kingdom of God?' Simultaneously, God also spoke to us through James 1:27 – '*Religion that God our Father accepts... is this: to look after orphans and widows in their distress...*'" Antoinette adds elatedly, "See how wonderfully these two parts of Scripture fit together. The one says you must search the kingdom of God and his righteousness; the other gives an example of how to do it.

"So, it was simple, really, just a 'God-thing' – that we started feeding, John and I... Listen, this is important – two 'old' pensioners, now over 70, who don't have an income (we each draw a state pension), feed 2 000 children every day, five days a week, and we've done it for 12 years. I mean, *really*, I don't have to say, 'Give God the honour' – I don't even have to *say* that! It's there, it's out there! It speaks for itself. How can two old people do what we're doing? So, the whole thing, from the beginning, was from God, with God.

> "If you consistently do what is best for the greater good, it will also always be best for you in the end."
>
> Francois van Niekerk

"Thus, out of that process of John being obedient, God has blessed us and I just had to come to the point where I also had to be humble and go to God and say, 'God, You are right and I'm *sorry*.' And it's just amazing how God had *formed* us in the process."

Then we asked, "You experienced God's guidance through Scripture; was there something else that inspired you towards the step that you took in faith?"

Antoinette continued, "Together with the inspiring friendship of Bishop Motaung, there was something else we've experienced with them. When we had the fruit and vegetable business we used to take some to them personally, and I remember Linah, his wife, always sang so beautifully every time we came there. She insisted that we don't offload before she sang and knelt on the ground to thank God for the food... They inspired us, Bishop Joseph, his wife Linah and son, Michael, to help them."

John added, "What you sometimes don't realise, is how God's Spirit in you inspires you. You walk the road, but you don't realise the inspiration and the strength you're getting as you do what you have to do. I often stood in front of the congregation, and in witnessing I could see what it means for others, to hear about the things you were able to do with God's help. Antoinette and I are just the instruments that God uses, but many others are also instruments, for example, the donors and the ladies who help at the churches."

A small beginning expanded

"How many children benefit from this?" we asked.

John replied, "We started with 26 kids on January 6th, 2006, with a little bit of fruit and 'mealie pap' (maize porridge) together with children's ministry, but within weeks we were talking about hundreds. So, over the years it has been growing – every year bigger and bigger. That was the pattern at every place where we started feeding and it is the same kids that have been identified by the church, who keep on coming back. The one thing I've continued praying for during all the years is *honesty*, and that we have had. This is amazing, considering that between 30 to 40 people are doing the cooking and feeding every day."

"You also extended the kitchen facilities at the church we've seen in the Masoyi area," we said, and John added, "At most of the churches we built a little kitchen, and in Masoyi we extended the church to make a place where the kids can sit and eat. One of the donors also built toilet facilities for them. At the other places, we put up covering and the sides with corrugated iron and provided the pots and utensils. Therefore, when it rains and it is unpleasant, there is covering for the women to prepare the food daily.

"Currently we are feeding about 2 000 kids a day and we now have seven places where we are feeding. Recently we opened one at Pienaar and we also feed children at an orphanage at Msholozi outside of White River. We provide food five days a week. We have cash donors and others who donate food which I collect every week. Initially, I did all the collecting and delivering, but now I have people who help to share the load in delivering. I spend much time during the week in the vehicle fetching and bringing in the food – we are talking about tons that are going out weekly. And it's remarkable – *there has never been a day in the 12 years that we haven't been able to provide the quantity of food necessary* – never been a day." And Antoinette confirmed, "Absolutely."

John continued, "And I have to mention that all the time, the volunteering women at the various churches had remained loyal – they've never been paid (though we've sent a couple of them to attend Bible schools), and they've been there for 12 years, feeding those kids on a daily basis. And that's important, the fact that *we do it as the church* and that we want the church to be seen doing the feeding, *and not John and Antoinette* or whoever."

God stepping in

"How are you experiencing God in all of this? Have you ever seen God stepping in?" we asked.

John replied, "We've seen it often – to this day God still multiplies. But I think Antoinette should tell you the story", he said with excitement before Antoinette continued:

"One doesn't realise that you see multiplication. But one day, my son Derek accompanied me to Masoyi and there was a long line of children. That was when he turned to me and said, 'Mom, we have approximately 200 plus kids in that line – they're not all going to get food from those pots.' And my words to him were, 'Let us stay here and you will see, every child will be fed. And it was like that – *every* child was fed that day from those two pots that we had in front of us! And they all had more or less the same amount of food. It was only as we were driving home that I realised – what we have seen today, was multiplication! And subsequently, we've seen it quite often.

"Once we received clothes and shoes from various churches and organisations which we sorted so we have enough for one venue (we know more or less the number of children and women who work there, the ages, etc.). When we had enough, we made up parcels at home for the children at the Masoyi base, who numbered 300 to 400, and we took it there.

"At the church the children started to come in and we let them sit down. But the word spread and within minutes there were many more children. I said to Pastor Michael, 'Before we start, we must pray that God will multiply the clothes so we have enough for all the children.' After we prayed, we started handing out and they continued coming in, and eventually we had just a little pile of plastic bags. I said, 'Let's start opening the bags, that if there's a pair of pants and a shirt, we just give one to each.'

"After a while, I went outside and stood behind the last child, praying, 'Lord, I don't have the faith. There's not enough for all the children.' I knew what was waiting inside and did not believe there would be enough. I stood there, helpless! Eventually we were inside and there were only a few little presents, and a few children. When we got to the end, there was a young boy of about seven, at the back of the queue. As he came nearer, they said, 'Sorry, there's nothing more. Sorry.' I said, 'No, search! Open up everything, all these bags.' And then we found a brand new soccer ball!"

John added, "And we've seen it at the other places, with the clothing, and with the food. It's regular, since the amount of food many times does not match the number of kids turning up. And at all these feeding points, they could always give the last child a plate of food.

"Another example is the *prayer that is done* for the supply of food. After one occasion when we prayed, I approached a firm that supplied maize and some other food. On arrival, I met the person in charge for the first time, and he said, 'Come along, I will see what I can do...' I expected perhaps a bag or two of spaghetti or something like that – I left there with two tons of spaghetti, macaroni, mealie-meal (maize flower), samp, you name it! And that was in the days when we did not have all the donors that we have now. It was all done by pure food donation only. Nobody donated money. *That* was multiplication, and it was necessary."

> "God's work done God's way will not lack God's support."
>
> Hudson Taylor

We asked them about financial constraints, and John responded, "My background is finances. I run the books, and I always check if there is enough as people need to be paid, and I pay no later than the next day – that's my policy. You do not compromise on those sort of things, because the people are good to you. Now, it was during March and I had to pay bills – but there was only R13 000 (already committed) in the bank account, and bills of R15 080 still to be paid! So, I checked the reconciliation again – and found that costs had increased by R11 000 a month!

"During quiet time and on my knees, a lady's name came to my mind. I experienced it as from the Lord and I called her. But as she was very busy, she promised to call back within a few days. The next Tuesday she called and said I must come and see her, she has a cheque for me. When I got there, I couldn't wait to see the cheque – it was R15 000!

"And from then we had another problem as we were trying to cut costs and get food cheaper without reducing quantities. However, to stop feeding was not an option. Then a friend of mine said to me,

'John, I have a new business that I started and want to donate a tenth of my profits to your ministry every month, though it will fluctuate up and down.' It wasn't two hours later when my phone went 'peep-peep', and there was a transfer. When I looked – R20 150! And ever since then, that is the sort of money he has been giving. This is just one example of how faithful the Lord has always been. The main thing is to *stay humble* and *in prayer with faith in God*."

The effect on them and others

"What impact does the work have on you and those who help you?" we asked.

John responded: "Our faith and our trust in the Lord has grown. I believe the Lord has taught us and improved our lifestyle, so that we can do this today as state pensioners while our son and daughter help us. We also find that friends are very generous to our financial wellbeing."

Then Antoinette said, "What makes a deep impression on us is the wives of the pastors and the women at the churches, some volunteers who prepare the food and the ones that evangelise the kids. They are not paid, but have been there for the past 12 years, because the principle, all the years, was that you do not do it for yourself, but for God and the children. *These* are the people who have inspired and motivated us." (John confirmed with a nod.) "*These* are the people that have changed us. *These* are the people that have shown us the face of God, if I can put it like that. Truly."

John added, "You know, as a result of this, we had many people who came to stay here and got involved, also with evangelisation outreaches – groups of kids and adults from everywhere, even from overseas, who couldn't grasp what was happening. The kids of one group even gave up an opportunity of a day's outing to a pleasure resort to go back to the scheme and continue evangelising there – incredible! And when this group saw for themselves what is going on, they were so touched, saying, 'We are going back and will do the same as you.' Therefore, the multiplication here leads to multiplication elsewhere.

"And some of the most wonderful things to me are that we can pray to our Father in Heaven, but you don't always know where it will end up. Therefore, praying and being obedient produce the fruit which is beyond expectation."

We then asked them what their toughest experiences or greatest disappointments were.

John replied, "Sometimes we've experienced a lack of commitment from people. And yes, we learned from our mistakes not to do it our way, but to go to the Lord in prayer. Sometimes you get tired, but it remains a pleasure because you achieve what you are supposed to do. We have good relationships with the people who donate and they are a blessing to us."

"What is next?" we asked.

Both of them agreed, "To keep doing what we are doing until God redirects us. All the glory to God for his mercy and grace."

Email: jdr.asif@gmail.com

Chapter 4

From engineer to 'father' of a city

In the twenty-first century, the agonizing social evils in society
will have to be faced as an essential component of mission,
and not just the proclamation of personal salvation.

- Patrick Johnstone

TJ Maré is one of those high achievers with an unsaturated passion
to develop viable and lasting solutions to the plight of homeless and destitute people in the capital and
surrounding towns of the Mpumalanga province of South Africa. As founder and CEO
of Nelspruit Community Forum, he is altering
a culture of unhealthy dependency into
autonomy. Eventually, his focus expanded
throughout a network among other cities and
towns.

TJ Maré

But he's also quite an eccentric advocate
for his course. We once saw a sloppy tramp
at a traffic light, near the venue of a special
breakfast for business and community leaders of the city of Nelspruit we attended, just to hear and see this guy later entering and
disrupting the event. He turned out to be the well-known TJ, as an
invited speaker on the challenges and opportunities which the homeless and jobless poses for the area!

When we asked what led him to a change of focus, TJ told us
how, after 16 years as an engineer in electronics and communications
in the corporate sector, he went through a difficult time in his life. At
the same time, he went on a church outreach to India during which
he experienced how God's presence set him free and healed him
from areas in his life where he was struggling.

He continued: "Over there, I was touched by the circumstances of the so-called *untouchables* and *that* has changed my life, totally. If God speaks about the *crown* of his creation, then it also includes these people and we cannot deprive them of such grace.

"I came back to South Africa, and immediately resigned from my job and agreed with management to stay on for three months, allowing them to find a substitute, while my wife Brenda and I continued to listen to the Lord. We found clarity of, firstly, being called for the cities of the world, and secondly, Ecclesiastics 11:1 spoke very clearly to us: *'Cast your bread upon the waters, for after many days you will find it again.'*"

The adjustments and cost

"That was a drastic decisive point. It surely asked for adjustments in your own and your family's lives," we suggested.

TJ responded, "Yes, it costs us some of our friends and even today some people say to me they can't understand why I've made such a 'stupid' decision. Even our oldest son, nine years old at that time, said to us, 'Why? Mom and Dad both have nice cars, we live in a nice house and we can stop at places and buy whatever we want. Why do you give it up?' But we shared the calling on our lives and our firm conviction and motivation, as well as our calling into city ministry."

"How did you prepare yourself?" we asked.

He continued, "We enrolled at Africa School of Missions near White River while Brenda still had a job to provide for food on the table, but during our second year of studies, that opportunity was closed. We also knew there was no turning back and that this was our test to trust God completely – and God provided. We managed to put our children through school. We never went to bed hungry, but have numerous stories of how God provided."

(John Piper says about such a choice, "It may not be loving to choose comfort or security when something great may be achieved for the cause of Christ and for the good of others.")[1]

"You were convinced of your calling, but tell us how your ministry started and developed?" we asked.

TJ explained, "After our studies, we did two years practicum in urban missions with Pretoria Community Ministries in the city-

---

[1] John Piper, *Don't Waste Your Life (Group Study Edition)*, Crossway, Wheaton, Illinois, Text updated 2009, 80.

centre of Pretoria. However, as the day drew closer for us to move on to where we must serve, we realised that it's not about air tickets, a foreign language and culture. It was clearly on our hearts – South Africa also has cities. So we had to communicate it with all our supporters – it's not India, and that the Lord had convinced us of the need right here and opened opportunities for us here in the city of Nelspruit.

"At that time some faith communities and businesses were busy caring for the destitute in different ways. Then three churches, as well as some of the ministries, invited me to address them on how to minister to city tramps. And that, on December 2004, was the beginning of our ministry here, in association with the different denominations within the city.

"So, to me, the context was very clear. I believe *there's a parallel between calling and contexts, the relevancy of what you're called for*. But we had to design it. We've seen models, and there were good ones, but not the alpha and omega for every situation. We couldn't duplicate it – we had to develop our own model."

TJ then explained how Nelspruit Community Forum (NCF) was established in 2004 in response to the many people living here on and from the streets of Mbombela, capital of the Mpumalanga province of South Africa (including Nelspruit). As a collective and central service point, NCF is benefiting the society in general, including men and women, boys and girls of all races, educated and uneducated. NCF is an NPO registered with the Department of Welfare as a Public Benefit Organisation and with the South African Revenue Service (SARS), with Article 18A status (for tax exemption to donors).

Passionately, he continued, "But instead of just feeding a problem, we have decided to take a further step – to *transformation*.

NCF accepted this challenge of helping and ministering to these people, also as an opportunity and part of community development and empowerment. We facilitate rehabilitation, regeneration and reconciliation within the Mbombela geographical area that also spreads further into other districts, planting satellites in all the neighbouring towns and even further into other districts, networking and communicating with other interest groups in other cities. This led to a name change and the establishment of Mpumalanga Leadership Foundation (MLF) in June 2011."

Instead of just feeding a problem, take a further step – to transformation.

Learning from one another, globally

"Were you influenced by some experiences or relationships along this road?" we asked.

TJ replied, "We had a very valuable time at Pretoria Community Ministries, to experience their model to help a person, in Christ, to be welcome in the city. We could also share and debate our thoughts, as you cannot copy anything just as it is.

"I also had to see what other city ministries are doing, not only in South Africa but also in Kenya, Ethiopia, Egypt, the DRC, Mozambique, etc. These people from all over the world have inspired me and all of this led to the development of the Leadership Foundations.

"Eventually, Nelspruit Community Forum is now a programme within Mpumalanga Leadership Foundation, and out of this network we started to take hands across the globe. In South Africa and abroad, ministries in different metropoles share skills and ideas, forming networks and enriching one another. Consequently, Leadership Foundations Africa was founded. We look at best practices and visit each other if possible to see how certain things are being done elsewhere. You keep on looking around you and learn from it.

"Thus, we had the calling, we determined the core, and then we had to define how we should do it here in our city with its state of affairs."

A picture coming together

"Looking back to before this change, was there something that God did in your past that now fits into your current role – the purpose you are now serving?" we asked.

He recalled, "I've learned about financial management and budgets and how to implement it from my directorship at the last company I've worked for. On the other hand, through my experience in computer science, we could develop a database and system to regulate the food supplies, distribution and usage – exactly who receive what and how much.

"I'd been in drugs myself, but by God's grace; He pulled me out of it before I went deeper into it. Brenda grew up through adversities in a poor family, but became a wonderful mother and today we can understand the person in the gutters. So, in that sense, we could somehow become a father and mother for the city, even for those in high positions with important titles, but in their circumstances also

44

marginalised and destitute. By God's intervention in our lives and that of others, we can witness today how the Lord developed people and put them in positions in our city, even for me, without a business of my own, as chairman of the business chamber.

"And now as things develop, we can see how God is always busy preparing new ground for us. The Nelspruit City Improvement District (CID) is a new phase, and because of the value and influence I can add, I was asked to serve on the Human Resource Development Council of Mpumalanga."

"Tell us more about the CID?" we asked.

TJ explained, "The CID is also a Non-Profit Organisation working on the improvement of the city, but still focused on the people. Furthermore, I also manage a team of people running several programmes with contracts in place – cleaning, security and *public space management*, and so on. All of this gives me the opportunity to stop at the guy begging at the traffic light or on the pavement and to interact with them – and for me that is part of the Gospel.

"It's incredibly rewarding. Walking several kilometers per day up and down Anderson Street (a well-known street for drug abuse and prostitution), I bump into those guys who want to do business with you – it's a wonderful opportunity for ministry."

Then we asked, "It may seem to be a stupid question, but what is the purpose eventually?"

TJ replied, "The purpose is twofold. When this role was given to me, the fact that I'm a pastor was important for the panel. But I do not preach on the streets. *The purpose is to model.* It changes people. There are people whom I regularly pass, who say, 'Thanks that you stop by me,' or, 'I have not seen you for three days, and I've missed you.' That's what it is about – there's interaction, and that's how the love and the message of Christ breaks through, causing lives to change. We walk the walk and show people another *Way*. And at the same time, you can walk, pray and proclaim. It's another way of ministering which God had set up. And I thoroughly enjoy doing it."

"When you saw the need, what did you do to get the involvement of the business leaders in the area?" we asked.

TJ explained, "We had to run an awareness campaign to show them what was happening and what it looks like – the all-inclusive picture of the city with a bigger problem than what most people realise (with all the homeless people, street children, women caught

in prostitution, drug lords, etc.). We also showed them how it could
be, towards what they could participate,
and what the benefits for the city could be
– and how *they* could benefit from it. Now
many are participating without even
wanting recognition."

> *There's interaction.*
> *That's how the love and*
> *the message of Christ*
> *break through, causing*
> *lives to change.*

At this point it was worth pondering
international award-winning philanthro-
pist Francois van Niekerk's answer to a question, "How do you view
the future and how do you see your heritage?" as he responded:

> I hope to see global progress toward a vastly improved and
> more equitable upliftment of the destitute 70 per cent of our
> fellow human beings. For this to be realised, each business
> corporation will have to promote a balanced form of co-
> operation between the church, business and government in
> its local operations.[2]

Poverty, street children and broken families

Then we asked, "How do you minister to a culture of poverty and
the challenge of street children found in this area?"

TJ answered, "When you look at poverty, there's a sequence that
you have to break. And it is important to know where it started,
because children become what the parents were. It did not start with
the person in front of you, but with the person who has been there
before – a father, mother, grandfather, or other.

"However, to break this cycle is not very easy. Firstly, you have
to model something better for them. And it is only by God's grace
that a person will tell you himself, 'I don't want to be like my parents
anymore, I don't want to roam around being dependent anymore, I
want to break with it.' Even then, you have to guide and encourage
them to keep to the decisions they took themselves and do not run
away from their responsibilities.

"The other thing I had to do at the founding of Mpumalanga
Leadership Forum was to focus on the people alongside them (family
or friends) and put energy into building into them and *reconciliation*
among them.

"For example, I can mention our huge challenge with street
children in the city.

---

[2] Francois van Niekerk, *Doing business with purpose... Beyond success to significance.* Christian Media Publishing, Durbanville, 2015, 115.

"After a year, we discovered one kingpin, one boy, who knew the whereabouts of other children with problems, who left their homes and families. He would get hold of them, give them shelter under a highway bridge and take advantage by abusing them – but he made them streetwise and a month later you have a 'converted' little tramp who starts sniffing glue and steal, working himself up in the ranks.

"We paid him a 'home visitation' one night underneath the bridge (after walking through sludge and 'what else') and befriended him, understanding his needs as being a child himself. We invited him to our shelter and asked him to show the other children he will encounter within the future, where they also can get a meal, and *that* turned it all around."

"What happened at the shelter?"

TJ explained, "Immediately they found not only food but also love and understanding. We knew they left home because they have been rejected – because they did wrong in their communities – that was the model. But here was care and share. Here they could cry and be a child that cannot help himself but knows there is someone who cares and wants to help.

"They need love – they will sometimes even injure themselves slightly, just to get that little bit of love, personal touch and care from you. They long to be touched, and together with it, you need to *model real fatherhood* for most of them. Here they can be clean, eat a good plate of food, receive medical treatment, get some skills training and go to school. They can be boys, becoming young men who even-

> There's a sequence to be broken. Know where it started, focus on the people alongside and model something better.

tually can do something productive. And at that stage, we can start to draw in their parents, because they start to search for their children because of God's powerful gift of love."

A Damascus farm project

"You also help adult people to develop from dependency to independence and sustainability," we said.

TJ replied, "We run a small farm project where we accommodate about 30 people in a family context and teach them to manage themselves. It is about seeing the ability in others and helping them discover and develop *their* capability.

"The people we work with actually had to have a Damascus experience to discover how God created them and what is good inside each one of them, because they've heard all the time how bad they were – 'too bad to succeed, too useless to work, to be a husband or a wife – you're a wayward, unruly child'. We had to convince them that's not how God had made them and see them, that God has dreams and plans for them because He loves them. You have to bring it to them in all 'languages' and dimensions so that they can realise it. *And the moment they realise they have value and are not bad and useless, the change inside them begins.* Then you can evaluate with them to understand what they've brought unto themselves and what was caused by others or something else."

"So, now that you've helped them to discover self-worth, you also have to lead them to take up ownership of their lives and responsibilities," we said.

TJ responded, "As a matter of fact, the growth from feeling useless to the point where someone can start to take ownership is sometimes just a millimetre long. However, *you cannot generalise and have to evaluate each one.* And from discovering their value and strong points, you have to guide them all along the road of healing and development. You have to cultivate the sense of ownership to those who never had it before and you help them to fit into a job and society according to their strong points. When the *old person* shows up again, you have to address all the excuses, even accusations against you, and guide them to understanding and further

> It's about seeing the ability in others and helping them discover and develop their capability.

commitment. It's debatable, but not interchangeable. And yes, we also learn from every situation."

Then we asked, "What is necessary to make a success of it?" to which TJ replied, "We believe the important thing in making a success of such a ministry is to *lay down the rules, the set of values and disciplinary codes, based on God's Word, and help everybody to conform around it.*"

It's a multileveled, multidisciplinary system

TJ continued: "Together with it, no community can exist without a kind of community service centre.

"There's a desperate need for it. It needs to be a multileveled, multidisciplinary system and they cannot stand on their own; they need to cooperate within a network drawing from each other's skills and expertise, and I want to expand it."

"And if we've heard you correctly, not only networking in different areas of the city but also among other towns and cities?" we asked.

"Oh yes," said TJ, "People move from one place to another, and so also those whom we work with.

"Therefore, in networking, we build sustainability amongst the organisations that network with one another. We have a *cloud application* which we can use when a person ends up in need in another city. By only using the person's ID number, we can trace that person's history. So, with the help of a team of professionals, we can then resume with his or her rehabilitation and guide the person to take further decisions and commit him or herself again to an individual development plan. And when there is an initial lack of cooperation, we take it further the next day because God's Word doesn't say you're useless.

"But we are dealing with fallible human beings. You do get the failures – those who still die on the pavement – but by God's grace, we win the majority."

Rewards and meaning

"Do you have a testimony of someone whose life was changed and who thanked you afterwards?" we asked.

He answered, "There are so many people all over South Africa and even internationally, who went through these processes. We received a postcard, saying, 'Thank you so much for caring so much for me. I'm back in the UK. My family loves me. I'm OK. God bless you.'

"But even more – they become part of the ministry. Many were so-called 'clients', but after a while, they start to help in ministry – peer to peer, because they understand."

"What does your role mean to you personally?" we asked.

TJ replied, "I can answer this with my response to the question that comes to us in other words – 'How do you survive (while we have to go through the pressure of caring for nearly 10 000 households at this stage)?' My answer is simple: When I sit down in the evening in front of my TV, I am very satisfied with the past day because I have made a difference and have done my best. So, I can rest."

> "At the end of every day, one more box in the calendar has been shifted from the future column to the past column, from possibility to history."
>
> John Ortberg

"What provides you with the greatest fulfilment in your ministry?" we asked.

Again, TJ replied with passion, "The greatest counter achievement and satisfaction that you can get, is when somebody realises who he or she is and starts to work on it. When I move in the city and such a person calls me, shouting, 'TJ, how are you?!' and he or she is working for someone, I can see the joy and satisfaction on that person's face because he or she no longer is in the situation of six months ago."

"What dreams do you have for the future?" was our next question, to which he replied, "Firstly, we have not yet arrived, and we will continue to develop. I'm still learning all the way because I still haven't reached the best of myself. With the help of a number of lecturers we now also have a Bible College where we train people in sound theology, enabling them to understand how all the 'blocks' come together, from Old Testament to New Testament, to the present, to reach out to others still on the *outers* of the communities."

"And your toughest duty or responsibility?" we continued.

"To say *No*," he said, "When you understand the situation, and a mother stands in front of you and you don't have any more room, or when you have to tell someone to leave because he or she has violated the principles that we stand for. It makes me cry. It's very, very difficult."

"Lastly," we asked, "What do you experience as difficult times and lessons, and how did you counter it?"

With a serious note in his voice, he answered, "To become sucked into these voids, and if you don't make a decision before you fall through the hole, you've dug your own hole. You have to take care of burnout. My doctor warned me and showed me how white my nails were. I had to slow down a bit and take up a hobby. So, nowadays I'm angling again and can boast with a 20.4 kg carp! This makes my nails pink."

Website: www.nelspruitcommunityforum.org

Chapter 5

Anti-missions corporate manager became theologian in Missiology

> God is calling forth an army of leaders who will love,
> nurture, teach, and lead local churches
> into the exalted role He has ordained for them.
>
> - George Miley

We met Frans Hancke in the mid-90s as the director of Pro-Christo Global Mission at one of their Bless the Nations conferences in Kimberley, South Africa. These conferences, with participating international mission leaders, played a leading and influential role in mobilising people and churches for missions during those years.

Married to Elize, a music teacher, and sharing a love for music and ministry in song, this former financial manager of major corporate institutions proved to have his feet firmly on the ground, with his heart and mind strongly focused on the Lord and his plan for the church and its mission to the nations.

Frans Hancke

This focus later led him to become the founder and executive director of *thePLAN*, with an additional role as part-time lecturer and research associate with the University of the Free State, South Africa. Here he was awarded a Master's (Cum Laude) in Theology in 2002. His thesis was awarded the Dean's medal for the best master's study in Theology. In 2006 he followed up with a PhD in Theology (Missiology) at the same university and his research is considered by several theologians as unique and of the highest international significance. Frans has authored various articles and publications and is currently also preaching and teaching in various congregations and countries.

When we asked him how his journey developed from a highly successful career in the corporate sector towards missions and theology, Frans shared his heart with us:

"Since being a young child I had an inner feeling that one day when I'm grown up, I will become a pastor – a thought with almost a short-lived foothold in my heart, which I succeeded in suppressing and ignoring during my school and initial university years. After a B.Com, I became a teacher. I was also a deacon in church but with a definite dislike in missions, subtly influencing people not to donate money for missions. Of course, I didn't understand it correctly, but that's how I was. Then after almost seven years as a teacher, I moved into the corporate business world where I enjoyed success in climbing the management ladder."

Seeing the *Light*

"But on May 11th 1992 all of that started to change. As financial manager at Eskom (power supplying corporation of South Africa) in Kimberley, I was ill in bed for a few days. At that time, Eskom launched an extensive project, called *Electricity for All*, with the vision to supply electricity for 3 million households who then didn't have it. So, I was deeply involved and the approximate 40 000 employees were quite psyched up with the idea.

"Meanwhile, a few friends, my wife and I started a ministry in song, called ProChristo, which was quite successful as pioneers in Afrikaans Gospel music. We performed weekly at various places in the country, recorded CDs and the music was broadcasted over Radio Pulpit.

"And then something happened that changed my whole life, totally, and that of many people along with me. As I was lying there in bed, thinking of light for all in their dark houses, it was as if the Lord spoke to me, saying, 'You are excited about a vision to change people's lives because of light in their houses, but you don't care at all about the millions and millions of people in the world where I, the true Light, am not, and where there is spiritual darkness. They live like this and die like this.'

> "Jesus started where people were – at their level of commitment – but he never left them there."
>
> Rick Warren

"And then I experienced a vision as if I was lifted up and could see most of the world in darkness, and as if in conversation with the Lord, I asked, 'But Lord, what can *I* do about it?' And the Lord said, 'I had given you a vehicle. I've created ProChristo so that you can use it as a vehicle.'

"I then also experienced several things about the strategy ahead. Firstly, I spoke to two friends, but it was as if they were not as excited as I was about my vision. The next Wednesday evening we had a Bible study group at our house with whom I also shared what has happened to me. One of them, a farmer outside Kimberley, then said to me, 'I am very glad to see that you have read Oswald Smith's book, *The Challenge of Missions*.' I said, 'No, no, no, I have never read such a book.' He said, 'No, no, I can hear that you've read the book. What you've told us tonight about what the Lord has said to you, you will find in *The Challenge of Missions*.'

"I did not know what he was talking about, but a few days later he brought me the book, and after I've read it, I understood for the first time what was going on. I found confirmation in my mind that what I was experiencing was similar to what Oswald Smith had experienced many years ago.

"All of this caused ProChristo to become ProChristo Global Mission. With the funds that people gave spontaneously at our performances, without us asking, we started to equip and support missionaries. And we started to grow so much in mobilising and guiding people into missions, that prominent mission leaders said that we were the fastest-growing mission organisation in the country at that time."

A bucket of ice-water

Then we asked Frans how his commitment to full-time missions developed.

He replied, "Around that time I was sitting with a well-known missions leader in our dining room, discussing strategies for the new missions organisation, when he asked, like a bolt from the blue, 'When will you commit full-time to missions?'

"A bucket of ice-water would have been less shocking. I stammered, 'What do you mean, full-time?'

"ProChristo's work is growing at a phenomenal rate," he said, "But it cannot expand indefinitely without your full-time involvement and guidance. The Lord has entrusted the vision and the responsibility to you. Others will become fully committed when you demonstrate your obedience to God's Calling."

Frans admitted, "I did not enjoy that discomforting conversation. But some weeks later, after a Bless the Nations conference, I was seeing another prominent missions-leader off from Kimberley airport. He was less diplomatic than his predecessor was.

'How much longer will you remain disobedient?' he asked blatantly, unexpectedly.

'What do you mean?' I demanded.

'You know' said he. And I did..."

Is it faith?

Frans continued, "It was as if the Lord was drawing his net closer and closer around my life. Sometimes it felt as though God was saying: 'So far and no further.' For the following six years, Elize and I have experienced more and more of the substance of his calling. There was less and less chance of escape – yet we did not even desire release. We welcomed the Lord's exciting intervention in our future.

"We knew what we were unswervingly aimed at. I've known it ever since my first moments of awareness – that the Lord wants me as his full-time servant.

"To resign my position and enter missions on a full-time basis was a radical decision. And that is how we've experienced it. There was no safety net of salary, investments, severance package or dividends. Knowing that this was a one-way street with no way back and without an open backdoor, evoked a strange emotion of freedom, but also one of threatening uncertainty.

"Can it work? It doesn't make sense. Such decisions go against all reason. The Lord gave us intelligence. Isn't this perhaps childish naivety? Or is it blind impulsiveness? Can it work? Is it faith?

"Four years of prayer journal entries, since February 1993, bear witness to the daily struggle: 'Lord, what do *You* want of me?' Sometimes I shouted in reproach because the Lord would not give me clarity regarding his will. Couldn't God just once, in plain words, tell me what to do? Just once... What if I resign my position and it's not his will? What then? What if I don't get involved full-time in missions and that is his will? What then?

"At times I asked humbly, at others with aggressive rebellious-
ness. 'Well, if You will not give me a clear answer that I can understand...' It nearly bordered on spitefulness. But I could never shake
loose of it; I knew what the Lord wanted to do with my life. It wasn't
that God did not want to lead; I did not want to follow.

"Truly, this was not an impulsive decision – it followed four
years of travailing labour. At last, I had to admit that the Lord was
talking to me. As I turn and review the past I can see his concerned
intervention like deep footprints on my life."

"And your family? What did they say?" we asked.

Frans continued, "They understood that we could expect,
at times, the same as our missions' predecessor, Paul – plenty,
deprivation; acceptance, persecution – but as co-workers of Christ
we will also experience the joy of millions who will hear of Christ's
redemptive work! My son Wagener probably summed it up best
when asked what he thought of Elize's and my decision: 'It doesn't
matter what I think; you cannot do otherwise – the Lord has called
you. I can see it.'[1]

"Then I resigned from Eskom on May 1st, 1997, before we presented the first Love Southern Africa missions conference in Kimberley."

Why such a long road?

"Frans, 'God's intervention like footprints on your life' – please tell
us more?"

After a short pause, he replied, "Over the years I've struggled
terribly with the question, 'Why did the Lord let me walk such a
long road, as a teacher, in a bank and through the corporate sector,
until God *caught* me in 1992 – why such a long time?'

"But I gained certainty in my mind that what developed my
ministry over the years to where it is today – each of those experiences, how short or how long – have prepared and equipped me more
to do what the Lord has called me for. I realised all that happened
before were not mere coincidence. Therefore, when young aspiring
missionaries or people who want to devote their lives to ministry,
come to talk to me, I would always tell them, '*Look back at your
story*, because your story is your journey with the Lord. And the
contents of that journey were meant for use in your future ministry.'"

---

[1] The sections "A Bucket of Ice-Water" and "Is it Faith?" were taken, with few
alterations, from a reflection which Frans himself wrote.

Further development, strategy and guidelines

While ProChristo Global Missions grew extensively, Frans started his studies in Theology and later became involved in research and papers he had to contribute academically. At the same time, he realised that his route started to change and that younger leadership was needed for the organisation, and handed over the baton. Concurrently, the head office then moved to Kabwe in Zambia. Three years later it was negotiated that ProChristo Global Missions become integrated with Operation Mobilisation (OM), focusing on Africa.

"What strategy did you use to develop and expand the ministry?" we asked and Frans started to explain:

"I don't want to sound saintly and I believe the story around 11th May 1992 confirms it – the point is – it wasn't me. I never had the faintest idea to start something like a mission organisation because, at that stage with Eskom and the dream about electricity for all and the singing ministry, I also had a stud-farm with cattle on the side-line. I had not even searched for a vision." With a smile in his voice, Frans added, "I had peace. I had a good corporate job, a good salary and a nice company car. I would retire one day and wanted to farm! So, I didn't search, neither prayed for a vision or a ministry!"

We all enjoyed his honest remarks with a little laughter. But out of the laughter, Frans continued more seriously, "The Lord did come and force it on me. So, if I'm talking about strategy, then it was a strategy that the Lord started; God starting with the ministry in song which gave us good exposure and led to a snowball effect."

"What guidelines have you implemented and are you following?" we asked.

He replied, "The single guideline that stands out for me, and with which I also struggle most, is *to listen; to hear God's voice and to discern*. I've been tested with it many times. For example, I've learned the hard way that the Lord's finances and mine, and what I've learned in B.Com, actually has fairly little to do with each other. God does things his way. And therefore, the 'be all and end all' for me is to hear and understand God's will.

"Through all the years, something else that was always very important for me when I had to interpret or be convinced about what or what not to do, was to keep an eye on 'the big picture'. I always try not to take the immediate circumstances as point of departure, but to see the big picture.

"*Integrity* always remains a very important principle in ministry. It also challenges the attitude of some who practise missions as a laid-back existence in which others care for them, never mind the outputs they deliver, how they do it and its quality. *Be professional in all you do and do it with excellence.* This is non-negotiable. When I have to do something for the Lord, I have to do it absolutely to the best of my ability." And we confirmed, "Those are the characteristics of the kingdom of God."

> "I know, my God, that you test the heart and are pleased with integrity."
>
> 1 Chronicles 29:17a

A child would lead the way

"How would you describe the meaning and impact of your ministry?" we asked.

"One would never know," he said. "Later years I ran into people who confirmed that they received their call for missions at some of our conferences. But again, it's not about me.

"I have to tell you this: Even after I wasn't involved with ProChristo anymore, they invited me a few times to be a speaker at their annual conferences in Kabwe. In 2016, they took a photo of all the missionaries who have been trained and were ready for the mission fields, as well as alumni already involved in Africa – about 120 of them. Amongst them was my eldest daughter, Johanni, who also received training at ProChristo.

"I was standing aside, looking at the group being photographed, when a pastor from South Africa said to me, 'You must certainly be very proud. Look what the Lord has started through you and what has developed from it – this number of missionaries, equipped and ready to go to the unreached people groups.' And I could say to him, straight from my heart, 'I'm not proud. Honestly. I'm stunned, rather than being proud. Because that daughter of us is physically disabled and ProChristo would never have been founded if it was not for that child living with disability. We would never have been in Kimberley if it was not for a disabled child. We had to move to Kimberley on advice that one of the best schools for physically disabled children was there. And really, it was the last place that I thought of because I had a good job with a top-class firm in the Western Cape Province. But because we knew our child needed to be there, Elize and I resigned and moved to Kimberley and found new jobs there.

"So, if it wasn't for Johanni, humanly speaking there was certainly not a ProChristo that I would have been part of and then I might have been retired and farming by now. Therefore, I often encouraged people that God can also use such situations in one's life to eventually bring the Gospel to literally thousands of people."

The PLAN

"Nowadays you are the executive director of *thePLAN*. How did it all start?"

Frans explained, "It started through research that I've done because I was puzzled why some congregations were making a greater difference than others? Why do some congregations seem to be actively involved in God's work, and others are mainly focused on themselves and even struggle to survive?

"So when the research was done, it was incorporated into training materials and two books and became pioneering material in South Africa regarding the missional character of the church. To summarise my conclusions – what we do is the product of what we are – *if the church rediscover who they truly are in Christ as his sent people, then the church spontaneously begin to live what they are*. Scripture as the non-negotiable basis for this rediscovery will generate new, enthusiastic vibrancy and the dynamics to fulfil their role."

Frans then emphasised the following: "Nowadays, I endeavour to help believers understand that *all* believers are principally meant to be in ministry – everyone is in *full-time* ministry as part of the body of Christ. To my opinion, this is the general view in the New Testament.[2]

Currently, the buzzword in Missiology is the *missional church*, and this has largely to do with our identity.

"Everything I have done around research in the past has always had one dominant goal – that the results should serve to help equip, encourage and motivate the church worldwide to LIVE as God's sent people. The traditional concept of be-

> *If the Church rediscover who they truly are in Christ as his sent people, then the Church spontaneously begin to live what they are.*

---

[2] 1 Corinthians 12:7, 18, 27; John 20:21; Ephesians 3:2; 4:1,7,12-17; 1 Peter 2:5,9; Revelation 5:9-10 etc.

lievers, that only *special people*, such as missionaries, are called and used by God, ought to change according to the Scriptures. More and more, I believe that the misconception about calling – being sent, *special* callings and the office of the believer – had an incalculable destructive and limiting influence on spreading the gospel. *All* are in full-time ministry."

"And now, this material is widely and successfully being used by many congregations," we added.

"Yes, in South Africa alone we've already facilitated courses and workshops at more than 150 congregations and the book was published in English and Afrikaans. With the first edition, the publisher initially wasn't interested, saying that missions are seen as a very unpopular subject. But then I said, 'That's precisely the whole point!' Afterwards, a version for India has also been released."

Then we confirmed, "Indeed, many theologians have noted that your research has 'practical feet' and does not gather dust somewhere on a library shelf."

When asked how many people are in his team at *thePLAN*, Frans replied, "Again, I want to say that it wasn't my idea to have another team or organisation after ProChristo. My idea was just to share the research material with congregations so that hopefully they could benefit from it. But again, the Lord added people who said they were led by God – theologians and pastors from different denominations, and the material was accredited at some seminaries for continued theological studies.

"Together, we wrote a Bible study guide, *Nine Weeks of Transformation*, also used by final year theological students at the University of the Free State and adapted for use in other African countries. In India, there are networks among more than 2 350 church leaders in five of the provinces in South India, who are using it. Our co-worker there is also establishing initiatives in Indonesia, Singapore, Malaysia and Thailand and another co-worker is using the material with church leaders in Nepal. We are blessed to see how people's lives are changed and how congregations are changing as a result."

The essence of experiencing God

"What gives you the most satisfaction in your ministry?" we asked.

Frans answered: "I don't philosophise anymore and any further than that the essence of my life is hidden in God and his plan and purpose with the world, and therefore also with my life. For me it is to see how God works in spite of me; to see the impossible becoming possible, repeatedly, in spite of our limitations and how the Lord is doing it his way.

"Many times Elize and I discussed the past years in ministry with our children (all three adults now), also asking them whether they would have preferred us to stay in the corporate world with all the security and money. Then all three of my children have always said that they would not have exchanged it for anything in the world, because they saw and experienced things they know their friends have never experienced in their lives. They've seen God at work in a way that other people only read about. We've experienced God's plan for us as priceless."

"What about your dreams and anticipations for the future?" we asked.

"Through all these years," he said, "I'm dreaming that the church, God's people, will begin to understand something of God's great restoration plan, culminating in Revelation 21. And I've seen so many times when Christians start to discover something of 'the big picture', it makes them excited and they will say, 'You helped me to connect the dots.' That's my dream – that the church as *Church*, and therefore also individual believers, will start to discover and understand their unique role within God's plan, and fulfil it. Because when the church discovers what it's meant to be, and starts to live accordingly, then we will see things happening what we've been praying for."

"It isn't our job to create the purposes of the church but to discover them."

Rick Warren

"Frans, we're talking about all these wonderful things, but what makes you unhappy – the issues you get discouraged about?" we asked.

He replied, "Discord, and vision spoilers – when people find it difficult to live and work in unity and to think and dream about tomorrow. Many times I have found people who somehow tried to steal or nullify my vision, saying to me, 'This, what you dream about, will never come true.' Unfortunately, it seems that most people in the world cannot see tomorrow today. They rather see yesterday today."

Frans expounded, "The church needs to be a *contrasting community* within our sick society. We cannot remain looking like the rest of the world, because then we have nothing left to show the world. We need to give the world a better alternative than what they are experiencing and struggling with. So, the *transforming patterns* of the church should result in outcomes which lead to transformation in communities, societies, towns, cities, countries and the world. And the challenge for the church today is to develop and display a lifestyle which reflects these missional patterns."

"Yes, the church is not a spiritual culture club to enjoy an entertaining and comforting time," we mentioned and we all mutually agreed. To this regard, Patrick Johnstone also said the following:

> Our reference point is not territorial or church growth aggrandisement, but building a kingdom that is not of this world, yet which will fill the earth as a contrasting alternative society... The twenty-first century may be the time when the alternative Church becomes recognized as the real Church... Christendom is doomed, but the future of biblical Christianity is bright.[3]

Calling does not retire

In conclusion, we asked, "What kept you going all the time and how do you see the road ahead?"

He answered with a few statements:

"Firstly, *the Lord*. Otherwise, I would have quit long ago. Secondly, and very important to me, is *my calling*. Because in times when I struggled as well as experienced people wanting to ruin my vision, and even doubt, I had to recollect my calling, every time – that I know I'm doing what I have to do because God called me. Also, *prayers* and other *people with constructive conversations* kept me going.

"So, about the road ahead – for me, getting older, an important perspective that one should stick with remains that *my calling does not retire*. In spite of circumstances (as in my case where I'm probably losing my sight), it means that God will give me opportunities to adjust, for example, to write even though I cannot see well. I can talk, even if I cannot see. I have to adjust in doing research, but the point is – my calling does not change.

[3] Patrick Johnstone, *The Church is Bigger than You Think.* Christian Focus Publications/WEC, Ross-shire, Great Britain, 1998, 263.

"Through the exposure and experience I had during the past few years, I've developed new and different perspectives and insights. There are also several new discussions and progresses globally developing in Missiology and our understanding of mission. I want to develop a broader perspective of how different churches consider themselves as God's sent people – and how their perceptions (*orthodoxy*) influence their being church in the world (*orthopraxy*). From this, I should be able to draw certain conclusions that may help us as the church in general.

"So, my calling does not retire and I have to motivate myself to it, because my diary for the year to come has few open spaces."

Website: http://theplan-dieplan.webs.com

Chapter 6

Called to serve on a ship became springboard for 'leader development'

Your personal purpose is your calling
- the reason you were created.
In the context of leadership, ...your individual purpose
in relationship to your influence on other people
must include serving their best interests
or it becomes manipulation and exploitation,
the absolute opposite of leading like Jesus.

- Ken Blanchard & Phil Hodges

After nearly 40 years of service through the mission organisation, Operation Mobilisation (OM) – mostly as part of the leadership

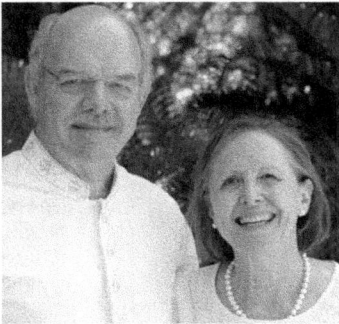

Francois & Karen Vosloo

– Francois Vosloo, together with his wife Karen, are now seconded to focus on 'leader development' with World Lead, an organisation started by a congregation in Boca Raton, Florida (USA). When asked about his current role and title, he replied, "I have no title – the congregation calls me *the missionary.*"

But the beginning of Francois' story with missions started when he took the first step in obedience to the Lord's calling upon him.

He explained: "All understanding I had of missions was to become a pastor. So I started my theological studies at the University of Pretoria, South Africa – that was the context in the church in which I grew up," he explained. "During those days, I was part of a group of students who visited the mission, KwaSisaBantu, where revival started in the KwaZulu-Natal province. This had a tremendous impact on my life, when I experienced somewhat of an *Isaiah moment*, confronted with the exaltation of the Lord, saying, 'Woe to me! ...Here am I. Send me!' (Isaiah 6:1-8).

"By reading about historical revivals, three outstanding concepts regarding all of them are always interesting to me, namely, *God's holiness, unconditional obedience* and *a focus on the nations* – and these also impacted my life, so that on arriving back home I prayed, 'Lord, here am I. Please also send me.'"

The calling and struggling

"After much prayer about where to, amongst other things, I felt the Lord's calling to serve Him on a ship. My reply was, 'Lord, I want to obey and there is no alternative, but sailors are difficult people and I really don't know how I will cope with them.' A few months later I received a prayer letter from OM, saying that they consider buying a second ship, the MV Doulos, and that they needed carpenters for alterations to transform it into a *ship for missions*.

"In our family, we had a furniture factory where I used to work during the summer holidays to pay for my university studies. So, when I discussed the possibility to serve on the Doulos with my parents, they were not very excited about it and said, 'You just want to follow your nose and see the world!' Mindful of the Word saying that we should respect and submit to our parents, I then said to the Lord that if it is his will that I should go, the Lord must also say it to my father and mother, because I would not like to go without their blessing.

"Then three things happened that made it very difficult for me every time I was confronted with God.

"The first was about not finishing my studies.

"I said to the Lord that I would like to finish my studies because that's what He called me for. Then I experienced the Lord asking, 'One day, if you have to give an account of your life, will I ask you how many years you have studied, how many degrees you have, or will I ask you if you obeyed when I called you?' Knowing the obvious, I then said, 'But Lord, please also speak to my parents, because I can discuss it with You, but it doesn't make much sense to them when *I* talk to them about it.'

"Then a second thing happened. My family asked if I would like to take ownership of the furniture factory.

"Wow! I was initially so excited because I thought I could earn much money to give to missions. Again, the Lord asked the same kind of question: 'Would I one day ask how much furniture you made, or if you obeyed when I called you?'

"Therefore, I just realised, *this* is what it is about. *It's about the Kingdom, and it's about the Lord.* I then had to go back to my family and say I do not experience this is what the Lord has in mind for me – God wants me to go.

"Then they sold the furniture factory and bought a farm. I grew up on a farm and I loved the farm – and then they told me it's my farm and I can stay and manage it. Wow! I was excited about it!

"But I'll never forget – one day, as I went for a walk on the farm, and being somewhat away from the house, the Lord, for the third time, asked the same question: 'Francois, would I one day ask you how many sheep and cattle you fattened, or did you obey when I called you?'

"Just there I burst into tears and cried like a child. I walked home and just realised I will have to go.

"And again I said to the Lord, 'Lord, here I am, send me. I have said it to You, but You must please talk to Pappa and Mamma about the matter.' And one morning very early, my mother came to me while I was in the room spending time with the Lord and she said, 'Last night, the Lord spoke to your father and me from Acts 23 verse 9, and we realised, maybe God had spoken to you.' My parents turned 100 per cent and asked how they could make it possible for me to go.

"I then applied to Mary Wiles, who was part-time at OM and handled the applications of prospective missionaries. She confirmed that they still needed carpenters for the ship. But a month before I had to start, she informed me that they had enough carpenters and that I did not have to go anymore. I said that I already bought my plane ticket and made all the arrangements, so she said that in that case, I would have to go."

We then asked him: "You were a young man who had chosen missions as your first profession. What were your further experiences to get going?"

After some pondering, Francois responded: "It's now 40 years that I'm involved in OM and I speak now from our context during those years. The concept *missions* was then still strange in the minds of most church members; for them it had to do with people in Africa – to reach *them* with the gospel. One would go to one of their *homelands* or one of the countries where there is a mission of the Dutch Reformed Church – that was our concept of missions, and world evangelism was also a strange concept.

"One's experience was that there was very little understanding from the church and the people around you regarding world evangelisation. At that time, when I asked my congregation to send me, I felt they were not willing. I had to go to another church where the minister had a vision for the nations so that they could send me. It was very sad to me, but it was the reality of the day and I blame nobody for it. The most precious of this is that two years later, my parents became involved with OM and they continued working in South Africa."

Hold on and press on

"Francois, what adjustments did you have to make to do what the Lord asked of you?" we asked.

He replied, "I was 23 when I became involved with missions and I remember that at times it was very lonely on the ship. After about a year I just got fed-up of everything: I did not like the food, I did not like the people, or the leaders – everything was just negative. Then I went to the leaders and said to them, 'Thank you, it was great to work with you, but I think it's time to go back to South Africa.'

"But we had a brilliant leader. He then said, 'Do you know, you've always told us so much how the Lord led you to come to the mission, wouldn't you just get your journal and show me how the Lord has led you to return to South Africa?' Well, of course, there was nothing about it and I realised I had heard correctly that the Lord wanted me there and I just had to press on and get on with the calling God had given me."

God preparing me for the task

"God used your earlier experience in carpentry. Was there something else God did or what happened to you, which contributed to your role?" we asked.

Francois continued: "After I had been on board the Doulos for six months, a Dutch carpenter in The Netherlands made his factory available to us to build the bookshelves needed for book exhibitions on board the ship. I was then asked to go, as the carpenter could not speak English while I spoke Afrikaans, which is very similar to Dutch, so we could communicate. I stayed with them for four months and it was a special time. Years later, when I was serving in Africa, he and his wife sent a container with equipment to Mozambique to support us with the work there.

"So, these are the type of things you are exposed to and the Lord uses it over and over again."

"Together with this, was there also something along the road that impacted your way of thinking?" we asked.

He reflected, "Other than my initial struggle, being understood when sharing my calling with the congregation, I had been at OM for a year and a half when one of the leaders of the ships came to me and five others, telling us that he sees leadership potential in us. He asked us whether we would meet with him weekly, as he wanted us to further develop the gifts the Lord has given us. This made a big impact on my life – the fact that someone recognised the gifts the Lord has given me, and specifically spent time with me around it – *that* was very special to me."

"Francois, how long have you stayed on the ship? When did you return and what happened since then?" we asked.

He replied, "I was there little over a year when I went to The Netherlands for four months to make the bookshelves. Then I went back to the ship for a short while, and they asked if I would go to America to help with mobilisation for missions. OM would be hosting two Operation World conferences, following Patrick Johnstone's book *Operation World* – one in Richmond, Virginia and the other one in Rochester, New York.

"However, my answer was 'No' – I did not feel it was right; they had enough believers; there is plenty of God's work, so what difference could I make in America? And I had many arguments against it.

"Apart from going to America, there were two more invitations – one to the Amazon forest and the other to Vietnam, apart from the option to remain on the ship. I immediately eliminated America. But the Lord kept prompting me and said I must do the conference.

"Again, I was not very impressed with that, but obeyed. We facilitated the conference and on the last day of the conference, 40 people were standing up to say, 'Lord, here am I, send me.'

"Then the Lord tapped me on my shoulder and said, 'You see, that's why I have sent you here. You could have gone to the Amazon or Vietnam or remained on the ship, but you would have made only a single impact. I have sent you here as 40 other people will be able to do much more than you if you continued on your own.' This was a very interesting experience for me."

Francois emphasised, "It's just the whole dimension of his ways are not our ways, and obedience is to do what the Lord asks of us and not necessarily cleverness on our part about what we think may or may not work.

"I was then asked to go to Mosbach, Germany, where the ship's headquarters and also the OM German headquarters were established. The two teams worked together and they asked me to lead the team.

"Two years later, I finally had to return to South Africa to do my two years' compulsory national military service. To my delight, I was appointed to work at the Chaplain General's headquarters. General Naudé was extremely well-intentioned towards missions and authorised me to attend OM's overseas conferences – something that was unprecedented. In March of the following year, I married Karen, upon which he said to me: 'Missions is one thing, your wedding is something else – so you have to work back your honeymoon time, but not the times spend on mission conferences.'

"At that time, the people involved at OM South Africa worked on a part-time basis and when I was in my second year of military service, OM International asked whether I would lead the work in South Africa on a full-time basis. We accepted the offer and we led the work officially on a full-time basis and it grew under the Lord's blessings and mercy." (It is notable to mention here Francois' referring to him and Karen as a team, in using "we" or "us".)

'Home-schooling' development of leaders

"Later, when we started in Africa, I realised that the main bottleneck we will experience in our work on this continent will be to develop leaders.

"We then invited ten young people in whom we have seen a lot of potential in terms of leadership, to come and live with us for three months in our home while our two sons slept on mattresses with us in our room. Karen and I just decided to be very open and transparent with the young people.

"It was very significant when we evaluated the impact over time (one month, then six months and a year later), that during this period we have learned more than they did.

"After a month, they said that the *community living* was great, rubbing shoulders, giving input into each other's lives, by people who came to teach and train them in leadership principles. Though, the further we continued – a year later – they made an eye-opening comment, saying *the things that meant the most to them, were our mistakes*.

"This was a revelation to me, because being embarrassed about it, we are so inclined to hide our mistakes and not talk about it, and yet that's what the Lord used most in their lives to form them throughout the whole process. We just decided we would tell them about all the mistakes we have made in our leadership and our walk with the Lord, and I realised I have to walk a lot more in brokenness.

"Interestingly," Francois continued, "Karen and I were recently invited to a university in America where we had the privilege of attending a weeklong segment of a doctoral course for Leadership Development, and we enjoyed it a lot. We realised again that the Lord looks at the one who is broken of heart and has reverence for his Word – to be broken and lead in brokenness. Even in leadership, *the Lord never invited us to come and lead; Jesus always invited us to follow*. If you are too big to follow, you are too small to lead. In leadership it is about following Jesus – it's his world, his plan. Don't try to figure out everything on your own – follow Christ Jesus and then get all the other people to follow you throughout the process."

> "True success in servant leadership depends on how clearly the values are defined, ordered, and lived by the leader."
>
> Ken Blanchard & Phil Hodges

Short-term outreaches and results

"Would you like to share something that stood out during the time you've served in South Africa?" we asked.

He replied, "A special development in our ministry occurred at that time because of the war in Mozambique, which resulted in more than two million refugees in South Africa.

"It presented a huge opportunity for the church to engage in short-term outreaches to them. In the past we told the church, 'Give us your people, we will send them abroad.' *That* concept of missions wasn't very popular, but when we brought it closer to them – that people could be sent out in the short term and get the exposure and experience – they said, 'Wow, that's what we want to do with our lives! The Lord speaks to us; we would like to get involved in a long-term basis.'"

Francois continued, "Statistics show that 80 to 90 per cent of people involved in missions received their calling when the Lord spoke to them while being involved in a short-term outreach. We started 11 congregations among the Mozambican refugees. But I think the concept of getting missions closer before taking it further, brought forth much of fruit."

Being noteworthy that OM showed remarkable growth in their expansion throughout Africa during the 1990's, we asked Francois about that.

He expounded, "So when Mozambique *opened up* after the war, we appointed leaders to start the work there. Then followed Zimbabwe, Namibia, and Angola, and because of this, from 1994 onwards, I was asked to become the Africa coordinator for OM.

"Initially, those were the countries where OM worked in Africa, and in 2009 we merged with ProChristo Global Missions and the countries where they already had missionaries were added. With the combined staff complement, the work then expanded to Chad, Zambia, Malawi, Madagascar, Tanzania and the Lake Tanganyika area, as well as Ghana. When we passed the baton in August 2016 – after 22 years – OM Africa had 700 missionaries working in 14 countries in Africa."

> *Statistics show that 80 to 90 per cent of people involved in missions got their calling when the Lord spoke to them while being involved in a short-term outreach.*

Lessons learned

Any kind of development and growth of such extent meets its challenges, and so we mentioned to Francois, "Surely, throughout all the development and expansion, you most probably encountered many teething troubles and other obstacles as well, and learned many lessons through this."

He responded, "The second thing that happened when we started training missionaries in South Africa, was that we had a large return of missionaries who did not complete their terms and we found that the reason was threefold:

- They did not have enough prayer support – the church sent them and forgot about them.
- Their finances became depleted.
- They went with a lot of personal 'baggage' – as they did not work through their spiritual and emotional issues before they entered the mission field.

"Then we required that prospective missionaries have to go through a six-month compulsory training before leaving for the mission field. The workers that were then sent out were well prepared, sorted out, and because of South Africa's diverse cultural composition they could get along with other people, as we grew up cross-culturally – something that made a huge impression on other teams internationally. So much so, that in 2017 OM celebrated 30 years of training of missionaries in South Africa with more than 3 000 trained and sent.

"There is another aspect to the work that wouldn't be possible without so many people praying for us! One elderly lady, for example, wrote to me saying she is writing down all her prayers since her mind was wandering too much. She would then from time to time send me pages of her prayers. It was wonderful that we were merely the hands and feet God used to answer her prayers.

"It was the same with donors and friends who lifted our hands as Aaron and Hur did for Moses. Without their encouragement and generosity, we would not have been able to see God at work in such remarkable ways. Our Board members also played a major role. I will never forget when we were growing so fast, one of them warned me, saying that you can grow yourself to death. That was a new concept to me and I asked him to journey with us to make sure we don't do that! We are a team and we need the body to work together!"

Other roles

Serving for 40 years as a leader means that in such a period you most probably will have to fulfil several roles.

In 2001, the Doulos ship was scheduled to visit ports of Africa and OM International asked Francois and Karen to be directors of the ship for two years, since having the Africa coordinator on board could be valuable for the work in this continent. This caused Francois, Karen and their two sons to serve in this capacity on board the ship for, in Francois' words, "a very special time to live with 350 people from 50 different nationalities, through which we also learned much."

He continued, "In 2003, when the founder and international leader, George Verwer handed over the baton, a new international director was appointed and the leader of India and us were asked to become the two Associate International Directors. We served as such until 2013. In August 2016, we handed over the baton to the new leadership in Africa."

Guidelines, principles and values

"Francois, looking back at your time with OM, what guidelines did you follow and on which principles and values did you build the work?" we asked.

He replied, "Firstly, *Jesus* – it's about God and his kingdom. *Prayer* plays a very important role for us – many days have been spent in prayer and fasting, seeking the Lord's guidance and honouring God, paying tribute to who God is and what God means to us. The relationship with the Lord remains a top, top priority.

"Secondly, *to spend time to choose the right leaders to work with you and to work as a team*. From the beginning, it was very important to me – it is not about Karen or me, but about the Lord, and about a group of people who have to lead. We drove to Lusikisiki to invite Christopher and Jeanne Agenbach to work with us, and to Polokwane to invite Marius and Christine Genis. They were some of the people whom we had the privilege to work with.

"Another aspect that has always been extremely important to me is to *invest in the next generation*. The church is just one generation away from extinction, and we now have the privilege to work with two or three generations. You have to invest in the next and the next generations," he emphasised again.

"Leader development is another very important aspect," he continued. "A year before we have completed our responsibility in Africa, we took five weeks off, just to become quiet and to ask, 'Lord, what is the next step?' and to listen. Once again, God confirmed it so clearly in our hearts – developing leaders for the way forward.

"Essentially, it is basic discipleship – nothing fancy – it is discipleship or 'leader development'. It is not 'leader*ship* development', because that focuses on skills. Leader development emphasises *character, spiritual formation* and *skills* that are necessary to be able to lead. Those three components have always been extremely important in leader development.

"Together with that, from the earliest days, we believed in *strong relationships to see the work succeed* – strong relationships and accountability with the Board, strong relationships with the local church and strong relationships with the business world.

"Also, *a vision for the kingdom of God*. People join you, full of the vision the Lord has given you, and they must be able to associate with you regarding the vision. Our vision for Africa was to see 350 of the most unreached people groups in a process of transformation."[1]

The millennials

Nowadays we often hear people say that it seems impossible for the youth to become involved in missions on the same basis as we did. So we asked Francois about his experience with the younger generations and their participation in missions. His response came with much insight and wisdom:

"Successive generations being different should not deter you – we just have to adapt. It's just like different cultures that one has to get used to, but you should not be put off by it. I'm positive, excited and hopeful for the next generation – there is a passion and zeal for missions among them. They do it differently, so let us make the playing field equal for them to do it differently. I say again, I am very excited about the next generation.

"The generation that came after us has been a much bigger challenge for me to co-operate with. But the biggest blame is on our generation who clung to things and was much more authoritarian. There were all sorts of characteristics of our generation that were not very positive, but the new generation, the millennials – wow, what an amazing generation! Yes, there is complexity, just like our generation who was, and still is, very complex. If we can see ourselves through their eyes, you will get a new perspective. Many very fantastic young people are willing to lay down their lives for the Lord Jesus."

---

[1] In Christianity, an "unreached people group" refers to an ethnic group without an indigenous, self-propagating Christian church movement. Any ethnic or ethnolinguistic nation without enough Christians to evangelize the rest of the nation is an "unreached people group". https://en.wikipedia.org/wiki/Unreached_people_group Also compare: https://joshuaproject.net/help/definitions

"Do you find eagerness with them to seek authenticity and value and make a difference?" we asked.

Francois answered, "They would like to spend their lives purposefully, and if you include the other components you just mentioned, that's exactly who they are. They also want to do it in community – in community with other people, in a team. Where our generation was much more individualistic, they would like to do it in community with others. These are precious values that you also get in Scripture – and let us help them, let us come alongside them to be successful."

Not statistics, but community transformation

"Francois, looking back, what impact and difference do you see as outstanding?" we asked.

He replied, "I've mentioned some statistics, but I am not very numbers-focused in the ministry. I learned a serious lesson from David who counted the people and was punished by the Lord (2 Samuel 24; 1 Chronicles 21), and I just realised one isn't there to count the people – just do what God has called you to do.

"Probably one of the greatest encouragements for me was when we had finished our previous role and asked God about it and the Lord said, 'You did what I asked you to do – in other words, you are done now and you have to get out of the way so that other people can take it further.'

"One of the major mistakes I have made at the beginning was a short-sighted focus on church planting. I can take you to a few very beautiful *monuments* we have built, but where there is currently nothing going on, absolutely zero. The big difference is, we did not focus on *community transformation* – we focused on church planting.

"The new model works just so much better. Yes, there is no transformation without Christ – you get people to love Jesus and follow Him, but then you also should facilitate in

> *"During the reformation of the church, the reformers wanted to make the Word of God accessible to every believer. We now live in a time when God's leaders recognize that we must make the work of God accessible to every believer."*
>
> George Miley

various other areas of development (health, education, small businesses, agriculture, social justice, to get out of child slavery, pre-school training, etc.) You have to start training a whole new generation, and how else do you do it than to start with the children?

"Since this has become our focus, we have seen communities change altogether and then the neighbouring community also wants what they see. You no longer need a missionary from the outside to accomplish it; that community goes to another community and offers the same process there. This transformation model takes between three and five years to bring about such a change in a community."

Thinking back

"Francois, when you are alone and become quiet and think about this, what does it mean to you today?" we asked.

He pondered a few seconds and responded with sombreness in his voice:

"You know, I experience that the church is at a very, very difficult place. This is a great generalisation, but there is a great deal of nominalism, and also lukewarmness in the church. And if it is there, there is also no passion for the nations – if there is no passion for the Lord, there is no passion for the nations.

"A third dimension is that we then have no place for God through his Word, and we begin to believe in all sorts of other nonsense. I so much like the New Living Translation of Colossians 2 verse 8, saying, 'Don't let anyone capture you with empty philosophies and high-sounding nonsense that come from human thinking and from the spiritual powers of this world, rather than from Christ.' It makes me very, very sad when I'm observing it because you realise there is so much of it – we are busy rationalising everything very beautifully and then excuse ourselves so easily."

"What makes you excited about the ministry and which of the experiences gave you the greatest satisfaction?" we asked, and immediately he replied:

"What makes me very excited is the new generation – their passion and devotion and the privilege we have to train leaders – to see the transformation in their lives, and the desire to be trained as leaders. I think we come from a generation where we did not have much discipleship, nor had mentors. This new generation wants to have mentors and to be discipled, and for us to walk this road with them. This makes me very excited."

Talking with enthusiasm about them, and a little joy in his voice, he continued, "What also excites me is that you can do it from a neutral level without having a title or a position. You just do it from a non-leadership position as one of them.

"The Lord blessed Karen and me with two very precious sons, Francois and Philip. God always included them on the way He walked with us, and in the process we learned so much from them!

"We learned about his Fatherhood – when Francois Jr. was born, we loved him with our whole heart. When Philip was born, we wondered how would there be enough love in our hearts for him too. We then realised that we could also love him with our whole heart. Thus, we could understand a little bit of God's heart – to love us all with his whole heart.

"We learned about God's provision – to trust Jesus for all our needs, and to see how he provided in the same phenomenal way for their studies. They could study without any debt, as the Lord provided every year in extraordinary ways – transportation (a car for each), accommodation (as the Lord gave us a beautiful house), and the list just goes on and on!

"The church is just one generation away from extinction! They are the next generation and we take lots of courage and hope!"

The next season

On that note, we asked Francois, "What would you still like to see happening through ministry?"

He answered, "Our passion and focus is on the unreached to hear the gospel – there are still around 6 000 people groups who have never heard the gospel of Jesus Christ, and I would very much love them to hear the gospel and to help prepare leaders to go and do it. *That* makes us very, very excited."

"Lastly, what is next?" we asked.

He replied, "We are currently developing leaders and we experience it to be the next season in our lives. It lies on many different levels – Karen and I also have a great passion to train leaders in the congregations, because many people received a gift to lead, but when they go for leadership development, the focus is usually mainly on developing their skills and not on character and spiritual formation.

"We strongly feel that these three aspects together – *leadership, character* and *spiritual formation* – are very important so that they can make a much bigger impact in the world. We do not want them to leave their professions as teachers, doctors or wherever they are involved, but we only want to equip them much better to make a greater impact and difference for the Lord Jesus Christ in the various areas of life where the Lord has placed them."

Hearing this reminds us of what Ken Blanchard and Phil Hodges said:

> The fruit of great servant leadership is realised when a leader seeks to send the next generation of leaders to meet the challenges of their season with all the wisdom, knowledge, and spiritual resources he or she can provide.[2]

Francois concluded, "So, we are working on that, to improve it even more."

Website: www.om.org; www.worldlead.net

---

[2] Ken Blanchard & Phil Hodges, *Lead Like Jesus.* Nashville, Tennessee, Thomas Nelson, 2008, 111.

Chapter 7

From a military background to training pastors and missionaries

When you influence a leader,
you influence all who look to him
or her for leadership.

- John Maxwell

Shai Mulder 'retired' as inspector-general of the South African Army in 1995 and was then seconded to Armscor (Armaments Cooperation of South Africa) for the last three years of service. During this time, his wife Elreza retired as a lecturer at the College of Education for Further Training at the University of South Africa (CEFT-UNISA).

Shai & Elreza Mulder

Ministry blood, however, was flowing in their veins since their youth. After Shai's conversion as a teenager, his father tried to convince him to become a pastor, although he knew it wasn't his calling and believed God wanted him to become a soldier.

Elreza grew up in a parsonage with soul-winning parents, passionate for missions and praying for missionaries while involving their children. They frequently accommodated visiting missionaries, even from elsewhere in Africa and overseas, when they shared about their work at the congregation. No wonder she eventually had a brother as a missionary and a sister as a pastor's wife.

Listening to how they shifted from his military background to training pastors and missionaries to serve in various African countries, one soon realises that since their youth a strong focus on ministry and missions became interwoven in their hearts and minds, like a golden thread through their course of life. God was continually preparing them to take the step towards Back to the Bible Mission (BBM) at Barberton, South Africa, when it was much needed.

Praying for missionaries

After Elreza finished her studies, she realised that she wasn't called as a teacher in the mission fields, but that she should continue to cherish her great love for missions and to pray for missionaries. Through the years, she continued attending nearby congregations where visiting missionaries shared about their work. She also continued receiving their newsletters and encouraging them.

She met Shai on a boat trip organised by the church youth association during her early years of being a teacher. He was the strict army captain who then didn't know yet what a missionary was, and therefore asked her to explain. They became friends and one day he asked her, "Those missionaries whom you are praying for, may I have a list of their names? I want to join you in praying for them." He was the first man ever to ask her this question and she realised the Lord was showing her her husband to be. Even before they married, they also joined in listening to missionaries wherever they visited. Later, as a military couple, they started to host many missionaries when visiting their city.

They were blessed with four sons whom Shai asked to join in praying for the missionaries – each equipped with a file having letters and information of 'his' missionaries from various global regions. The family became known among Christian circles as *that military family praying for missionaries*, daily at six o'clock in the mornings – a tradition still followed by their grandchildren.

Elreza quotes the following poem in her book, *Praying for Missionaries:*

From Your Missionary

Because you prayed...
God touched our weary bodies with His power
And gave us strength for many a trying hour
In which we might have faltered,
Had not you,
Our intercessors, faithful been and true.

Because you prayed...
God touched our lips
With coals from altar fire,
Gave Spirit-fullness and did so inspire
That, when we spoke, sin-blinded eyes did see;
Sin's chains were broken;
Captives were made free,
...because you prayed...!

- Unknown

A prelude to missions

Over the years, Shai advanced through the ranks in the military and Elreza became lecturer at CEFT-UNISA. Responding to our question about their step from the military to the mission, Shai shared two stories portraying the *missionary blood* in their veins.

"I served as inspector-general of the army until the beginning of 1995 when I was seconded to Armscor. I then had the opportunity to market the anti-mine equipment of the South African Army, travelling globally."

Elreza added, "Every time, I gave him some Bibles to hand out."

Shai continued, "When I had to represent us at an international exhibition of arms in Malaysia, she gave me 30 Bibles. Even though I was quite busy at the exhibition, I was continuously aware of the Bibles.

"On the last night, I had to attend a dinner with all the delegates and had to take a taxi to the venue. As I got into the taxi, I saw a little cross hanging from the rear-view mirror – in that part of the world, seeing this, you know this guy is a Christian.

"So, I asked him, 'Are you a Christian?' 'Yes, I am', he responded. 'OK, you know what?' I said. 'I brought some Bibles that I wanted to give away to some of the people, and tonight is my last night in your country, but I was so busy, I just couldn't do it.' He replied, 'But is it possible that you give *me* the Bibles?' I said, 'Yes, do you want one?' He said, 'No! How many do you have?' I said, 'Thirty.'

"And then he said, 'Glory to God! You know what, Sir? We've been praying for thirty Bibles for almost a year! Is it possible that we can go back to fetch the Bibles?' 'Yes', I said.

"Back at my hotel room, as I took the Bibles, he asked, 'Would you mind if we first go to my pastor to tell him that the Lord has answered our prayer and to hand him the Bibles?' I said, 'Yes, let's go.'

"When we arrived there, he got out, found the pastor, and said, 'The Lord has answered our prayers about the Bibles!' 'Thirty Bibles?' the pastor asked. 'Yes! Here it is,' answered the driver. 'Where does it come from?' the pastor asked. 'South Africa, from this gentleman,' the driver said. The pastor asked, 'Did you bring it for *us*?' I replied, 'No, I just brought it here and happened to be in the taxi with this gentleman.'" Shai added, "So, *this* was just wonderful to me."

Then Elreza reminded him of the very high official from a Middle Eastern country (Shai was hesitant and we decided not to mention the detail).

He continued, "It happened that while I was with Armscor, this person came to South Africa and the head of the army asked me to take him on a trip through our army. As we both are paratroopers, I then took him to the parachute battalion, where we jumped together. And from there we went to other units and ended up at Sun City.

"That evening he asked me, 'General, is it possible that we can have a late supper tonight at eleven o'clock, in my room?' And when I got there at eleven o'clock, he asked me, 'May I give you a gift from my superior?' I said 'Oh yes.' Then he gave me a golden watch, inscribed, 'A gift of...'

"Then I said, 'Sir, I would also like to hand you something from my King.' He asked, 'Is Mandela a king?' I said, 'No Sir, it's from my King, who is the King of kings.' I didn't say any more and passed him a very special Bible, in English and Arabic, with a genuine leather cover. He asked, 'May I open it?' And when he opened it, he said, 'It's the first time in my life – I never had a book like this in my hands. I promise you, Sir, I will read this book.'"

Shai continued, "At the end of 1997 I finished my term at Armscor and retired from the Army, and for two years I joined one of my sons in the building industry, while Elreza was our chief marketer. But earlier, we had made a promise to the Lord that when we retire, we will become missionaries. However, as we didn't do it, we found ourselves in a situation where the Lord spoke to us in various ways."

Entering missions – with some lessons

"Then in 2000, mindful of my military background and MBA, Murray Louw of South African Action for World Evangelisation

(SAAWE) asked me to help them bring order and sort out procedures and administration in their ministry, while Elreza was involved in their prayer department. However, after two years we realised that our task had been completed. We also realised this had been our first step into missions.

"During this time, we experienced a few dramatic incidents. On one of this, we were on our way to a congregation when a kudu jumped onto our car, which then had to be written off. Both of us were admitted to a hospital with major injuries, I being unconscious for two days.

"There we had an extraordinary experience. Walking to the bathroom, I was complaining terribly to the Lord: 'Lord, I cannot believe that You let this happen to me! I'm now a missionary and am working for You, but my car is written off; we are badly injured, and look at our faces! What is Your plan? What is wrong? Are we at the wrong place? What must I do?'

"Coming back from the bathroom (quite a distance), a man was walking next to me, asking: 'Has your wife died?' I said, 'No.' He asked, 'Have you died?' I said, 'No.' He asked if I will be able to replace my car. I said, 'Yes.' He asked why am I complaining so much and whether I know how many paraplegic and quadriplegic people are lying here in hospital because of accidents, and how many widows are here? I said, 'No, I don't know.' He said, 'You are complaining too much. *Now, shut up!*' (Just like that, army style.)

> *"Hear my cry, O God;*
> *...I call as my heart*
> *grows faint;*
> *lead me to the rock*
> *that is higher*
> *than I."*
>
> *Psalm 61:1-2*

"I looked at him again, and he was gone, just gone!

"Back in the room, I told Elreza what happened and she responded that God has sent me an angel to tell me, in army style, that I have to stop complaining. That came as a shock to me and I then realised how important it is when I say something – the words of my mouth, my moaning and my objections.

"Quite a while later, I asked the Lord one day, 'Lord, please tell me, why did this happen? What is it all about?'

"Then I experienced the Lord telling me, 'I just want to bring you to the ground level in My army. In My army, I am the general, not you. You do not determine what is being done. I give you instructions.

You execute my instructions and you do not complain about it.'

"I could only say, 'Thank you, Lord. I've learned my lesson.'"

The transition to Back to the Bible Mission

Shai continued, "Back at home, while sharing with friends that we experienced our role at SAAWE was fulfilled, the phone rang. A friend, who started a Bible College in Barberton, was sick in Malawi where he started another mission. His wife called and asked if I could manage the college, just for three months. Immediately, I knew the answer."

"The move from the military to the mission circumstances must have been quite an adjustment," we said.

"We started at Back to the Bible College, beginning of 2002," Shai continued. "Circumstances were not good – meagre funding for the 30 students from four countries; electricity and telephones were already cut off. The board asked two pastors to consider it as a future calling, but none saw their way open."

Elreza added, "It was really difficult times to deal with all the new challenges and to learn how to lead by serving, because the Lord, and not you, is in charge. All of a sudden, the two of us, from two different career worlds, were now together, full-time. Fortunately, Shai makes room for my talents. He had to adapt from where he was in charge of thousands of troops to where he is now leading an average of 120 students – people from Africa. We also had to adapt to different cultures, personalities and diets.

"Together we studied a book, written by George Müller, to learn how he served in faith. We had to start on our knees. We were in a position where we had to cry out, 'Lord, please help us!' We needed financial and material support, food for the students and staff, and more. And it was significant how God led us, step by step, and provided – for example, nearby farmers and even a mine that are supporting us now for the past 16 years."

Shai added, "Since we are in missions, it was important for me to learn to accept gifts – to let go of my pride. One of the most difficult situations to adapt to was when someone handed me money, and to be able to accept it. I remember, right at the beginning, when a good friend gave me R1 000, saying, 'You are now serving the Lord. It belongs to Him. He will show you what to do with it.' To me it was difficult to adjust after doing things myself, thinking – *I* can pay."

Then they also shared how God opened a door at the Afrikaans radio programmes (RSG) of the South African Broadcasting Corporation, where they could record short programmes and later also sermons for Sundays – a way of making their work known to the public, that led to some support.

Shai and Elreza also realised their need to be better equipped for their academic role, which led to a point when he told Elreza, "We are going to study Theology." He continued, "And so we started our studies at the University of KwaZulu-Natal, at the age of 60! Eventually, and with the grace of God, we both obtained our PhD degrees at age 67. Even though it was hard work, continuing with all our responsibilities at Back to the Bible Mission (BBM) and even working through our holidays, we enjoyed it very much, as we did it together and could encourage each other."

Serving at BBM

"You receive students from various countries, some where there are very difficult circumstances – war, extreme poverty, hunger," we mentioned and then asked, "Given this background, how did you succeed in helping those who needed it, to overcome their distress?"

They expounded, "The foundations of BBM are *The Word of God, Prayer* and *Outreaches*. As part of their theological training, we also cover all the books of the Bible, *with much emphasis on the Word and how to preach it*. Every Monday evening is a high-light when about six students present sermons and are evaluated – and *this* builds them up, as they get to know the whole Bible.

"Music also plays a major role. They perform choral singing in the different languages of their countries, and with the support of a professional from the music industry, they make CDs every second year. This also adds to build their character.

"A further part of it entails that the student council exists of 12 cell group leaders. These cell groups include staff members who are there for support, but are led by the student leaders. Each group has a specific task, for example, a group for fulfilling library duties, others for the chapel, prayer group programmes, kitchen duties or attending to the security, and so forth.

"God is guiding us through all of this. One day, during our quiet time, we experienced God saying to us, 'Involve your students in praying for the missionaries whom you are praying for. Give each student two or three missionaries to pray for.' So, until today they are also praying for the missionaries.

"Their character and leadership formation as future pastors and missionaries are also developed during outreaches – in the nearby surroundings and their own countries during holidays, as well as on their knees, praying daily for the missionaries."

Then we said, "The people whom you are training are going to be pastors. What is your heart's desire – what should be their spiritual fruit?"

Shai replied, "It is our dream and heart's desire that when we send them out, they will lead disciplined lives and serve the Lord, at all cost. We pray and guide them that when they are back home, they will fit into a congregation and will know their place as junior pastor, and that they will not try to impress the people with a paper on the wall, but that their way of life and their preaching will really be like Jesus Christ for the people." Elreza added, "That they continue to pray for missionaries and teach their congregations to send missionaries and pray for missionaries. Many of them even visit the missionaries for whom they pray."

> "Absolutely nothing is more critical to the completion of God's purpose on earth than the formation of the inner person before God."
>
> George Miley

Not a career, but a calling

"When the two of you are back home in the evening and you talk about the work, what does it mean to you, being in the ministry?" we asked.

Shai responded, "For me, it is now a calling, not a career. I had my career in the army, but what I am doing now is a calling for which God has prepared me. Before, I was working with young people, teaching them repeatedly, many times without seeing the wanted results. But I simply had to carry on doing it. At a stage when I got tired to reprimand the students about their discipline, the

> "Endure hardship as discipline; God is treating you as his children. For what children are not disciplined by their father? If you are not disciplined – and everyone undergoes discipline – then you are not legitimate, not true sons and daughters at all."
>
> Hebrews 12:7-8

85

Lord reminded me, 'How many hours have you talked to your sons about their discipline?' And I thought – many times, thousands of times! Then I experienced God saying to me, 'These are now *My* children and you are responsible for them. In the same way, you've persevered with your four sons, you now have to do with these students – simply carry on. Don't become tired of it.' And since I have started obeying God, I have inner joy and I am at ease, just *doing* it! I am doing it, knowing everything I do is for the Lord, and I enjoy doing it at BBM.

"So, when I go to bed at night, I go to sleep with a good conscience, knowing that what I did, I did for the Lord, to the best of my ability, knowing that there are still many things that must be improved.

"What is wonderful to me, is when the alumni let me know, 'Baba (African word for father), thank you for the discipline – to be on time, and taking responsibility to clean up the campus. Thank you, I will never forget it.' Or when they quote something that I've taught them, for example, 'Train hard, fight easy – if you are very well trained, it will be easy out there.'"

Elreza added, "We receive mail from them and they keep contact with us, many times referring to what we've taught them – 'Your walk with God is more important than your work for God.'"

She continued, "Being at BBM is the fulfilment of my life – in music, song, prayer – correspondence and prayer for more than 300 missionaries, prayers of other people across the world who tell us, 'We are now praying for *you*.' *That* is extremely important to us – also the sacrificial kindness of the people – people who carry you like an Aaron and Hur, upholding you. We also appreciate communicating with the alumni, and our interaction with the community around us. I believe the people of God inspire you to persevere.

"The cross of Calvary urges us on – every time when you think life is too burdensome, God reminds us to persevere (also with the five-metre white cross identifying BBM from the main road). Inside the chapel is a painting of the crucifixion with the following inscription: 'This is what I've done for you. What do you do for *Me*?' These words teach us to focus on what Jesus Christ did for us."

Then she leaned over to Shai and continued, "I thank God for my life-partner – my husband Shai – and that we can pray and work together – *that* keeps me going." (And Shai nodded with a smile, "Uhm.")

The way forward

"What does the future hold?" we asked.

Shai replied: "The fact that both of us are now 75 years old, doesn't mean that we have to retire. I've said, 'I want to die in my boots working for the Lord.' The Lord himself will provide the right people at the right time. Success without a successor isn't success. We must make sure that the baton is passed on and that it is done correctly.

"As we see it now, we would also love to broaden and expand our outreach terrain wherever God calls us. We believe the Lord showed us to focus on the alumni and to support them where they are serving now – to encourage them, give refresher courses, further training in leadership, and to uplift them. In doing so, we should also collaborate in partnerships and establish networking. We have already talked to a few leaders of other organisations.

"On our BBM emblem, we have these words: 'Fix your eyes on Jesus!' (Hebrews 12:2) – We believe that the best is yet to be!"

Website: www.bbmission.org

Chapter 8

Government minister called to be an advocate for children

If you want a sense of mission to burn brightly in you,
spend some time feeding your divine discontent...
Allow your emotions to become deeply engaged,
and carry with you that fire that things must change.

- John Ortberg

When we met Shiferaw Michael, memories returned to what the son of the founder of an international mission organisation shared with us on servant leadership during devotions at a conference: "At the end of my father's ministry, his desire was to serve again as an *ordinary* missionary at a mission station," he said, continuing, "Some people thought he was out of his mind, saying, 'Where have you ever seen a bank manager finishing his career as a clerk?' My father's response was, 'But I'm not working for a bank.'"

Shiferaw Michael

Shiferaw's life in public service of the Ethiopian government covered different high-level roles, spanning three governments – of Emperor Haile Selassie's, the government of the so-called Derg (the military junta), and of the subsequent Transitional Ethiopian Government under which he served as Minister of Justice.

He obtained degrees in law from the Haile Selassie University, Addis Ababa (where he later taught in the Law Faculty), Columbia Law School, Columbia University in New York, and has a master's degree in Organisational Leadership from Eastern University in Pennsylvania.

Integrity, wisdom and sincerity, grounded in faith and prayer, are some of the outstanding characteristics shining from this man as you get to know him better. No wonder that when he realised the essence of his life's purpose was not fulfilled in his role of serving as minister in government, this led, as earlier with his decision to serve there, "to another time of fasting and prayer, wrestling with God over the issue, until finally my wife and I felt that I should resign, which I did."

A hunger from the deepest of his heart

Often, steps towards change start with an experience or exposure which creates a deep concern.

So, we asked Shiferaw, "Were there experiences in your past, which under the guidance of the Lord, gave birth to the urge to make a difference through government and other means?"

"Yes," he replied, and we could sense the felt pain and drive in Shiferaw's heart as he continued. "Africa is a continent that is so immensely blessed with natural resources. But poverty reigns. It seems ridiculous to me that Africa is poor, as far as resources are concerned, because all forces that rob the dignity and wellbeing of humanity are here: Together with poverty comes malnutrition, poor sanitation, disease, lack of proper education, including human rights violations, corruption, and more. My early years were ridden with extreme poverty and injustice enforced upon our family when people with authority simply grabbed my father's land. I have experienced poverty, and I hated it.

"Therefore, my sincere dream was that if I was given the opportunity, I would help the people and the government itself in keeping the dignity and rights of people. In the full sense of the word – to see people who understand their own purpose and opportunities as human beings, and because of this, to see the interests of others as human beings. This also included the marginalised people groups in the country. So, respecting others, the rights, the dignity, and then in the process, the equality of all Ethiopians – these were the things I put on paper as well."

God's underlying plan

However, in retrospect of his resignation from government, one would see underlying building blocks in God's plan for Shiferaw's future ministry.

After finishing his university education at the Law Faculty of the Haile Selassie University, Shiferaw was advised by his spiritual leaders to join the Kale Heywet (Word of Life) Church. Kale Heywet Church (KHC) is the biggest Evangelical denomination in Ethiopia, planted by the mission organisation SIM, and in his own words, is "an excellent nursery for my faith in Christ". As a member of the KHC, he not only learned more about love but also about the church being the *Body* of Christ, where he served in much of the work of the church. This led to later opportunities in serving at the highest level of leadership of this denomination, including as the Board Chairperson.

He continued explaining his resignation from the government: "When I resigned, I didn't have any plan of what the next step for my life should or would be. For seven days I sat before God – seven days, not knowing what to do – no law firm; maybe going back to teaching, so many possibilities."

He laughed a little, "But then, as I was still in prayer and reflection – you will be amazed – the licence to act as a lawyer was sent to me from the office! You know, sometimes my tears come when I talk about this. It was just amazing, I did not have to go to the numerous institutions that needed to check different things before clearing a person to engage in legal practice – everything was already processed! So I took that as God saying to me, 'I have opened this door of legal practice for now; go into it.'

"It was immediately after my resignation from the government, that I was put in a direct leadership role in the Evangelical Churches Fellowship of Ethiopia (ECFE). Neither my denomination nor I was prepared to enter into this role. But it was as if I was ushered into the Board leadership of ECFE by *the wind* of God. I was asked to share the Word of God at the General Assembly meeting of the Fellowship, which I did. After that, the members went into electing the Board members and my name was not even suggested for election before the meeting, which was the usual way of doing things. Later on, it turned out that they included me in the newly elected Board. I served two terms as the ECFE Board chairperson.

"At that time I felt that the Fellowship needed to focus on greater things, like missions and social issues facing the society, and not only on the requests of its member denominations. But we did not have the money for such developments. We had to trust God for it – if He wanted us to do it, God would help us.

"Therefore, probably one of the most memorable and impactful actions we took on during my leadership was the work we did in partnership with Pastor Charles Blair of Calvary Temple Church of Denver Colorado.[1]

"Pastor Blair came to Ethiopia to start his own church here. He had already approached the Municipality of Addis Ababa for land for the construction of the church. I was practicing law at that time and he came to me to help him register his church and ministry in Ethiopia. As we were discussing the issue of registration of his church, I felt the moving of the Holy Spirit in my heart to the effect that I told him it was not God's will for him to start the church, but that he should work with the Fellowship. I boldly shared what I felt with him and he took a day to pray about what he heard.

"The next morning he called and told me that the Holy Spirit confirmed to him that he should not pursue the idea of building a church in Addis but instead work with the Fellowship, saying 'I want to serve what the leadership of the church of this country wants to do, without precondition.'

"Because of this, Pastor Blair entered into a partnership agreement with ECFE for the training of missionaries, and as a result, we were able to train and send 150 Ethiopian missionaries to the unreached people groups of Ethiopia. Through the ministry of these missionaries, about 600 churches were established in the country in only one year. Later on, we were able to train and deploy 27 Ethiopian missionaries to Israel and some to other Middle Eastern countries as well as some to India."

The transition to a focus on children

"From law practitioner to children's ministry – how did this change occur?" we asked.

Shiferaw explained: "At that stage, I was the founder and CEO of a vibrant and prosperous law office in Addis Ababa, when the three most senior leaders of Compassion International, accompanied by

---

[1] More about the work of Dr. Charles Blair in Ethiopia can be read in https://petrosnetwork.org/about/story/

another senior staff member of this organisation, asked me for the legal service to register the ministry in Ethiopia. I accepted the offer and studied the foundational documents of this ministry. Besides, I also recommended to them several people to be interviewed to lead the ministry of Compassion in Ethiopia.

"At the same time, my wife began reading these documents out of curiosity and fell in love with the mission and vision of the institution. Then she started praying that God may speak to me to leave my legal practice and join Compassion! When she was bold enough to share her ideas with me, she presented it to me as a prayer item. We prayed and fasted about it together and were convinced that the Lord wanted me to join the ministry.

"During those days, a panel of senior officials from Compassion started interviewing people that I recommended for the position of Country Director for the Ministry. So, eventually, I went and knocked at the door of the room in which the panel was working and told them that I also needed to be interviewed. After they prayed over my strange request, they felt that I was to be given the chance. I was interviewed – and they selected me as the director."

Hearing and understanding God's calling

Knowing Shiferaw as a person who walks closely with God in prayer, we asked him to share something about his experiences in coming to this conclusion.

With a little laughter in his voice, he said, "Let me try... You know, we are all different. Even with the advice we get from or give to one another – the mystery of being a unique person would always lead a person in very unique ways. I never found it easy to hear God and understand what God says. On several occasions, I've encountered such challenges and always in different ways than before.

"But two things are clear to me: First, there is an emotion in your heart – inside of you there is a movement, a commotion – you don't understand what it is; there is just a 'movement' inside me."

Then, distinctly, Shiferaw described how he waits and listens to the voice of God:

"When things like that happen, what I usually do is to be alone for as long as is needed for the thing in my heart to become clear to me. I even ask my wife to leave me alone. I don't even speak out words from my mouth. I see it as my inside speaking to God. I just sit and sit and sit and sit – you understand what I mean? It is like converting all the parts of my body into ears, eager to listen to God. You just sit before God as if to open every organ to his voice.

"Now, you hear God, but then, sometimes you may not even understand the words or thoughts coming to you – for example, words like those of Jesus, when he said, 'Follow *Me*.' They sound simple, but what does 'Follow Me' means? I could never immediately find the type of clarity I hungered for, in what I heard from God. It usually took me a long time before understanding what I have heard.

"And sometimes the clarifications come from a person that you did not expect – some of them don't even know me. That person might be talking about something different, but in the words they say, would come a clear message that is a direct affirmation, and you just hear – Aha, this is it! It just clicks.

"I cannot explain it, but the clarity can be through or from so many things, so many people – it is even when you walk, and you see something. Most of the time the little things I hear, the little things I see – it does not come in clear shapes, but always build one on the other. All of these would go back to what you've heard God saying. Then they put light and strength in you so that you say, 'Oh, OK!' And after that, I can tell you – inside me, I become a solid person – that is to say, I decide; I determine to follow through with what needs to happen.

"So, when my wife and I were convinced that I should join Compassion's ministry, everything unfolded and seemed to be falling into place at the same time – this ministry that has resources; this ministry that wants to help poor children; this ministry that wants to work with the church, the *Bride of Christ.*

"It was also strengthened by the way I grew up – I never knew three meals a day. In spite of living in extreme poverty, I grew up in a family of love. Love was in abundance when I grew up. My parents always shared the little we had with any visitor to our home. Our home was a place where the hungry and the thirsty came and found nourishment. The sick came and rested in our home – even mentally sick people frequented our home to eat, drink water and rest. These memories always make me see poverty as the biggest enemy against which I will invest all my energy to fight.

"So, what I read in the documents of Compassion, together with my childhood memories, stirred up my desire to give hope to children whose hopes were taken away from them by poverty."

The greatest asset of the church and Africa

At this point, we asked Shiferaw how this background influences the way he values children in today's reality.

He replied: "I see children as the greatest asset of the church, of my country and the continent of Africa; the only chance the continent has to get out of the ills that it finds itself in for centuries."

With emphasis, as from his innermost, he continued, "*I see children as the solution to all or most societal issues facing Africa.* Indeed, we need to see every child as an individual with God-given potential. We need to see them as God sees them. Every issue we face on our continent, whether it is poverty, corruption, injustice, ethnicity – everything, in my opinion, would be solved, provided we follow God's Word and God's heart in raising and nurturing children in the family and by the *Bride of Christ*. We need to nurture them as we should.

"Children could be Africa's greatest natural resource with approximately 50 per cent of Africa's population under 15 years of age. With so much potential, I think there isn't a more important area of investment in Africa than investing in our children. Because the investment will grow in the heart and mind of the child – and will cultivate a sound value system with the greatest impact *if* we do and model it right. What is sown in children, grows. The little you do for a child brings about so much change.

"Neglecting this is neglecting the most helpful and profitable resource of Africa. *And this is why I see the role of the church as critical. This is in the hands of the church!* Therefore, there is this burning eagerness inside me to share this with the leadership of the church: to focus on building the family first, and then, its direct ministry to, for, with and through children.

"So, for me, these are the driving forces of my life. If I don't help my country – if I don't help Africa on this, I am not helping my country and I am not helping Africa at all. If there is to be change in Africa, this huge young population has to be encouraged, inspired and challenged to say no to the sad realities of the continent."

> *I see children as the greatest asset of the Church, of my country and the continent of Africa.*
> *There isn't a more important area of investment in Africa than investing in our children.*

No ambiguities

"You faced a demanding calling and circumstantial challenges to adjust your lifestyle, needing wisdom in exactly how to lead the ministry in Ethiopia," we mentioned.

Shiferaw responded: "During our prayers about me joining Compassion International, the Lord shared his heart with me how He wanted the ministry to operate in Ethiopia. There were no ambiguities about *what* God wanted me to do and *how* He wanted me to do what was needed to be done.

"One of the key ideas the Lord revealed to me was to *'start children's work in the hearts of church leaders and not in church compounds.'*

"I had to spend many days in prayer – alone, and with my wife and our prayer team members – to decipher this phrase. It became clear to me that God doesn't want children's ministry to start in good looking church compounds, in nice facilities, only. But the most important thing was that the church leadership should understand what children's ministry means – *that they understand God's heart for children's ministry*. This was confirmed to me by a verse in the book of Amos: *'Do two walk together unless they have agreed to do so?'* (Amos 3:3). Later on, it turned out to be what is now known in the whole of the Compassion family all over the globe as a 'vision casting' process.

"First, my immediate supervisor did not like what I have shared with him, because the consequence of accepting it would mean changing the way they had been doing things for 37 years in many countries. A little while later, during my orientation in Kampala, Uganda, I had the opportunity to meet and pray with the second-highest person in the leadership of Compassion International. This person asked me about the church and children's ministry in my country. He also asked me, 'Shiferaw, did God tell you anything how He wants you to run children's ministry in your country?'

"When this question came from this senior person, who did not know anything about the struggle I had with my immediate supervisor regarding children's ministry projects, I was very sure God was behind what I heard him saying. Then this man took out of his pocket a small tape recorder and recorded everything I said. So, this idea entered into the ears of the senior leadership of Compassion International who loved and embraced the initiative. The response was: 'Shiferaw, we will follow what you've said.'"

A new way of doing ministry

Hence the first-ever "vision casting" workshop for Compassion's ministry was conducted in 1994 in Debre Zeit, Ethiopia, and a new way of doing ministry started, which quickly became the modus operandi for Compassion globally. This enabled the ministry of Compassion to grow very fast and in about three and a half years of operation, Compassion Ethiopia became the second largest country office for Compassion Worldwide, surpassing countries that were in operation for over 20 years.

Shiferaw was also instrumental to share the profound importance and necessity of giving greater emphasis to children's ministry with the leadership of ECFE in 1997 – if the church was to survive and thrive during this era of global change.

About 700 church leaders from all over the country gathered for the first time in their history to have a meeting on God's heart for children, the Biblical mandate of the church for children, the state of children and the threats to their wellbeing in the country of Ethiopia. God touched the hearts of the leaders, causing a turning point in the history of their church when they started to see children, started to mind the children and include them in ministry. "It was a great breakthrough on children's ministry and a real turning point in our country," said Shiferaw.

Start children's work in the hearts of church leaders and not in church compounds.

After this successful development, he was then sent to start a new country office for Compassion in Tanzania, which became another pacesetter for the work of Compassion International country offices in many ways. Later on, he was appointed Compassion's Africa Director for child advocacy, which opened up the whole of Africa and even further abroad for him – by God's grace, a humble servant, willing to step down from a senior position in government to a greater calling in God's kingdom.

Shiferaw concluded, "Therefore, one of Lord did in my life is Him leading me to the ministry of Compassion International. Although this meant a significant reduction of income to my family, I got great internal satisfaction and fulfilment be-

"Make my life count for something more than comfort and worldly success – something God-exalting and eternal."

John Piper

cause of saying yes to God's voice and will. I was able to serve God in something that was the hunger from the deepest of my heart and I could not have been in a better place. *I found the rare and unique opportunity of working with God's two most powerful instruments to transform the world, namely, the Bride of Christ and children.* It made me experience maximum fulfilment and meaning of service, and life in and through this ministry."

However, there was yet again a further step in faith and obedience to be taken.

Unacceptable matter flows deeper and wider

Five years after founding Compassion International in Ethiopia, the Lord started to speak to him about *"something that I was not able to understand and describe clearly at the beginning."* He expounded further in a way that many of us can identify with and learn from:

"There were times that I felt as if God literally deserted me – as if a dark cloud of doubt moved into my soul, which made me even doubt whether or not I truly heard God regarding the vision – times of loneliness, lack of encouragement, lack of the means to execute the vision, misunderstandings by people that I looked up to for support and help, the government bureaucracy. There were many sleepless nights, days of confusion, desert walks... I had to spend long hours before God, not in prayer as I knew it before, but just sitting and waiting for God to come and clear the cloud in my mind about what He was saying or trying to say to me.

"I found myself returning to my mind when I just sat before God with my confusion and doubt. When I say *sitting* before God, I literally mean sitting, most of the time saying nothing and at times only uttering words of complaint to God. I think my *stomach* or my inside did the talking and perhaps it communicated better to God than my lips. There were times when sheer perseverance, anger against my doubts, the determination to go and finish the task I started, were the things that helped me out of my doubts.

"With time the picture of what God wanted me to do, started to take shape in my mind. But I quickly discovered that getting clarity of vision was no solution for me. The matter which God made clear was totally 'unacceptable' to me. It was too big and needed so much money which I could not dream of getting. It also seemed that it would take a long time for me to establish, which I thought might take longer than the balance of my life on earth.

"I thought the proper handling of the vision needed a younger and a more intelligent and wealthier person to spear it. I had none of these qualities. Besides, we have a son who needed to be cared for because of his mental illness. I also felt that I had started many new ministries and even where I handled already existing ones, like in the Ethiopian Kale Heywet Church and the Evangelical Churches Fellowship of Ethiopia, the overhauling done during my leadership was enormous and needed lots of hard work and prayers.

"Therefore, I said to God and myself, I needed to slow down, spend more time with my family and focus on teaching and writing and enjoying retirement.

"These arguments seemed not to matter to God. They were probably irrelevant information to Him. In a way, He was and is right – because each of the reasons focused on me and not on Him.

"He continued to work on me unceasingly. As time went by, I discovered that everything belonged to God, including sleep and peace of mind, which seemed to me He took away from me for a prolonged time until this issue between Him and me was settled. God filled the whole time and the whole space – ultimately there was no hiding place for me from God, no escape from God. Truly, heaven is his throne and the earth his footstool. He fills every space and time!

"I had to say *yes* to Him to have my peace, and in 2005 the sometimes exciting, sometimes confusing and sometimes doubtful journey establishing the Child Development Training and Research Center (CDTRC) with God began.

"The CDTRC is a child-focused, faith-based institution and as such strives to create a new generation – modelled after the life of Jesus Christ, equipped to be agents of transformation, helping to create a healthy, developed and peaceful Ethiopia and Africa, doing it within families, the church, community and government.

"Its dual mission is to transform and equip the hearts and minds of people working directly with or on behalf of children and to influence leaders in both church and society so that the nurture, development and role of children are given greater priority in Ethiopia and other African countries.

"In so-doing, CDTRC offers training to children's workers (also those serving in orphanages), Sunday school teachers, teachers and child advocates and works in partnership with *all Ethiopian churches*, schools, and other child-focused organisations, such as Petra Institute of South Africa, Compassion International Ethiopia, World Vision Ethiopia, International and Global Transformation Network, OAK Foundation, Global Children's Forum, Logosdor, Sports Friends Ethiopia and many others."

Since its establishment, CDTRC led workshops to create awareness for over 5 000 church leaders, civic and faith-based organisations and governmental agencies; conducted hundreds of training programmes for teachers and child advocates; trained more than 200 children workers at diploma level and gave short term training to nearly 10 000 children workers. This caused more church denominations to start many more children's Sunday school classes in thousands of their congregations, as well as for the construction of child-friendly classrooms to be built in many churches. They also produced books, resource materials and DVDs on the significance and potential of children for Ethiopia and for promoting social justice and positive social and political change. Also, many parents started to understand their roles concerning children.

After seeing this institution growing as a significant ministry, Shiferaw had to take another step in faith when he handed over the leadership of CDTRC at their 2016 conference, themed *Succession in Leadership*.

But God intended him for more. As part of leadership teams, Shiferaw could share in the grace of God by starting and shaping four other big worldwide movements regarding children in the last two decades – Viva Network for Children at Risk, the 4/14 Window Movement, the Child Theology Movement and the Global Children's Forum.

"What are you doing nowadays and what more is to come?" we asked.

Shiferaw replied, "I plan to write several books, about eight of them, for which I already have outlines prepared. So, my priority desire is to write. I also want to be mentoring young people, including the CDTRC staff. I want to spend more time with my wife and our mentally ill son. Spending longer time with God and reading are also on my radar for my last days on earth."

We can conclude in the words and a quote from Scripture that Shiferaw himself used in a public address on his life's journey to a SIM History Conference in 2013:[2]

"I am glad I am a Christian! Glory to God in the highest!"

> *"You make known to me the path of life;*
> *in your presence there is fullness of joy;*
> *at your right hand are pleasures forevermore."*
> *Psalm 16:11[3]*

Facebook: https://www.facebook.com/cdtrcethiopia/

---

[2] Shiferaw Michael, *The Touch that Became the Riverbanks of My Life*, Prepared for presentation at SIM History Conference, Addis Ababa, Ethiopia, 9-13 July 2013. Apart from our interview, this document and other personal notes supplied by Shiferaw served for the storyline.
[3] The Holy Bible, English Standard Version. ESV® Text Edition: 2016. Copyright © 2001 by Crossway Bibles, a publishing ministry of Good News Publishers.

Chapter 9

Towards a new post-atheist Albania

So many of our dreams at first seem impossible,
then they seem improbable,
and then, when we summon the will,
they soon become inevitable.

- Christopher Reeve

Gesina Blaauw-Secka was born in Amsterdam in The Netherlands, but is living and working in Albania as a missionary ever since the doors of Albania *opened* in 1991 – a dream for her and many other believers that came true. (Albania used to be the only self-declared atheist country in the world.)

We met Gesina in 2003, a pastor with a huge vision, in her own words: *"My vision has always been that Albania will become a missionary sending country."*

Currently, Gesina is president of God Loves Albania Ministries International and Stichting Henoch Zendingsprojecten.

Gesina Blaauw-Secka

The foundation of her remarkable and specialised ministry in Albania originated from her childhood years, because of her physical disabilities and difficult experiences she had. We asked Gesina to tell us about her childhood and how the way she grew up affected her life.

"When I grew up, I had a very hard time as a child, especially as a teenager – *the hardest for me was that I grew up without my father*. Besides, our family suffers from a hereditary disease where the joints are not formed properly through a lack of cartilage, especially in the hip joints. It also affected me and when I was six and a half

101

years old I underwent surgery, and for almost four years I spent time in hospital or a rehabilitation centre."

Then she explained its impact on her life:

"If they didn't intervene, I would have had serious problems later in life. I had surgery on my hips, knees and back during that four-year period. Several decades later, I had more advanced surgery, hip replacements, a correction of the shape of my legs above the knees and surgery on one knee that was affected by arthritis. As I became older, I developed problems when walking too long distances, or standing still.

"I am also shorter than normal, which to me has not been a problem, but other people make it a problem when pointing at me or ridiculing me. It only meant adapting some things to make them functional and more comfortable for me. In fact, my mother and grandfather were my role models as my mother was even smaller than me and had bigger physical problems. In spite of this, she was a social worker and had been a teacher during the war in Indonesia. My grandfather had the same problems but he was a bank director in Amsterdam! I therefore never limited myself in my mind.

"However, not knowing my father and being hospitalised for so long, influenced my whole life. I became a very bitter person, not because I felt unhappy in hospital, but because of what I saw around me – especially the many children suffering from a disease that disabled them and eventually led to their death. Nobody dared to show any feelings, so they all covered up their emotions by using bad language and being very rough. All of us got that attitude – we were no longer able to show any hurt."

Pulled out of the deep

"So how did you come out of this?" we asked.

Gesina responded, "There was no spiritual counselling, no emotional help. During all the time in hospital, only three or four times someone came to tell us Bible stories, but that made an impact on my life! So, when I was 14 and had a real crisis in my life, the story of the Good Shepherd came back to me during a stage when I was full of hatred and was about to give up on the idea that there was a good God. I did not know about salvation – all I heard was the story of the Good Shepherd. I wanted to change, but tried in my own strength and without being redeemed.

"It was indeed the Lord's wisdom to enable me at the age of 18 to spend one year in the USA, away from my language and in another culture. There, for the first time in my life, I met people who said that they believed in the Bible as the Word of God and that their lives were changed by the Lord Jesus. I felt the message was foolish. To me, it was just plain nonsense, but I could see Jesus in these people and I could see a reality which created a desire in me.

"After attending church many times and listening to the message (because I was obliged to go with them), the message one day penetrated my spirit and I surrendered to the Lord. It was wonderful – as if the Lord was standing there with open arms, saying, 'Who are you to refuse my love if I have given myself for you?'

"From that moment on God's peace and joy and purpose filled my life and it was bigger than anything I could ever expect and I kept thinking, 'Why did nobody tell me before?' I did not know any born-again person in the whole of Europe and I did not know of a Bible school in Europe, but I *did* know that the Lord has called me, and as He called me He would also show me the way."

She paused, and then continued with sincerity in her voice, "God became my Father. *That* was very important. I still remember the very first time I prayed to Him and using the word *Father*. It was something very emotional for me. It made a big, big, big difference because I had been looking for my earthly father – therefore I even made a trip to Sicily. But from the moment I met the Lord, He filled that emptiness and instead of looking for my father, I decided to share forgiveness with him. Very graciously, the Lord allowed me to do that later on through a letter. We never met. Just before he died, he received my letter and I heard many, many years later that it made a great impact on him."

The call to missions – a detour

"So when did the call to missions come, and why did you choose Albania?" we asked. And what then followed was like a pilgrimage unfolding.

Gesina continued: "It was almost immediately after my conversion. At that time, I kept thinking of Sicily and kept seeing the people in front of me whom I had met there during the search for my father earlier that year. The fear in their eyes and the oppression I could sense became a burden to me. Was God calling me to go there, I wondered."

Light-heartedly, she said, "But at that stage I had only read 18 chapters of Matthew. So I thought the Lord was making a big mistake to call me as a missionary. I said to the Lord, 'Perhaps social work?' It became a real battle inside me."

Then, more seriously, the story unfolded. "I understood that if what I was experiencing came from the Lord, and He was calling me, I had to obey and go – but if it was not Him, and just my feelings because of personal circumstances, then I could never be effective.

"My thoughts went around in a gruelling circle for weeks or months, until David Wilkerson prayed with me. He asked the Lord for a miraculous answer. The answer didn't come at that moment, but what did happen was that I felt perfect peace, for I knew He would answer. That peace of mind was necessary. My mind no longer went around and around with the same thoughts: 'If it's You, I must go; if it's me, it's nonsense!'

"About three weeks later during a prayer meeting, the Lord touched me and gave me a vision, and convinced me that it was Him calling me and his grace was sufficient. None of my excuses could stand before Him. *That little bit of Matthew's Gospel I knew, and which had changed me, was enough to change the lives of others as well.* I could share what I had received from Him – a new life in Jesus! And I said, 'OK Lord, I will say yes, but You have to fill it in as I have no idea how to ever realise this.'"

"If your knowledge of Jesus Christ is more than your obedience, be careful of hypocrisy."

Nati Stander

With confidence, she said: "God gave me perfect peace, but also such a certainty of his calling that I never worried any more how it was going to happen, and quite soon after that, somebody gave me some books – one was of Brother Andrew (God's Smuggler), and the other was of Corrie ten Boom. Through *God's Smuggler*, I found my way to the WEC Missionary Training College in Scotland from 1972 to 1974, and from there to Sicily.

"While living in Sicily, I became involved with people of Open Doors. Indeed, Open Doors Italy was started from our bookshop ministry that I started in the capital, Palermo, and they wanted me to visit communist countries.

"But I knew that there was the challenge of Albania being an atheistic country at that time. Any form of religion was prohibited and it was supposed to be closed. I also knew that many people there would understand Italian, as I by that time could speak Italian. It was the only place I desired to go to. So, I decided to go but did not know how and thought it would be a one-time visit.

"One evening I had to take books from our bookshop to a meeting on the other side of Sicily. To my surprise, the main speaker was showing slides of Albania. He was the first person I ever met who had been there. As we spoke, he told me about a communist group who organised a trip to Albania once a year. He gave the address of their agency and through them I was able to make my first trip to Albania in 1981, only for five days.

"But the Lord just touched my heart so much – for example, they took us to a kindergarten and primary schools where we saw little children who were given wooden rifles to play with during playtime – and the songs they were taught were songs like 'Uncle Enver, (the name of their dictator), he is our star, he saved us.' All the things we learned about Jesus, they taught the children about their dictator! This broke my heart and I started to pray for the children of Albania that they would hear the Gospel.

"On my third visit a young man I talked to, said, 'My grandparents are true Christians, but when they die, there will be nobody anymore who can tell me about God.' *I knew when he was speaking, that he was representing a whole generation and when his grandparents died, there would be no more testimony about God* – and it touched me very deeply. I also knew at the same time God was not going to allow that to happen. He will always leave a witness. For me, that was the start to speak more openly about Albania and to proclaim that God was going to open up the country soon."

Blacklisted – and a network of praying people

Gesina then mentioned how the Lord built up his network of praying people, how He brought them together and how they would encourage each other in what He had shown them.

One visit became eight visits until 1987 when she was blacklisted. But those visits helped her much to gain insight into the hearts and minds of the country and its people. Despite the setback, she believed that God would one day involve her in rebuilding the country.

For four more difficult years, she had to hold on in faith, keeping on preparing for some time in the future to live and work in Albania and continued to study the language and culture of the people.

At this point, Gesina's story reminded us of something in Patrick Johnstone's book, *The Church is Bigger than You Think*, that reveals more of God's earlier strategy concerning Albania:

> We need the simplicity and faith of children in our warfare against the strongholds of Satan. My late wife, Jill, was long burdened to write a book to help children pray for the world. Its title, *You Can Change the World*, came about in a beautiful way and illustrates this principle. When Jill began to write the book in 1990, she described Albania which was then a Communist hermit state proudly claiming to be the first truly atheist country in the world where all religious expression was illegal. At our mission headquarters in England there was a group of praying children who interceded for each country or people as Jill completed the chapter. These children took on their hearts the need of the children of Albania where the Gospel was banned and where there were no known believers. They prayed for religious freedom to come to that land. A few months later the Communist government fell, and freedom for worship and witness came. Jill had to re-write the chapter... their prayers were joined with others praying earnestly for the Gospel to have free entry to that needy land!... we know now there is scarcely a town in that land which does not have a group of witnessing believers.[1]

Gesina continued: "But during those years the Lord worked out his plan. As part of this, He also brought key people from Albania on my way – delegations of scientists, writers, diplomats and more. He did the impossible!

"In 1989 the refugees started to escape Albania on ships. Through the network we had by then, it was possible to provide thousands of Gospels in modern Albanian to the refugees in the various camps in Italy.

"During this time, I contacted a refugee in the USA who left Albania earlier and whom I had befriended. We nicknamed him Jonah, to cover his real name. He assisted us in correcting the Albanian New Testament. I told him that if his family was amongst the refugees on the ships, they could live in my home in Sicily until they would be reunited with him. He thought that would be impossible, but some days later, they were there! His baby boy,

---

[1] Patrick Johnstone, *The Church is Bigger than You Think*. Christian Focus Publications/WEC, Ross-shire, Great Britain, 1998, 274.

Steephy, was only 5 months old when he escaped, so Jonah didn't know his son, who was now five years old, was disabled. Steephy was the first Albanian child with a disability who I have met. His sister Romina immediately asked me if she looked like her father. I phoned him – and what joy to see them speak to each other!"

The new beginning – the *go-between person*

We asked Gesina about the time when Albania opened up and how she became involved with disabled people, and she told us the following:

"In 1991 God opened the door for me to go back and put me in a key position, totally reversing the situation. He took me from the blacklist and made me the go-between person to link the government with the incoming missionaries and organisations.

"During the first week of July, we were allowed to openly proclaim the gospel in the Stadium of Tirana. The stadium director asked us to put banners throughout the town to announce the event. To break their mind-set that God had forsaken them because they had turned their backs to God, the Lord put on my heart to get everybody's attention through proclaiming *Zoti e do Shqiperine!*, meaning *God loves Albania*!

"Also, the opportunity was created to serve the people holistically – equipping them with the message of salvation and God's Word, providing in their direct needs, helping them with skills development and restoring infrastructure. So, when we distributed relief supplies, the people spontaneously started to call us 'the people of God Loves Albania'.

"But in the beginning, when Albania opened up, the country was bankrupt and we needed to provide almost anything for everybody. There was such a dire shortage of food and clothes. We came to villages where for 25 years they received nothing – the people wore just patched-up clothes. The need was so big, you had to give to everybody otherwise they would fight. And because of the war in Yugoslavia, transport of relief supplies from the North West of Europe became very expensive. They had to take the ferry crossing from Italy. So, gradually we received fewer relief supplies and we needed to focus on smaller groups."

An adjustment in focus

"In 1995 God Loves Albania Ministries (GLAM), which started as a society, changed its status in becoming a foundation. Through prayer as well as experience, we knew the people with disabilities were marginalised and poorer than the rest. So we decided to focus our relief efforts mainly on them and their families.

"But then we realised we did not see any disabled people, we only saw their relatives. When asked, they said they did not have wheelchairs. So, the next step was doing advocacy in getting wheelchairs into the country.

"As we started giving the wheelchairs to disabled people, we realised that they were illiterate. Because there were no wheelchairs to go to school, and neither a suitable infrastructure with special toilets and so on, the disabled adults and children did not have the opportunity to attend school. This was made even more impossible with the roads that were so bad, while some places had no roads at all. Furthermore, there was also the cultural factor that they were considered mentally disabled because they had a physical disability!

"I then realised how many useful insights I had gained from my childhood years in the hospital. As I had seen so many children with disabilities being rehabilitated, I knew what could be done for them by creating adaptations and by stimulating them to do things they had not thought to be possible before.

"So I started creating awareness of the huge need as well as for a rehab and educational centre for people with disabilities. When a teenage girl who was paralysed from the shoulders down asked me to teach her to write with her mouth, like she had seen Joni Eareckson Tada do on a video we showed (already in the Albanian language), this became the start of our school and rehab centre. This is also how we started to train children and young people to integrate into the Albanian society."

Decades later

It is now nearly three decades later and GLAM's programme of activities increased significantly. They serve the Albanian people holistically with a wide range of therapeutic services, educational courses, spiritual counselling, children's ministry, and summer camps for people with disability and supporting some homeless people, encouraging the people both spiritually as well as materially. There have been moments of working in the background and other moments on the forefront.

We asked Gesina to recall some of the differences their work brought about. She responded with joy:

"Praise the Lord for these years of freedom for the Gospel – from no church to over 30 000 born again believers, and from no pastors to an Evangelical Alliance with mainly Albanian pastors now. There are Albanian missionaries abroad and also Albanian Christian NGO's coming into being!"

"So your dream became reality. Do you have some stories?" we asked.

Gesina continued with excitement in her voice, "One day when we were busy with a wheelchair distribution, an Italian nun came to me and said 'Please come with me. We have a desperate family and I see the love of God here. Please come.'

"So we immediately went along to this family. There was this paralysed girl to whom I referred earlier. Three years earlier, at age 14, she was sitting at her grandparents' home, when a stray bullet went through the window and hit her in her neck, paralysing her from the shoulders down (at that time there was a lot of shooting in Albania). Since then, Suela, who was one of the 10 best students in the country, was just lying in bed – there was no rehabilitation facilities, no wheelchair, no further education and for her and her family it became a time of total despair.

"The first thing we did was to get her a wheelchair so she could get out of bed and at least be around the house and maybe in the surrounding areas. Furthermore, the movie of Joni Eareckson was life-transforming for this family – in the beginning not spiritually, they only saw the practical things, the adaptations and integration, which they never saw before. They watched it many times and some days later, Suela called me and asked, 'Can you please help me to use my mouth to learn to write just like I saw Joni doing?'

"I told her I would give her an answer in a few days' time. So I tried it out myself with a pen or pencil in my mouth. I realised it was not that difficult and all we needed to do was to encourage her and to adapt certain things, such as giving her a higher table. We also involved a few other teenagers and had three sessions a week – which was the beginning of our school. The other teenagers had never been to school, whereas Suela had been to school until she was paralysed.

"We started teaching her English as well and it was wonderful to see how it improved. Additionally, we taught her to use a computer with a pen in her mouth and later with a headstick to press the keyboard. With her English that has improved, someone gave us a voice-activated computer programme. From then on, she could use her computer to write whatever she wanted and later enrolled with Oxford University, studying law through the Internet. This was a girl with no more hope who could prepare herself to be a good partner in society, and she is just one example."

A community's change of mind-set

"Another example is the story of two young people who became a couple through our ministry.

"The young man, Klodi, just had his driver's license and his mother had given him an old vehicle so he could make a living, but quite soon he had an accident that left him paralysed from the waist down. He was very depressed when he came to our centre, very melancholic. We invited him to our first camp, but it took him quite a long time to find the Lord. A while later, a young lady, Majlinda, who had fallen from a tree and was partly paralysed, was taken up in the centre. The two of them fell in love and they became the first couple with disability in Albania that got married!

"It was so special for Albania that it became an item of advocacy – we did not do it on purpose, it just happened. They invited the prime minister to the wedding which took place in our centre. The prime minister and his wife attended the whole ceremony as well as all the newspapers and television stations. We made the front page of the newspapers and it became the token in every shop – all over Albania people were talking about it!

"All at once they realised that people with a disability were just like them, with normal feelings and can also get married. This has done a lot in changing the mind-set of people who once thought that persons with a disability should be put away somewhere. Klodi and Majlinda are now elders of the local church in the village where our centre is, as well as part of our house parent team. Majlinda is also a teacher at our school and started studying to be a social worker."

"If we are to achieve a richer culture, we must weave one in which each diverse human gift will find a fitting place."

Margaret Meade

The tent's ropes lengthened into Africa

In 2003 'the ropes of Gesina's tent' (Isaiah 54:2) were lengthened and the ministry became "God Loves Albania/Africa Ministries."

She expounded: "In 2003, our social worker and I did a three months Children's Ministry Leadership course at Petra Institute in South Africa. Participants came from many different countries. During our evening prayer times, I always brought some prayer points from our centre in Albania. Two pastors from Malawi became very interested and acknowledged how they had never thought of inviting disabled children to their Scripture Union Camps. They wanted to include them in future and asked for our help.

"I shared this with Joni Eareckson, and her organisation (Joni and Friends) helped us to organise a camp in Malawi in December 2003. The two pastors, James Mandawala and Pearson Jassi, had invited 25 disabled children along with 25 other children. From our side, we came with a team of three from Albania. With me were Shqipe, a lady who lost her leg when she was a toddler, and Odeta, a girl who jumped from the third floor and broke her back.

"During this camp, we not only shared our testimonies, but also trained the workers as well as the camp children in disability ministry – what to do or to avoid, wrong language and attitudes, inclusion, accessibility, and so on. At the end of the camp period, the disabled young people asked us if we could set up something for them like in Albania. We encouraged the leadership to choose a committee and from them we formed a board to start a new Foundation. Pastor Mandawala became the leader of this new Foundation, which was called Christian Ministry with the Physically Disabled."

Future dreams

We concluded our conversation by asking her, "Gesina, what are your dreams for the future?"

"There are still many obstacles to conquer in Albania," she said. "My vision is to set up a small training campus, where we can train the disabled people, not only in life skills but also provide them with professional training in various fields, like business, journalism, handcrafts as well as in ministry to build them up and prepare them for the future. For Malawi, we desire to have our own property that can be a training centre and a campsite."

Indeed, a brave lady with a huge vision!

Facebook: https://www.facebook.com/God-Loves-Albania-Minis-tries149294635087792/

Chapter 10

Growing cattle and *growing* people

If you want one year of prosperity, grow grain;
If you want ten years of prosperity, grow trees;
If you want one hundred years of prosperity,
grow people.

- Chinese proverb

Growing cattle and *growing people* are synonymous for Willie du
Plessis, a seasoned commercial Jersey breeder from the Eastern
Cape, South Africa, who heeded God's call
for full-time ministry during 2008.

Willie is currently involved with Amadlelo Agri, an agricultural organisation where
many farmers from the Eastern Cape and
KwaZulu-Natal (KZN) provinces of South
Africa are involved in dairy farming projects
on under- or unutilised community land in
the former Transkei and KZN regions. The
projects consist of six farms where around
6 000 cows are being milked. Amadlelo

Willie du Plessis

supplies the cows and manage the projects, ensuring skills development and capacity-building to allow local community members to
manage their farmland.

Apart from agriculture, he became involved in missions with
Foundations for Farming and various other projects that flowed
from them, such as Crown Financial Ministries which are linked
with Foundations for Farming in Malawi. He is also involved with
Ebenezer College in Bulawayo, Zimbabwe as well as Turn Matabele
Land Green. The latter two projects are run by the Cunningham
family, who grew up in Zimbabwe. They have asked Willie to assist

with developing a dairy branch at the college and he moved some cows there and now visits them regularly to supply training and support. Furthermore, he is also involved with the Foundation for Cross-cultural Education (FCE) in Zambia.

When will you start working for Me?

"How did you become involved in missions? Was there any influence or impact through some friendships in your life?" we asked and Willie explained how he became more and more aware of God speaking to him; how he understood God's calling and his response to it.

"We have always been involved with the church, but around 2008, I heard God asking me, 'When will you start working for *Me*?' I gave the standard answer that I think many of us give: 'Lord, I am an elder in the church; I teach Sunday school – all the things that are being done in the community – I am involved!'

"But the voice kept coming back, 'When will you start working for *Me*?' I realised my total focus was to grow and expand our farming enterprise and my involvement with the church was done in my spare time. My whole life revolved around agriculture.

"During this time, I was exposed to the people of Foundations for Farming, in particular, Boet Pretorius who is based in Zimbabwe, but has done considerable work in South Africa. Boet lost his farm through the controversial land reform programme in Zimbabwe and became involved with Foundations for Farming.

"I began to realise we should look at life differently and that the Lord expected more of me than what I was doing at that stage.

"Boet and his wife Cecilia had a huge impact on our lives. It is inspiring to see how people who have lost everything, now have a rich life – rich in terms of their joy and quality of life. They now live with very little material things, but have enough to live with – they do not struggle. The life they live – the joy and outlook on life to serve God, has been a revelation to us. We also see this from many of the other Zimbabwean farmers with whom we are involved, as with Brian Oldreive, founder of Foundations for Farming as well as other staff members. Most of them lost everything and now serve the Lord full-time.

"Craig Deall (CEO of Foundations for Farming) once said, 'If I knew what I would have gained, I would give away what I had, to gain what I now have.'

"He used to be a very wealthy farmer, but hearing this, creates an understanding of a shift in values away from material things to spiritual things, where things operate on a different level. It is a privilege for me to experience this as we in South Africa are confronted with questions about the future and what will become of us if things go wrong. Where do you go to, what will become of you? I am now 59 – if I lose my farm tomorrow, where can I go and what employment opportunities are there for me? Then you realise that in the Kingdom there is a place for you to work and your age is of no importance."

I am not a pastor; I am a farmer and agriculturalist

"The hand of the Lord was clear in all of this, for while we were contemplating the matter, I heard that a Foundations for Farming conference would be held in Polokwane. My wife and I decided to attend.

"Understanding what they were doing, we realised this is where we belong. I do not want to become a pastor or a missionary that preach to people – I am a farmer and an agriculturalist. Foundations for Farming win souls for Christ alongside the training and guiding of people in the production of food and agriculture. So, I realised that with our background and knowledge, we can contribute here.

"A clear purpose not only defines what we do, it defines what we don't do."

Rick Warren

"After the conference, we spoke to Brian and others, and shared our desire to become involved and asked what we could do in South Africa that could assist them. They said with my background and involvement with the Jersey Breeders Society and other formal agriculture structures, I should use my ability to organise and coordinate their activities in South Africa and raise it to a formal level.

"Until then, many individuals have contacted them but they worked individually in their communities and there was no liaising or networking among them. We then prayed about it and asked them to give us time as it is easier said than done to organise something on a national level. After praying much about it, we were finally convinced this is where we belong."

Adjusting to God's plan and purpose

Henry Blackaby and Claude V. King, in their book *Experiencing God*, explains that one of the phases we go through when hearing

God's call, is to make major adjustments:

> Every time God spoke to people in the Scripture about some-
> thing He wanted to do through them, major adjustments were
> necessary. They had to adjust their lives to God. Once the
> adjustments were made, God accomplished his purposes
> through those He called ... Your obedience also will be a part
> of the action required. Your adjustments and obedience will
> be costly to you and those around you.[1]

Willie experienced this himself:

"And yet another reality struck me... I had to make other plans
with the farming as I could not farm full-time and coordinate Foundations for Farming in South Africa. I would be either an excellent
farmer and a poor coordinator, or an excellent coordinator and a
poor farmer, and this would not be to the glory of God. If we neglect
the positions we stand in, it creates a poor impression of kingdom-
work and would not serve the kingdom of God.

"I therefore reorganised the whole management team on the
farm and appointed someone to farm on a shared basis so they could
take responsibility for the day-to-day activities. I am still involved
with the administration and overall planning, but not with the day-
to-day activities since 2011.

"Since then, we were fully involved with Foundations for Farming, moving around South Africa and meeting with people Brian and
Boet previously had contact with, to get the ministry running on an
organised basis.

"Currently, we work with around 27 organisations in different
places. The model we follow is to involve churches and individual
Christians who then are responsible for the work on a local level.
We provide the training opportunities, have an annual conference,
coordinate and send newsletters out, liaise and give support for the
work of Foundations for Farming. The people on a grassroots level
work independently and conduct the work within their specific context. This model works very well, because if we are not available
for extended periods, people take ownership and the work goes on."

---

[1] Henry Blackaby & Claude V King, *Experiencing God*, Cape Town, Struik
Christian Books Ltd, 2000, 230, 231.

Breaking the shackles of poverty

The test of the work we do for God lies in the fruit it bears. We asked Willie about the effect of Foundations for Farming.

He explained: "The work is based on 1 Corinthians 3:11 – that there is no other foundation than Christ Jesus. And there are other Scriptures such as Isaiah 61 that speaks of freedom, release, healing, repairing – that is what we do.

"The shackles of poverty, hunger and misery are tremendous – throughout the world, but specifically in Africa. Africa, on the other hand, has been blessed with very fertile land, with natural resources – such a contrast. We see it as our calling to break these shackles of dependency, of people who are not able to take care of themselves. It takes away their self-respect, their dignity and creates many social problems. But it is such a satisfaction to see the joy of people when they realise that with the skills they have acquired and through their own efforts, they have been able to supply in their own needs – even though not all – and that there's a blessing on it.

"Often the community starts realising things have changed in this person's life and they start asking for guidance. *Then* is the opportunity to tell them, 'I have learnt what my responsibility towards the Lord is, was obedient and managed to start producing food. Are you interested, can I help you to do it, too?'

"When I work in Bulawayo with the young Matabeles and explain to them what the potential of a dairy cow is, their eyes shine with excitement. They drink in every bit of information and are so eager to know more. Some people believe they are nothing, not good for anything, poor and at the bottom of society – but to loosen them from this syndrome through empowerment and the Gospel – *this* is what drives us; this is what makes all the sacrifices, the effort, going through difficult times, worthwhile. Through this, they see the Kingdom, they see the freedom and release that Jesus said He would bring."

So, we asked, "Willie, the fact that you help the people understand they do not need tractors and equipment of millions to take care of themselves, brings release to them. What guidelines are you following?"

He responded, "When we start teaching someone about a garden, we start with Genesis 1 – the Lord has given you light, soil, water – the basic things you need. We are very strict not to give many things to people. We teach them that when God came to Moses, He asked him, 'What is in your hand?' When we go to a township, we do not take fancy equipment such as watering cans, with us. We show them how to use what they have – a tin lying around can become a watering can.

"When you come with your fancy equipment, people may think they cannot do the work without such things. You may hear, 'I do not have a watering can or fertilizer,' telling you what they do not have. We teach them they already have most of the things they need, and about making compost and so on. Just start, do something, be faithful and you will make a difference.

"We need to change people's attitudes and value systems. If you give someone from a poor community money, but you do not lead him or her to Jesus, teaching his value system and principles as well, you commit an injustice. If you take money into a poor community and they do not have the background to use it responsibly, you sometimes cause more harm than good, because this is where social problems start.

"The basis of what we do is to help people to come into the right relationship with Jesus. Flowing from that, we help them understand that they also have to take care of the environment and the consequences of not doing so, such as global warming. If someone's relationship with God is not in the right standing, his or her relationship with the environment will also not be, and people will see it as something to be used and abused.

"We also see that you cannot give training only once. There needs to be follow-up training and you have to build up people's faith, since you have just led them to the Lord. When we work in areas where we cannot build long-term relationships, there has to be a church or someone who can continue with the relationship to *guide these trainees to spiritual maturity*. For if they are on their own, who will help and guide them when they are confronted with all sorts of temptation or other influences? In other words, this is a long-term relationship you develop with those you train. You need to have enough time with people to *build and maintain deep relationships* to steer all involved in the same direction, especially in organisations and churches we work with."

> *The basis of what we do is to help people to come into the right relationship with Jesus.*
> *Flowing from that, we help them understand that they also have to take care of the environment and the consequences of not doing so.*

"Willie, can you share an example of someone who grew through this?" we asked.

He continued: "One of the beautiful stories is that of a man by the name of Makesure, who has been trained in Zimbabwe by Boet Pretorius.

"Makesure started training other people and later became so busy with training that he did not have enough time for his own gardens. One day when Boet visited him, he said, 'I made a plan: I chose 12 disciples, I am training them and each of them has to train other people.' Makesure and his group of trainers are currently training around 800 to 1 000 people a year in the rural parts of Zimbabwe."

We asked what other principles they use.

"On a management level, it is pertinent for us that everything we do, is done to the letter – administration, finances, control – everything is being done on a very high level of professionalism. The trustees working with me are people with much experience. We *make sure all control measures are in place* – not to be legalistic, but to *be accountable* for what has been entrusted to us. I think this is of utmost importance in the Kingdom – if we fail on this level, it is a very bad reflection on the kingdom of God and not to his honour."

Your heart will be where your treasure is

"Willie, people in general are striving to be successful in what they do, but when you look beyond success – how do you see meaningfulness or significance in your own life and those of others?" we asked.

He replied, "Our relationship with the Lord has deepened since we became involved with Foundations for Farming. The Zimbab-wean farmers that are involved have all gone through very hard times and many have lost everything they had. Yet, they have found richness in the Lord. Matthew 6:19-21 says, 'Stop storing up trea-sures for yourselves on earth, where moths and rust destroy and thieves break in and steal. Instead, store up treasures for yourselves in heaven, where moths and rust don't destroy and thieves don't break in and steal. Your heart will be where your treasure is.' We learned what really matters – storing up riches in heaven. In contrast, I see other farmers and businessmen – people who do not believe – who are embittered by their circumstances, whose marriages fell apart because of this.

"We recently spoke to our children about the work we do, and it made such an impression on them that they start to look differently at life. We live in a very materialistic world and those who do not see this biblical truth find it very hard to keep up with a worsening economy. They live in fear of what will happen tomorrow and what will happen to what they own and to their savings. We have been very privileged to experience the opposite.

> *Those who do not see this biblical truth find it very hard to keep up with a worsening economy and they live in fear of what will happen tomorrow and what will happen to what they own.*

"Something else that is very special is the hunger these rural people have for learning – they cannot get enough and keep asking questions. It's a privilege to link livestock and crops to the Kingdom and to see their openness – how they take in all that they learn, and to know that they come from very difficult circumstances and this is an opportunity for them to change – not only economically but as a new creature in Christ."

Subsistence farmers and poor people providing food

"Willie, what excites you; what do you dream about?" we asked.

Heartily he replied, "It is the immense potential I see in projects such as the dairy project in Matabeleland. In my mind, I see across Africa how subsistence farmers and poor people are producing food. I grew up as a commercial farmer – I still function in that sector, and there you see everything becoming bigger, such as mega farmers. *In comparison, it is surprising to see what the subsistence farmer can achieve*, and this excites me! In the world of organised agriculture, they will say that subsistence farmers cannot contribute to the production of food. That is not true! What a glorious day it will be when the subsistence farmers turn this around and commercial farmers understand the value these people can add to food production.

"With what I currently observe in Bulawayo and the rest of Zimbabwe, I am 100 per cent convinced of the potential locked up in these subsistence farmers. We must change our perspective and conduct. I am convinced that I can play a role in this: we who are in commercial farming can build a bridge between commercial and subsistence farming. We have to bridge this gap, but if you do not have experience of both, you will battle to do it."

We asked Willie what they do to get other commercial farmers involved.

He continued, "In Zimbabwe and Zambia there is to some extent good cooperation between commercial and subsistence farmers. Elsewhere, we have a few commercial farmers supporting us; however, some tend to see us as the solution to their labour problems. We cannot be that – a change of heart is needed. We have to build and maintain sound relationships with our workers – then many things will fall in place. We have to acknowledge that we have to solve the problems ourselves. Many times the biggest problem is *me*, not *my employees*!

"Looking back on my own life on the farm – I realise that I was the biggest problem, not my workers. It is your attitude, the fact that you are in control, make the decisions and have to give guidance. If you don't do it right, no one is going to succeed."

Stumbling blocks

We also asked Willie what his biggest obstacles were.

He answered, "Two things: Some people become involved for the wrong reasons – they are seeking a job and hope we will help them raise money to make a good life. They do not have the heart to serve – they have huge expectations, which in itself are not wrong, but should not be the driving force.

"Secondly, it is not easy to change people's hearts. *In raising funds, it is easier to raise money for hungry children – it touches people's hearts and they will give. But for our work, people will acknowledge the necessity of it, but not easily support it financially.* We do not have that emotional advantage on people to get the support. Perhaps when we approach it differently, we will have more success, but I have never felt comfortable to play on people's emotions..."

Do not lean on your own understanding

"The biggest lesson we've learned," he continued, "is to completely depend on the Lord. We often have made some brilliant plans and schemes, done some thorough strategic planning, but you progress a little and then the wheels come off. Then we come to a point where we have to say, 'Lord, we tried, but it does not work, what now?' Then, suddenly, the Lord opens the doors, or He helps us to look at it differently and do it in a better way. We have learned to be completely dependent on *Him* and to trust in *Him* and that we cannot do it by ourselves.

"Knowing where we come from and on *Whom* we rely – *that* has kept us going through the difficult times. Recently, we had to face a very difficult situation regarding the farm that has put us under much pressure – up to a point where we said, 'Lord, we are in your hands.' While we tried to solve it ourselves, it was very hard. Then we prayed and said, 'Lord, we give the problem to You, we cannot solve it, we do not know what to do, and we leave it in your hands.' Two, three days later, we became calm, and soon the problem was solved in a fantastic way which was much better than we would ever have done. *That* is what keeps us going – to know our help comes from the Lord."

Letting go and passing on

"Doing this work, certainly is not always easy – what do you find tough? What was dear to you that you had to let go of?" we asked.

Willie replied, "Being on the road so much is tough on your family. Secondly, my work took me away from being among the animals on the farm every day. The nicest thing in the world for me is to be among animals and work with them. I grew up with them and I can read an animal's body language like you read a person's body language. I can see from far if an animal is sick. Giving up on these things is hard for me."

"What are you doing to pass on the baton to those who have to fill your shoes one day?" we asked.

He responded: "We have not paid much attention to this in the past, but at a recent conference, we seriously discussed the matter. We want to draw in those who have not been so involved in the past – to develop a team. What helps, is that we have been working with a team of trustees since the beginning. Fortunately, this is not a one-man band, so we try to involve more people. We would like to have a big enough team, but also retain individuality where people can continue independently."

Focus on the future?

On this question, Willie concluded: "There are two issues we will be focusing on soon: one is to focus much more on developing training material for livestock farming, as there is a need for it. In South Africa, we are working towards establishing one or two permanent training centres of our own, and there are currently some interesting developments in that direction. By doing this, we will be able to equip many more people. We will continue with the current model, but would like to pursue the Zimbabwean model of having training centres where we can train many more people and guide them into becoming new beings in Christ."

Website: www.foundationsforfarming.org

Chapter 11

Obedient 'yes' of one man led to a global movement

On the far side of every risk
– even if it results in death –
the love of God triumphs.
This is the faith that frees us
to risk for the cause of God.

- John Piper

God often chooses the seemingly 'unlikely' person to do the impossible. The late Johan du Preez was such a person. As a minister of the Dutch Reformed Church (DRC) in South Africa, he became a trailblazer for children's ministry in Southern Africa.

One would envisage a person involved in children's ministry as a soft-spoken, easily approachable person. But God used someone different to put children on the forefront in mission circles, not only in South Africa and Africa but also internationally.

Johan's brother, Dr. Kruger du Preez, remembers him as a natural leader, a strong-willed person, a family man – someone with a burning passion to reach the world with the gospel of Jesus Christ and particularly the children of Africa. Johan was a passionate person, impatient with idle talk and things that did not serve the cause. His restlessness about what he believed God had placed him for on this continent drove him to think what is unthinkable and do what seems impossible to achieve.

Johan du Preez

Johan's vision for children's ministry was born during a visit with Rev. Chris Fourie to the islands east of Africa. He realised that children were largely overlooked by the church, and that very little was done to reach children who were not part of the church. *Oom* Chris (Afrikaans for Uncle Chris, as he was mostly known) encouraged Johan and his wife Aretha, to attend the training of Child Evangelism Fellowship (CEF) in Switzerland. Equipped with new insight in God's commands about children as well as skills and techniques to share God's Word with children on their level of understanding, Johan saw this as God's answer to addressing the spiritual needs of the children of Africa.

Immediately, he began dreaming of a similar institute for Africa – a dream that many shrugged off as unimportant and unattainable. In his quest to turn this vision from God into reality, Johan refused to be halted. Even the fact that he would lose his status as a minister of the DRC, did not deter him. Fortunately, the Uniting Reformed Church at Standerton called him and gave him the commission: Child Evangelism.

The birth of a movement

On 1 April 1989 – for some perhaps an April fool's joke – Johan's dream became a reality when he founded the Children's Evangelist Training Institute (CET) in Ermelo, in the Mpumalanga province of South Africa. One of the farmers in the area gave a piece of land to build the necessary facilities for the ministry, but this could not be done due to a lack of funds. A vacant South African Railway boarding house came to their attention and the application was approved... until it was discovered that 'non-whites' would also use the building. The offer was instantly cancelled, and other facilities had to be found.

A meeting with supporters was held in October 1989 to discuss various possibilities, one of which was a former hotel, Petra Mountain Inn, situated in the Mpumalanga Lowveld. The owners were contacted to arrange for a visit. "We will pray about it and let you know", they replied. In anticipation, Johan and his staff waited. A week later, they received the go-ahead. On 17 November, Johan and his wife Aretha, and staff members Laetitia Bull and Johan Snyman set off to the Lowveld to meet with Gerry and Mary Schoonbee, then owners of Petra Mountain Inn.

Johan shared his vision of reaching Africa's children with the gospel of Jesus Christ. Gerry later commented on this initial meeting: "Our first association nearly did not bear fruit – mainly because we had a vision for a ministry of reconciliation to all races and amongst all denominations in the body of Christ. And here in front of us on that Friday evening was a stern, rigid Afrikaner from one of the most right-wing areas of the country, and belonging to one of the conservative mainline Afrikaans churches. So, our first answer was 'NO! We do not believe that we have a compatible vision!'

"However, the Lord gracefully interfered in my judgements during the early hours of that Sunday morning, as He always will if we remain open to Him. Isaiah 11:3-4 says: 'He shall not judge by the sight of His eyes, neither decide by the hearing of His ears, but with righteousness and justice shall He judge.'[1]

"Jesus was not looking at Johan's appearance and circumstances, but at his heart. That morning, God revealed a glimpse of what He saw to Mary and myself – and that is how our association started – ever so small and insignificant at first, and it grew and grew as it was watered by the faithfulness of the staff whom the Lord added almost month by month."

On 7 January of the following year, the ministry moved to Petra Mountain, outside White River, and on 14 January started its first course of three months with eight students.

Johan had the gift of seeing the future as if it is the present. His vision was contagious, as his enthusiasm with which he worked to realise his dreams. He gathered several men and women around him to whom he imparted his vision. It was his pride and joy that the students and staff of CET would be able to continue his work. By faith and action, he turned his dreams into reality.

The focus of CET was to equip leaders in churches for children's ministry to the level where they could train others who could again train others. From the start, the focus was on leadership training and multiplication. And multiply it did!

But that did not impress Johan – he looked at the numbers of the unreached and was driven by the passion to reach the millions of unreached children in Africa. He realised the enormous latent

---

[1] Isaiah 11:3-4, Scripture quotations are taken from the Amplified® Bible (AMPC), Copyright © 1954, 1958, 1962, 1964, 1965, 1987 by The Lockman Foundation. Used by permission. www.Lockman.org

and untapped potential of these children. Africa, the scorn of the world, could rise beyond what the world made her to be, if only her children could be reached with the liberating Gospel of Jesus Christ. And through this, their potential could be unlocked.

Initially, most of the people trained were South African. Slowly but surely the work then started to go beyond the borders.

Johan has been involved in mission circles in South Africa, where he was a voice for God's command about children.

Pastor Willie Crew, founder and international team leader of World Mission Centre, said the following: "In a real sense, Johan was our conscience – when we as visionaries would want to run off in one direction, he would say, 'Wait a bit, what about the children?' Many times he was our conscience, and I believe, kept drawing the attention of the body of Christ to the fact that the kids are key in terms of missions."

Johan based his vision for children's ministry on Psalm 78 and other parts of Scripture, with its call to tell children about the wonderful deeds of God, so the next generations would know and pass on this knowledge to their children. He was convinced that this was the best strategy for world evangelisation and he saw the church as the instrument through which the world should be evangelised.

Murray Louw, well-known director of the South African Action for World Evangelisation, told of an occasion when, as they were planning strategy for world evangelisation, Johan stopped them in their tracks with these words, "Stop trying to be smarter than God! He has already decided to use the church to evangelise the world!"

CET as an organisation was also not to function apart from the church. He saw CET as an arm of the church, helping it to be effective in its ministry to children by training leaders from churches who had been identified and sent by their churches to attend the training courses.

Unwavering faith sorts out trouble with the bank!

John Robinson, a friend of Johan, shared the following story of his initial meeting with him:

"Reborn at aged 48, a businessman of the world and my business recently in liquidation – praise the Lord – for my walk with Jesus began! I met Johan du Preez – a man of true faith, and I experienced the need for obedience and faith. This was to be my first experience of trusting in the Lord, and little did I know then how this was to happen over the next 20 years.

"John Huisamen, a staff member of CET, phoned me mid-December 1993 in a *mild panic* about their bank account which was overdrawn by R26 000 and innocently said: 'We do not know how this could have happened – the bank has made a mistake'. Most of the staff were on leave, including the administrative lady. How could I help?

"My first visit to a Christian organisation was about to happen, and this was to lead me taking one day a week from my newly acquired business to help CET set up their administration, in me serving the Lord. The Lord has blessed me so much that it still brings tears to my eyes when I recall it.

"So, my first meeting with Johan du Preez – a true experience indeed – was imminent. After a few pleasantries, Johan said, 'Has the bank made a mistake?' and I replied: 'No! CET has overspent, innocently maybe, but no bank error.'

"After offering my services and expertise to assist in setting up proper administrative procedures in the new year, we realised a visit to the bank manager was required. Johan's face and eyes – a picture: 'What?! I sit in front of a bank manager!'

"We prayed and Johan said our problem would be resolved before the end of December, with a deposit of R28 000.

"Oh," I said, "How do you know?" He replied, "Faith."

"So off to the bank, where Johan and I sat before the bank manager and I could not believe that me, a 'finance man' was about to tell the bank manager: 'Mr. Bank Manager, the bank overdraft will be settled before the end of December without some form of guarantee.' 'Mr. Robinson, that is great. Do you have debtors or business income due at that time?' 'No Sir, we have prayed and asked the Lord in faith and trust in Him.'

"Johan was confident, with a smile on his face. I was sort of embarrassed, wanting to crawl under this man's desk. Guess what? The bank manager was happy with the arrangement but asked us to please ensure no more cheques to be issued, and in future to make arrangements with him if we wanted to overdraw on our account.

"We blessed him heartily and went our way – on 28th December the R28 000 was deposited and my walk of trust with Christ began. I praise the Lord for my small contribution and his love, for giving me the ability to have faith and trust in Him – be assured He has been picking me up as I fall all these years."

A new missions awakening begins

n 1993, the Love Southern Africa (LSA) movement started annual conferences in different cities of South Africa. This brought a new awareness of missions in the Southern African Church, and CET used this channel to focus the attention of the church on the biblical and strategic importance of children and ministry to and through them. Yearly, Johan and other CET staff facilitated training workshops at these conferences to equip people going on outreaches throughout Southern Africa, and to create awareness of children and children's ministry in the church.

In 1995, CET made a deliberate effort to market its courses to the church in Africa and more and more African church leaders attended the three-month training courses at CET.

Johan became involved in international missions conferences and in 1995, attended the Global Consultation on World Evangelisation (GCOWE) in Seoul, South Korea. Again, he urged the leaders of GCOWE to include children in their strategies and pleaded for a track focusing on children. At that stage, there was a combined track focusing on children and youth, but mainly focusing on teenagers and not children under the age of 15. As the approach to reach children differs from that of reaching teens, Johan worked hard to establish a track specifically for younger children.

During the initial planning for GCOWE 1997, the organising committee did not heed his call, but because of Johan's insistence, such a track was eventually included just three months before the consultation, and Johan had the joy and privilege of being the co-ordinator and chairman of it.

The conference, held from 30 June – 5 July 1997, saw 4 200 people from 135 countries congregate in Pretoria to discuss and strategize how to finish the *unfinished task* of the Great Commission. This truly took his ministry into the international arena. The message from this children's track went out to all of GCOWE. Mission and church leaders had to take cognisance of the biblical commands that children *should* be reached and of the enormous potential it has for the growth of the church – but beyond that, that children are already part of the church and should be utilised as part of the workforce of the church and given space to exercise their spiritual gifts.

During his final appearance at GCOWE 1997, Johan said, "Let us claim Africa for the Lord! Let us focus on the children. Not only should we bring them the message of salvation, they should also learn how to live according to biblical standards at all levels of society. I challenge you to become part of God's army for this. Let us help Africa to realise her freedom in Christ so that her children can become what God planned them to be! Let us look at the enormity and the so-called impossibility of our task in Africa in a different way – in God's way."

In a letter he wrote to delegates of the Children's Track after the consultation, he said, "We strongly believe that something very special happened during this consultation. That is not only in our own lives as people who attended the Children's Ministry Consultation, but also in the lives of many church and mission leaders. We are confident that the Lord manifested his special love for the children of the world in the spiritual realm. The GCOWE Children's Ministry Consultation is but a small symbol of the real manifestation.

"It may sound like a cliché, but I see the awakening of a worldwide interest in the needs of children, and the desire to disciple them, like a wave. I thought of myself as surfing or riding this wave. During this consultation, however, God allowed me to look over my shoulder. To my amazement, I saw a far bigger wave of the Spirit. This wave is all about releasing and utilising the children for practical ministry, intercession and missions."

In his book, *The Church is Bigger than You Think*, Patrick Johnstone mentions a few "greater challenges" the 21st century will provide as areas in which Christian ministry could and should play a major role, saying: "Looking back over the twentieth century it is astonishing to see how little ministry to children has featured as a major concern for mission agencies in recruitment, in discussion at international conferences and in deployment of resources."[2]

Referring to the eventual inclusion of a track specifically for ministry to children at GCOWE in Pretoria in 1997, as well as new attention by some organisations and individuals, he remarks: "At last the children of the world are becoming a major focus of mission. This gives greater hope for the Church of today as well as the Church of tomorrow."[3]

---

[2] Patrick Johnstone, *The Church is Bigger than You Think*. Christian Focus Publications, Ross-shire, Great Britain, and WEC International 1998, 251.

[3] Ibid., 253

Final baton to a great cloud of witnesses

A month after the GCOWE '97 conference, another Children's Ministry course was held at CET from August to October. The calibre of students attending the course was what Johan had dreamt of for so long – strong leaders from African denominations, who could influence their denominations to carry the baton forward and reach the children of their respective countries.

Every morning, Johan presented the *Christian Maturity* subject, building into the lives of these dynamic leaders. One of the students who became a full-time staff member, Rev. Enslin van Velden, commented, "I did not want to miss one of the *Christian Maturity* classes each morning. He spoke so much about your status and identity in Christ, and that you should live accordingly. Paul's letter to the Ephesians has gained much deeper meaning to me.

"On the morning of 5 September, Johan concluded this series. Dropping the chalk on the floor, he said: 'I taught you everything you wanted to learn. Now you have to trust the Lord how to carry the baton forward.' Little did I know it would not be long before his voice would be quiet forever, but his legacy lives on."

Later that morning Johan had an appointment with a business-person in Malelane, a town about 100 kilometres from White River. After completing his class with the students, he left. With him was his son, Johan. A drizzle fell during the overcast morning. Just outside White River, on a sharp bend on the Plaston road, Johan lost control of his car because of spilt diesel on the road. His car skidded and went under a heavy truck. He and his son were trapped in the car. Johan sustained serious injuries, and he passed away at around 5 pm. His son only had minor injuries of which he recovered.

The shock was immense – for his family, staff, students, friends and supporters. At his memorial service at the packed Dutch Reformed Church in White River, many local mission leaders spoke with great respect about Johan. "I want to pay tribute to one of the most outstanding leaders in the field of missions that I have known. I will remember his humility, his vision and his immovable faith. The Lord chose Johan to establish a phenomenal vision." (Dr. Frans Hancke, Executive Director, *thePLAN*.)

Dr. Johannes Malherbe took over the leadership of CET after Johan's death. In a tribute in the CET News, he wrote:

"Several people have referred to Johan as a visionary – one to whom God had given the privilege to see things hidden from the rest of us. Johan often emphasised the importance of vision. He said to his staff and the latest body of students, 'Vision, flowing from hope, creates in us the energy to do God's will.' With this, he pointed out that it all starts with hope, that irresistible, positive mind-set regarding whatever it is that faces you. It is God Himself who gives us hope for our world and, particularly, for the children of our world. This hope imparts vision – it allows you to dream and to plan. It also creates within you a divine discontent,

> "Those who preserve and arrive at an understanding of God's vision, and then devote themselves to implementing it, experience outcomes they never could have foreseen without God's vision as the heartbeat of their ministry."
>
> George Barna

which gives you the fresh energy to turn your dream into a reality. It is this energy one utilises to do the will of God. His will should not be only discussed or sought after – it should be done.

"Johan taught CET to dream about a world in which children laugh and play because they can freely enjoy all the good gifts God intended should be theirs. He also urged us to put to practical and effective use, the energy which God has created in us for this purpose.

"And now Johan du Preez is no longer with us. What will happen to CET? The answer is simple: CET will go from strength to strength.

"This is possible because CET is not the work of Johan du Preez. It is the work of God. He who has begun a good work here, will complete it. The dream, placed in our hearts by God, is beautifully expressed in Ezekiel 47:1-12 and Revelation 22:1-2. A stream of pure water runs eastward from the mountain of God and it brings life wherever it flows. On its banks are trees, which bear fruit each month and the leaves of which bring healing to the nations.

"CET headquarters have a prime position on top of Petra Mountain in the most beautiful surroundings. We dream that the Lord will, every month, produce good fruit through the ministry done from this mountain and that healing will be brought to many nations. It is our conviction that God wants children to play a very important role in this healing process."

Pastor Willie Crew, of World Mission Centre, said at the funeral the following about the future of CET:

"When I was phoned on Friday and subsequently on Saturday, the same thing came back to me: 'My son Moses is dead. Do not wear the shoes that he wore, but go and take the Promised Land.'

"I would dare to say to you this morning, I believe that word was a word from the Lord for the body of Christ around the world, but is prophetically being carried out in this nation in a very profound and almost hurtful way, and I dare to say this morning you and I need to understand that in front of us is the Promised Land. If we think we have seen results in the ministry of my brother Johan, I want to say to you this morning we are about to see much more than we ever had. And I want to say that to you as a ministry – if you think you have seen something in the past, watch what God will do in the future.

"We see in the Bible that unless a corn of wheat falls into the ground and dies, what will come of it? And I dare to say, don't think your ministry is going to go this way, but rather see in Jesus this morning that the ministry of CET is going to explode in a very positive sense."

Gerry and Mary Schoonbee, then working with Campus Crusade for Christ in Jamaica, responded to Johan's death in a letter addressed to his family and staff:

"In 1986, in July, we received a prophecy over Petra Mountain from the Book of Micah, chapter 4. Out of the many aspects of it, we felt the Lord reminded us of the second verse as we read the latest CET Newsletter, under the article 'Hitherto…' on page 5. The 750 students that have been trained and are working in 25 countries, of which 17 are part of Africa and its influence, can indeed testify to verse 2: Many nations will come and say: 'Come, let us go up to the Mountain of the LORD,… that He may teach us His ways (with children)…'[4]

"We cannot describe the thankfulness that arose out of our hearts, knowing that God has done it, not through us, but through a ministry under a leader that He chose, not even us! How exciting to thank Him for his faithfulness.

"And now… we are here in Jamaica, coping with the news that our beloved Johan has left us to be forever with the Lord, Whom he loved, and whose burden for children he so faithfully carried in his heart and his ministry. And to all of us, the writer of the book of Hebrews, Chapter 12, tells us in verses 1 and 2, 'Therefore we also,

---

[4] Micah 4:2, Amplified® Bible (AMPC), paraphrased by Gerry Schoonbee.

since we are surrounded by so great a cloud of witnesses (to Johan's love for the children of Africa), let us lay aside every weight (of any discouragement and invitation from the evil one to despair at our loss) and let us run the race (which Johan started and led us on) and that is (even now more importantly) set before us, looking unto Jesus, the author and perfecter (of Johan's) and of our faith."[5]

> "The enduring significance of our life and the legacy we leave for future generations will be achieved and enhanced by our conduct, magnified by the recognition of and obedience to God's presence."
>
> Francois van Niekerk

Johan was laid to rest on Petra Mountain on the Prayer Rock which overlooks the Peebles Valley. Fitting the mood, it was a cold grey day with rain pouring down. 'Truly, I tell all of you with certainty, unless a grain of wheat falls into the ground and dies, it remains alone. But if it dies, it produces a lot of grain' (John 12:24)[6]. True to God's promise, this grain of wheat that died, produced far more than could have been imagined!

From a kernel came a great harvest

Under the leadership of Dr. Johannes Malherbe, the organisation underwent many changes regarding the way leaders were trained from the many nations, not only from the African continent but also the Middle East, Europe and the Far East. The name was also changed to Petra Institute for Children's Ministry. In January 2005, Rev. Dirk Coetsee took over from Dr. Malherbe as Managing Director.

The Institute focuses on raising mentors in children's ministry which resulted in the establishment of large children's ministry training centres such as the Child Development Training and Research Center (CDTRC) in Ethiopia; Eye on the Child in Egypt and Children Mission in Ukraine, training mentors from various Russian speaking countries and expanding throughout Central Asia. It also expanded through the Baptist Church and Scripture Union Singapore to other regions of Asia. The Church of Pentecost in Ghana (with

---

[5] Hebrews 12:1-2, The ESV® Bible (The Holy Bible, English Standard Version®), copyright © 2001 by Crossway Bibles, a publishing ministry of Good News Publishers, paraphrased by Gerry Schoonbee.
[6] John 12:24, International Standard Version®, Copyright © 1996 – 2012 by The ISV Foundation of California

a network of congregations in more than 90 countries) has made children's ministry part of their theological studies as a result of the training they had from Petra Institute and realising the strategic value of children's ministry for the growth of the church. An ever-growing number of international training partnerships are still coming into being, taking this vision and command of God even further.

The following word from Ken Blanchard & Phil Hodges correctly sums up Johan du Preez's life:

"A truly great and enduring vision will extend beyond the leadership season of any one individual and be carried in the hearts and minds of those to whom it has been entrusted."[7]

---

[7] Ken Blanchard & Phil Hodges, *Lead Like Jesus*. Nashville, Tennessee, Thomas Nelson, 2008, 111.

Chapter 12

Farming couple find fulfilment in farming and ministry

Fulfilment is discovering our own uniqueness in Christ,
using our gifts and talents to edify others
and to glorify the Lord.

- Neil T. Anderson

Bernard Joubert is an export grape farmer from the beautiful Hex River Valley in the Western Cape Province of South Africa. One would think that Bernard, being a successful farmer and business-person, and enjoying life with his wife Chrismaré and sons, would experience fulfilment in his life. However, there was a time in their life that something was amiss.

We asked Bernard about this time and the way God changed not only him and his family's lives, but also that of thousands of adults who were trained, and children with their families who were reached with the Gospel.

Bernard & Chrismaré Joubert

"Both Chrismaré and I experienced a part of our being not fulfilled only by farming," he said. "I enjoy farming and I wanted to do it, but there was not complete fulfilment. We asked our cell group to pray with us that the Lord would show us exactly why we felt so unfulfilled.

"During this time, our congregation wanted to appoint someone who could work with Amos Agrimin (Amos), a ministry to farmers and farmworkers. I was part of the committee that appointed Rev. Deon Koegelenberg and his wife Charlotte. The committee decided they should attend the children's ministry course at Petra Institute for Children's Ministry in White River.

"Deon and I visited Amos to see how they operate. What stuck in my mind was the way the staff of Amos ministered to the farm children. We learned from them about the training Petra Institute presents. At that time Deon and Charlotte already applied and were approved to attend it, and I realised Chrismaré and I also had to go."

Chrismaré took up the story from there: "I was unaware of the existence of Petra Institute. Bernard was involved in the meetings with Amos, and I was involved in my own things. At that stage, I had a coffee shop. Both of us had the desire to have more than two children, but I realised that an additional child, as well as the coffee shop, would not work – somewhere something would go wrong!

"I was about to extend the shop and Bernard lent me money to do so. Still, I had this huge struggle in my heart – we both knew we would like to have another child, but with the shop – how could I tell Bernard I do not see my way open to run it *and* have another child!

"One Sunday evening, as we returned home from the cell group, I still wondered how to tell Bernard that I did not want to continue with the shop. Unexpectedly, he asked how I envisaged the shop in a year's time, and if I do not want to continue with it, I had to tell him as soon as possible.

"This was my opportunity to share my feelings! When I told him I would like to sell the shop, he told me, 'In that case, we are going to Petra Institute for three months.' This was the first I heard about the institute, and that we would go there for *three months*! I still remember the exact spot on our way home where he told me! We got the ball rolling to sell the shop and prepare to go to White River, and everything just fell into place."

At the beginning of August 1997, the couple and their two boys, Pieter and Richard, left the farm to attend the course. On their return home, Chrismaré was expecting their third son, Berno.

Finding a mandate

Bernard continued: "After completing the course, I went back home with a mandate and mission to coordinate training in the Western Cape. I saw it as my responsibility to coordinate it there, and we started presenting courses in the area. Staff from the institute mentored us in presenting the training up to a point where they were satisfied that we have mastered it. With our focus on a widespread region, we also trained several tutors who could present the courses – and more and more communities began asking us to equip leaders for children's ministry in their congregations.

"As a group of tutors, we decided to start a training campus for the Western Cape Province and people from the community then became involved. The old prison building was vacant as the projects they had there, ended. However, a crèche at the prison buildings continued with its work. A community forum managed the facilities and we approached them with our request. They approved, with the understanding that the crèche could continue using the part of the facilities they occupied. We accepted the offer and started to upgrade the facilities to our requirements. This was not a dream we had – it just so developed that this was the best facility, with huge potential.

"We presented the basic courses for three years as residential courses, but as many people find it hard to leave their jobs and families for an extended time to attend, the team at De Doorns took the training to them instead. The facilities still serve as staff accommodation and offices, and occasionally as a training base. But from here, many communities in the Western, Eastern and Northern Cape provinces receive training in various courses by the De Doorns team, continuing to make a huge impact on the lives of adults they train and children they minister to."

To the ends of the earth

However, the ministry expanded much further than several provinces in South Africa. We have come to know Bernard as a visionary and practical person – typical of being a farmer.

With the fall of communism in the early 1990s, many South African congregations became involved in the Commonwealth of Independent States (CIS – previously member states of the USSR). Bernard accompanied a group who went to Ukraine as part of the Ukraine Hub that endeavoured to link South African congregations to congregations in Ukraine to support them. Some of the group members also helped to present a cell church conference.

Bernard explained, "As part of this conference, we were allowed to present two sessions on children's ministry. In preparation, we

trained a Ukrainian woman, Inessa van Rooyen, staying in Fransch-
hoek (also in the Western Cape Province) in the basic course. She
then made a summary of each booklet and translated it into Russian.
She accompanied us to Ukraine and acted as an interpreter so the
correct terminology for children's ministry training could be used.

"The conference had a busy schedule, but the participants were
free for Friday afternoon. We thought some people might be interested in how to lead a child to Christ and invited them to attend
the Friday afternoon session. And 50 people turned up! As we went
to Ukraine, I was not sure if there would be a need for children's
ministry training. The turnout that Friday afternoon partly answered
that question!

"During this time in Ukraine, God gave me a 5-year plan to
establish a ministry among Ukrainians and take it to where they
could function independently.

"Back home I spoke to several groups. First, I asked the CIS
Hub if we could use their administrative channels as they had an
office in Ukraine and could provide invitation letters for our visas.
Secondly, I negotiated with Petra Institute for permission to translate
the training material into Russian and to bring people from Ukraine
for training at the institute.

"Then I spoke to Murray congregation of the Dutch Reformed
Church in De Doorns as well as the Uniting Reformed Church of
De Doorns and asked for support through prayer and finances. All
parties agreed. Thereafter I wrote to Rev. Koos van der Merwe, who
was a minister in Ukraine, saying we want to train four Ukrainians.
They had to speak English, love the Lord, love children and should
be available.

"They identified four young people and apart for one of them,
who helped with interpretation when we were in Ukraine, I met the
rest for the first time when they arrived at the airport in South Africa.

"When we arrived at Petra Institute, I spent some time with
them and asked about their dream for the children of Ukraine. All
of them had very small dreams – reaching a few children in their
church, hopefully… One of the participants, unfortunately, had to
go back for exams and missed doing the tutor-training course. After
completing the course, the other three came to De Doorns, and again
I asked them about their dreams – it was much bigger than initially!"

Mentoring for growth

Bernard explained his strategy for their development: "On their return to Ukraine, they had to do further translations of the Petra Institute material and prepare worksheets for use during training. We would conduct four 10-day courses they had to organise and get participants to attend.

"A few months later, my family and I went to Ukraine for three months, presenting these courses. The first one was mainly presented by Lyuda Bryn, trained in South Africa, and myself. We then divided the remaining three courses into three blocks and with each course, each of the three who completed training had to present a different block, so that by the time we were finished, all of them presented all parts of the course.

"The mentorship process we followed was very important. I expected that by the third course, each one of them would be able to present the subjects on their own, without any help from me. I realised that because I was in class all the time, it was easy for them to fall back on my help and guidance. So, one day I excused myself from class, without them knowing where I was going, and left them with a list of principles they had to follow to make a success of the workshop.

> "Leaders should influence others in such a way that it builds people up, encourages and edifies them so they can duplicate this attitude in others."
>
> Bob Goshen

"That afternoon I took them to McDonalds and explained my expectation that from then on they had to present all the training on their own and shared the principles with them.

"It is one of the stressors of mentorship – I was not sure they would feel up to it. The first thing I asked the interpreter the next morning was what they were talking about that evening after our meeting, and if they would be prepared to facilitate the training themselves... and fortunately, they were!

"At the fourth course, I only presented the Spiritual Formation session in the mornings and left for the rest of the day. In the evenings, they gave feedback – the next step in the mentorship process.

"During the tutor-training course that followed later, we used the same process. I again presented the Spiritual Formation session that focused more on leadership and then left. At lunch and in the evenings, they shared what they were uncertain of and I coached them on what to do.

"The important part of the process was mentoring them – sometimes when you are not available, they are forced to find solutions themselves.

"Later on, they would sometimes write an e-mail asking for guidance, but because I was busy and did not see the e-mail, they would find the solution themselves. The assurance that I was available to assist and guide, as well as the fact that I returned every year, gave them the courage to continue. Initially, we had to mentor many people, but now, our focus is on mentoring Lyuda and the leaders of the other countries as part of the ministry, *Children Mission*, we have registered."

The Lord's light to the world

When we asked Chrismaré how she experienced all of this, she responded with a smile.

"When Bernard and I got married, he told me that if I have the desire to travel abroad, I can forget about it, as he does not have any desire whatsoever to do that. He is not a tourist. Therefore, the day he asked me if I would be fine if he joins the group of pastors going to Ukraine, I was blown away!

"Without me knowing what lies ahead, the Lord worked in my spirit during the time Bernard was away, asking me if I was prepared to go to the mission field. I said it is fine, as long as the Lord does not tell me today I have to go to China tomorrow, as this is not me. So when Bernard returned after three weeks, saying we would go to Ukraine for three months the next year, the Lord indeed gave me enough time to prepare myself – He created me, He knows my nature."

"What significance does this have for you?" we asked.

She replied, "I think to trust the Lord unconditionally, knowing that He knows the long-term road ahead. Looking back to the day we married, I vowed to support Bernard in everything and all circumstances, not knowing that Ukraine would one day be part of it. However, there is nothing I regret, knowing the Lord is using us as a couple.

"When we got married, we wrote a little story that we would become one and like a candle burning closer to the candleholder – symbolising the Lord – we will be his light to the world. Perhaps we were naive, but that was our desire, not knowing the Lord would use it so powerfully! You have to trust the Lord unconditionally – even in situations that you are not comfortable with. He takes you through it and provides for every day.

"When doing the course 19 years ago, I did not know where and how I would apply it. Today I know that through the course, I discovered I have the gift to work with sick children and that the Lord used the course to equip me to connect with them as a nurse."

"So Bernard, where did the extended vision for all the Russian speaking countries come from?" we asked.

He recalled, "I guess it was in the back of our minds right from the start. During the first tutor course we presented in Ukraine, it was part of the vision that not only Ukraine but also all the Russian speaking countries would be reached. Currently, Children Mission has trained people in Ukraine, Russia, Armenia, Moldova, Georgia, and Latvia. Some networks working in the other nine countries invited Lyuda to a conference, and training also started with people from those countries. Funding the training in those countries remains a challenge, but the Lord will provide."

Spiritually prepared to take ownership

We asked the couple how they went about building the spiritual development of the students and workers, and how they then took ownership of the work.

Bernard continued, "Right from the start, we used the Spiritual Formation course – written by the late Rev. Johan du Preez – with the students and it helped them out of a place where they lacked creativity and self-confidence, to believe they can. For the first few years of my ministry, the best part was not so much about children's ministry, but to see the light going on in someone's eyes when that person realises, 'I am good enough and I *can*, and the Lord can and wants to use me!'

"It is a holistic approach. We spent sufficient time on their spiritual development. It is not enough just teaching people skills without making sure they have a good grounding in the Word of God and understand there is a calling on their lives – *and* that God is calling each individual. It wasn't by accident that they've done a course or that their pastors sent them there. Hence, we spent much time studying chapters such as Judges 6 about the calling of Gideon."

Letting go hurts

"Bernard, you have prepared the Ukrainian people for seven years to take the baton, but letting go meant giving something of yourself away," we remarked.

After pondering, he told us, "Helping people to take ownership is a complex process you have to manage through the grace of God! The process we followed with the initial four courses presented in Ukraine, was the first step for the group to take ownership, and it developed gradually through the ministry of Children Mission.

"After seven years of our involvement, I shared with the Ukrainian team that we have done our part – it was now up to them to take it further. It was a very emotional experience – for them and me. I thought handing over the reins to them would be a relief for me, but in fact, it was extremely emotional. I experienced a sense of loss for a few days.

"However, I told them it does not mean they will never see me again, as I came to love all of them – and even if they do not invite me, I would still come to visit them. Since then they successfully trained tutors and mentors, and in this way have grown the ministry. Indeed, they took ownership and ran with the baton."

Involving the local church

"It is not so simple to support people living on the other side of the globe – how did you do it and motivate them?" we asked.

Bernard responded: "When we started in a new area, it was important to spend time with the pastors of the ministry leaders, building good relationships with them. We explained what we intended doing in the area and that this includes mentoring these leaders in ministry, but they need someone who can give them spiritual guidance and care, which is the local pastor's responsibility. This support meant much for the expansion of the work.

"Once, when I mentioned the name of a specific woman to a pastor, his response was 'How can she be a 'master teacher' – she only recently accepted the Lord.' Nevertheless, he supported her, and we went back every year to visit him. Later he introduced her to the pastors fraternal of the city – one of the biggest cities in Ukraine – and *that* has gained her the trust of the pastors, opening the way for her to work in that city.

"The fact that we have good relationships with the pastors gave

142

us the freedom to visit them any time, and if there are problems, to have an open conversation.

"Therefore, we uphold this principle, because we cannot take care of the spiritual welfare of our leaders from here in South Africa. The team also continues doing this when they train tutors. At the end of the course, they invite the pastors to attend the certificate ceremony and inform them about what the tutors can accomplish with their new skills and where they will be working. The children's ministry workers are part of the local congregation, and the church is involved in the work they do."

Credibility and sustainability

Chrismaré continued, "After the fall of Communism, many people came to these countries to introduce their ministries and training programmes, and then left. The congregations listen to it and forget about it, as next week there is someone else with their 'answer' to the local people's problems. They leave and never come back again. The fact that we returned every year, and that Bernard made an effort to meet with the pastors, made an impression on the congregations. Without us knowing it, the Lord used this to bring trust among the pastors, Christian communities and the ministry."

We asked the couple how the ministry has been financed, as money often becomes an obstacle in ministry.

Bernard responded: "Funding is always a challenge. The congregations of De Doorns contribute to the income of key leaders – the rest of the people involved are volunteers. From the start, we encouraged them to raise support from the local churches, but this was a long process. However, more and more congregations are becoming involved financially. We also taught the leaders to use money wisely."

New generation of leaders raised

As the saying goes, 'the proof of the pudding is in the eating'. We asked Bernard and Chrismaré what fruit they see after all they have put into this ministry.

"What makes me extremely excited," Bernard replied, "is that among the current group of tutors in Ukraine are people in their 20's. Some of them came through the Sunday school system of the churches. The result is that many of the churches have no problem finding well-equipped Sunday school staff, as they are sourcing young people and teenagers that came through the system and they understand children's ministry. The group of leaders in Ukraine is a very healthy mix of people between 20 and 50 years of age. Within these churches, a new generation of leaders has been raised.

"Another aspect is that some people who have been trained are also involved in pre-schools, and they apply the principles of children's ministry there. The principals or other teachers see the fruit of this, and also want to be trained. Many pre-schools are not Christian schools, but their staff is trained by us and with the training, they also receive the Biblical truths. Many within the school system are becoming aware of the success of this approach, and there is a move towards using it. We will have to see how it plays out."

Bringing hope to Stofland

Bernard and Chrismaré are also involved in their community in the De Doorns area. We asked them what they were dreaming about concerning Stofland (Afrikaans for Dust Land), a township on the outskirts of De Doorns.

Both their faces lightened up and Bernard explained, "Each of us has different dreams. In some areas, development takes place as people replace the shacks with brick houses, but in the other areas, there is hardly any development. This is where Chrismaré wants to become involved to assure that these children receive the correct nutrition, medical care and inoculations up to the age of six, so they can optimally develop – physically and intellectually.

"It's a huge area and there are many other needs as well. We would like to get involved in early childhood development. The question is how do you change the DNA of our community in the next 20 years? I believe this is a 20-year project as there are no quick fixes for the dire poverty and social breakdown there.

"We dream to establish proper crèches and pre-schools, where children will receive the correct stimulation for their specific age, together with proper medical care and nutrition to prepare them to be school-ready. Chrismaré already started weighing children at various crèches, but we have to make bigger inroads in the area.

"Another aspect is guidance for pregnant women. We are involved with the government and the church in the First 1 000 Days project

"Education is the most powerful weapon that you can use to change the world."

Nelson Mandela

(a campaign to raise awareness of the crucial first 1 000 days of a child's life). In this way, we believe the DNA of our community can change in the next 20 years.

"We often speak about economic empowerment – if we want to empower the pre-school children of Stofland economically, we have to start now. If we do that, the people of Stofland can also become doctors, lawyers, and scientists within the next 20 years because the children will not enter school with a huge backlog – a backlog that can never be wiped out."

"Do you receive financial support for this?" we asked.

"From churches and local businesses, yes," said Bernard. "There is also the SmartStart project (a social franchise providing quality early learning to three- and four-year-old children) that is financially supported by the Dutch Reformed Church, working with groups of six to eight children each, giving them the correct stimulation."

One life and its influence

"Bernard, your involvement with missions takes much of your time – in what way has this involvement enriched your life as a farmer and a businessman?" we asked.

He answered, "It took some time to realise there is only one life you live – you do not live in compartments. No matter what I am busy with, I remain a child of God, and I serve Him. If I am busy with business or missions, I am serving Him and the one is not more important than the other or a higher calling than the other. If I am pruning the vineyard today, am I busy with a lesser task than when training a handful of people tomorrow?"

We also asked Bernard how other business people are influenced by his involvement in missions.

He replied, "I think I live from who I am and what I do, and I believe it influences the people around me. This is something I wrestled with. When I became forty, I often wondered if I should continue farming or become involved fulltime in ministry. When I recently became ill, I again asked the Lord what his plan is for my life. Each time I received a very clear answer that I must do both – I farm and I do ministry – it is not one or the other. For me, this is how the parcel looks, and I work with the whole parcel."

Chrismaré added, "When we left the farm for three months at Petra Institute, it was a huge issue for the community; some thought we totally lost it, it is irresponsible, and you just do not do it. Gradually, they realised the farm didn't go to waste. Some say they cannot imagine how he keeps up. However, I think people admire him for doing it and I see in a younger generation that something is being awakened in them in terms of becoming more involved."

Bernard continued, "I found my calling there – to be an advocate for children. This brought so much peace in my life when I was able to say *no* to what was less important, and suddenly saw much fruit on the work I did for the Lord. Before, I would attend about 50 meetings annually, but looking back at the end of a year, there was very little fruit to show."

Growing fulfilment through *growing* people

"I also experience a further calling towards more involvement, in time to come, in helping people find their calling. After the recent harvest, and being involved with Deon Koegelenberg's ministry on farms, we had a discussion group with farmers about what the Lord is calling us all to do. In so doing, I enjoy helping a person to find his or her calling and then

> "The Christian is called out of insignificance into significance – a man's greatness lies not in himself but in what has been given him to do."
>
> William Barclay

guide him or her along the way, because I can speak from my own experience."

"What inspires you to continue?" we asked.

Bernard answered, "Initially, being part of the CIS Hub that came together yearly, where we could share about the different ministries within the Hub. The same is true with Petra Institute as the support group in South Africa. These two groups gave us much new energy, as both are actively involved in ministry and their staff accompanied us to Ukraine and Russia to assist with training. There was continuous growth and development, and the same goes for the other CIS countries not been reached yet – there is an expectation and it is part of a dream that has not yet fully come true.

"Also seeing people staying true to their calling for the past 30 years inspires me. I see its value also in the fact that I have stayed true to my calling for the past 20 years, still focused on children, and still having the same vision. This energises those who came after me."

"In my case," Chrismaré adds, "it's a love for the country and its people, as well as the unfinished task. In addition to what Bernard said about role models – I want to mention people such as Francois and Karen Vosloo of OM who played a huge role in our lives, and the fact that people just continue with the work because they love the Lord and are committed to what He laid on your heart."

"Other dreams?" we asked.

Chrismaré answered, "As explained earlier, we both dream about Stofland – helping them reach their Kingdom potential."

Bernard adds, "As for the CIS countries, it's still our hearts' desire that all the countries of the former Soviet Union will have independent and autonomous children's ministry."

"What gives you the greatest fulfilment?" we asked.

Chrismaré answered, "In seeing how God uses ordinary people, there where you are, to bring change to the lives of children. I do not need specialised equipment; I must only be available and make a difference."

Bernard continued, "It excites me that one can equip people with basic principles and see what happens in and through their lives as God uses their gifts, talents and passion.

"My biggest joy and fulfilment is to support and guide people to grow to the point where they can experience the joy of understanding their calling and what it means to stand in a ministry. With the basic principles and skills we teach – the little we give them – many establish huge and successful ministries. It is so remarkable and gives us joy and fulfilment indeed!"

Website: www.petra.co.za

Chapter 13

From glorifying Lenin to equipping people to glorify Christ

Joab has made a strategic decision for the cities of God,
and he did not know how it would turn out...
He had to make a decision on the basis of sanctified wisdom...
and he handed the results over to God.

- John Piper

We met Lyudmyla (Lyuda) Bryn for the first time in 1999 when she and three other Ukrainians came to South Africa for a course on children's ministry.

Lyuda Bryn

An English lecturer by profession, her soft-spoken nature hides leadership qualities she applied from a young age. Since that initial meeting, we have seen, with great joy and admiration, how these qualities have been put to great use in the kingdom of God in several countries of the Commonwealth of Independent States (CIS), through a ministry she was part of from the beginning – Children Mission. She also became the Regional Coordinator, Eastern Europe for the 4/14 Window Movement (focusing on children up to age 14).

But from the context in which she grew up into this role, it was an unexpected, rich and interesting road travelled.

"I grew up in a non-Christian family," Lyuda started sharing. "This was during the Communist movement, and as a child I never heard the name of Jesus. We grew up believing that Lenin is the one who cares for children. We were not taught to pray to him, but always to exalt him, chanting 'Glory to Lenin, glory to the Party who makes our lives so nice.'

"And I remember how I, as a child, felt pity for the poor children somewhere on the streets of Africa and in the United States who did not have enough food, because the Soviet propaganda made these stories and pictures look so real. We were taught that the only way we could help those children was to introduce them to Communism."

Meeting Christ

Asking Lyuda how she heard the Gospel and about her conversion, she replied:

"It was only in my first year at college that the Soviet Union collapsed, and the truth about the Word of God started to come out. Many people received it at once, but I remember how, during the whole of my first year of history classes, I would defend Lenin, saying he was a very righteous and good man, which is not true if you look at history!

"Somewhere during my second or third year, a group of American exchange students attended the college and they started a Bible study group, although they did not call it so. As it turned out, they were associated with an organisation called International Fellowship of Students. They then organised a conference which some of my friends and I attended, and there God touched my heart."

How can I teach the Bible to children?

"Having been an English lecturer, how did you become involved in children's ministry?" we asked.

She told us, "When I became a believer, and because I was at a teachers training college, I thought 'I love the Lord; I love the Bible, so how can I teach the Bible to children?' I helped as an interpreter at several camps that were held by an overseas team, and at first, I thought, 'Oh, this is good! The children seem to be excited about God.'

"However, the next year, when the same children returned, I realised that they forgot everything we taught them the previous year, and on top of that, their behaviour became worse than before.

"That left me with many questions I asked God. With an inner desire to be involved in ministry, investing my time in something that really influences people, and specifically children – why did our efforts not make any difference, even though we were trying very hard? If the ministry was effective, the lives of those we ministered to should have changed.

"So I asked the Lord to guide me to where I could be trained how to share knowledge of the Bible with children, and guide them effectively to meet Him."

God opening the way to his workshop

"Towards the end of 1998, while I was praying about this, I received an invitation from a group in Kiev, saying they were looking for four people to attend a children's ministry course in South Africa. To my surprise, I was invited for an interview!"

With a chuckle, Lyuda continues: "I went there the last day of the interviews, and I was chosen! And so, the decision was made in one night. My pastor explained the situation and said, 'Well, why not?'

"Then I called the head of my faculty, who said, 'This is a unique opportunity! Three months in a foreign country, speaking English – just agree and we will make a plan on how to substitute you.' So, she was the most excited one of all the authorities I had to ask for permission to go.

"However, I had some hesitation asking my two older sisters to take care of our father during this time. To my relief they phoned early the next morning, saying they were willing to do so.

"I thought this seemed like the answer from the Lord, as I was very disappointed with the camps and not sure if I should continue with it or with children's ministry, as nothing was making a difference. Based on this, I decided I should go. I applied and received my visa, and everything was arranged at the academy where I worked.

"Then, at the airport in Johannesburg, I met Bernard Joubert for the first time. I believe it was important that he met the other three persons that were also invited and myself there and brought us to the institute a few days before the course started, so we could share our thoughts. Also important, was that Bernard shared what problems he saw in Ukraine concerning children and his vision for us.

"At some point, he said, 'I believe God has brought you here because we prayed for people to come from Ukraine. But please feel free to spend time with the Lord and listen to what God says to you. If you say 'No' after this training or somewhere during the course – you do not owe me anything. I will not charge you your airfare or for anything else. Just be open to what the Lord will be saying to you and how He will touch your heart.'

"For me, it was a very important time with the Lord, as I had my questions and was eager to hear from Him.

"Since the first week, every day had a huge impact on me, as something big was growing inside of me. Previously, I thought I was such a good teacher, such a good person loving children. But then I saw how people at Petra Institute treated their children – how freely they could come in and out of the classroom and how adults respected children.

"I read what the Bible said about children, and by Friday I realised I'm not such a good person I thought I was."

Laughing, Lyuda said, "You see, deep inside, I thought I was this very important adult and all these children have this huge honour that I come to see them, giving them something and teaching them something. However, in God's eyes, this was something I had to repent of. This was the most important part of the first week of the course for me. I just sat and cried and repented before the Lord, saying, 'Lord, I want to be like You and have your heart, not being so arrogant and proud about myself, for no reason at all.' This was the first step of what God was doing in my life regarding my future ministry."

That's why it did not work!

"As the course progressed," Lyuda continued, "I realised that I was receiving the answers to my questions – why we were not successful with the children. First, our attitude, because I realised that as young people we participated in the camps for children, not for their sake, but for the sake of being together as young people, spending 'good time, serving the Lord', ...but not really.

"We also didn't know all these methods – how to speak and use language that children understand. Realising this, I was so excited, wanting to change all the mistakes I have made. Already, I had the whole plan on how to present a great camp and great children's ministry in the church in Ukraine."

A vision to answer the prayers of others

"In fact, until then the only thoughts and questions I had were about children's ministry and children's camps. I had no thoughts about Ukraine or other countries or anything else. I had my own problems and I was very happy God was addressing it.

"But then somewhere towards the end of the course, during one of the morning Spiritual Formation classes, the principal drew a mountain on the board, saying, 'You are now here, but it is time you start seeking God's will in what to do next.'

"At that moment, I received a vision! Suddenly I could see a map of Ukraine, and the focus was zooming in on a city with many villages around it, then jumping from one part of Ukraine to the next, and the next.

"In those villages were flames of fire. When I saw that, I realised those were the prayers of the people inside the cities and villages, who prayed the same prayers as I have before I came to South Africa.

"And so, when I experienced that vision, I suddenly realised in my heart that everything I'm learning here is not only for me, but to develop my ministry back home. Moreover, it was also for other people back home who cannot speak English, and for all the other reasons they could not come here. I also realised God wanted me to be the answer to *their* prayers – it is not about me, but all about his plan.

"Therefore, during the tutor course, I already had that picture and put in all effort to gain as much as possible from the course, for I wanted to be a blessing to all those people back home.

"On returning to Ukraine, Bernard and his family also came here, and together we presented four courses from June to August, in different parts of Ukraine."

Quite emotionally, Lyuda concluded our question, saying, "At the end of every course there were one or two people who approached me and shared their testimonies of prayers, the same as what I've prayed before. For me, that was a miracle – them saying, 'You are the answer to our prayers.' This was God's plan and I was receiving a calling and his revelation."

God's hand at a crossroad

"When you became aware of your calling – that training in children's ministry would become your full-time ministry – you must have realised you're not going to earn a salary. Your circumstances would also change. How did you experience the adjustments you had to make, and what thoughts and emotions did you have?" we asked.

She responded, "Already during those first four courses we

presented in Ukraine, I realised God is in this, and more had to be done, as people were thirsty for this training. They were already asking what to do next and how we could train more people. Also in other churches, people started seeing the need for this training and material, as they would surely benefit from it.

"So, by the end of that summer, we realised that the need was huge. I continued for one term as a lecturer at the university, but it was very intense. I would go there in the mornings, and in the afternoons, after classes, I went to the office to translate material for Module 1 in Children's Ministry.

"On Saturdays, we visited the groups we have trained in different regions during summer, to see what was happening in their lives. Additionally, we had a group we trained on Saturdays in Kiev. This meant that I did not have any days off, as on Sundays I was busy with children at the church.

"After six months, by Christmas and New Year, I realised I wouldn't survive at such a pace. But I had two groups of students in their second year of an English training programme, running into the new year before their exams. It would have been unfair to them if I left them in the hands of a new person in the middle of their academic year, so I had to continue until the end of it. Also, the funds which Bernard was raising for us from South Africa weren't enough to support me full-time.

"My concern, on the one hand, was the next semester at the university. On the other hand was the financial implication of leaving my work and that we would not have an official registered organisation in which I could apply my qualifications. At that time in Soviet countries, it was as if I was ruining my life, since I would not have an official job, saving money for my pension fund. Socially, it was not accepted well.

"I also enjoyed teaching English and I enjoyed my students – young people with whom I spent time. So, I started to evaluate – if I stay at the university, what would be the fruit? Will I be influencing future leaders and entrepreneurs in Ukraine, as they were preparing to become the future business people?

"However, if I choose ministry through Children Mission, I can influence many adults – and they can touch many children's lives, not just for a better future for Ukraine, but also for eternity. In the end, my main motivation was what would be more important for eternity.

"Realising the big need, we had books translated and printed by the end of the year, so in the summertime – when I have holidays – we could train our first tutors in Ukraine. They could then start training children's workers the next year, otherwise, we would not train as many children's workers as needed for the church and the country. However, they would not be able to train on their own yet. We still had to be with them to mentor them."

Lyuda continued, "With all this in mind, I phoned the head of faculty about my decision. She was very sad, but said, 'Well, at least you have enough time during the whole summer which is vacation time, paid by the university. By the end of August, you can sign all the papers.

"But then, before I could sign the papers, I received a call from the head of the faculty who was quite confused, asking, 'How did you know?'

"I said, 'What should I know?'

"She said, 'the situation at the university – they reconsidered the English programme – how it should be taught and by how many lecturers.'

"My position was cancelled because I was the last one to be appointed in that faculty team. Therefore, as it coincided with my decision, I experienced it as God's affirmation that I made the right decision. So, I said, 'Don't worry; I see God's hand in this.' *That* encouraged me much, and I was inspired by the fruit I saw – the changed lives of people, the changed lives of ministries and children who were influenced.

"Yes, it was a sacrifice. I sacrificed my social position and people started asking questions about what I was doing. Being on my own and training some people in the churches was not seen as so important. I also realised I would not be able to give private classes in English anymore because there was no time left for this, which was sad. I enjoyed teaching."

Leadership qualities honed by perestroika

"Was there something in the past that prepared you for this role and purpose you are now serving?" we asked.

"Well," she said, "as I grew up, I was quite active in social life in the Soviet set-up. I have some leadership abilities and was practising it as a child in those situations created by the school and government.

"When perestroika (restructuring of the Soviet political and economic system) began, I was in my teenage years. Suddenly people started to discuss all the secrets from the past, and you had the right to have your own opinion. At school, we had several boycotts and situations where we stood up against the administration of the school, as we did not agree with them about some subjects. And they had to change it, which would not have been possible before. However, because it was perestroika, they had to listen to us as young high school students. We respected adult people, but we thought that we can change some things and we have the right to speak and influence openly.

"I think that was something inside of me, and why I was not afraid to become the leader of a ministry at 25. So I see it as a way God was preparing me for my current role", she said with a shy smile.

Facing the challenge

Asking her about the problems that children in Ukraine faced during the times of change, she replied:

"At that time Ukraine's economy was very bad, which resulted in unemployment, affecting families and children. The parents, mostly between the age of 30 to 40 plus, didn't know what to do, as they grew up in a communist society with no free business or undertaking and they were used to somebody else deciding or providing jobs for them. They knew how to live in a government-ruled country, but when the country became free and many government-owned factories, businesses and enterprises closed down, people did not know how to generate work for themselves. This obviously influenced children.

"Furthermore, people were very eager to get hold of literature and information about Christianity, as it was forbidden to preach and openly learn anything about God during communism.

"This resulted in churches growing very rapidly, and noticeably, parents brought their children to church. With many children in the churches, we experienced parents were still very young in their Christian walk – still being 'children' themselves in their faith. Most did not think of passing their faith on to their children, as they were eager to find answers to their own questions. On the other hand, they also did not know how to share their faith with their children. The majority of people in the church did not have parents who taught them about the Bible when they were children. So, it was a paradox."

People, ready for training

"Did you struggle to make people aware of the necessity for training in children's ministry?" we asked.

She answered, "When Bernard initially came to Ukraine in 1998 for the conference in Dnipropetrovsk, one of the biggest cities in Ukraine, God showed him that this training was needed. He was allowed to present a seminar on children's ministry, but on a Friday afternoon. And being in English, he didn't expect many to come.

"But what happened? There wasn't enough room for all the people, about 50, who came for his seminar! From their questions, he realised that although there were some children attending church, the parents and church lacked knowledge and skills to minister to them. Some people already had burnout and were at the point of leaving after only two or three years' trying some ministry to children. Neither was there any support from the pastors or other people.

"So, when we started in 1999, we sent invitations to the pastors who were already connected to some South African churches, and we had enough people in every region for those first four courses. For the first five years, we did not advertise, because the work of Children Mission spread by word of mouth. People would call, saying: 'We want a workshop, what should we do?' We only needed wisdom to decide which cities and regions we should go to; whom to select; and to organise and coordinate the training.

"Even nowadays, with our whole network, it grows mainly through people telling one another. So, there's no need for advertising – God is leading us to people, churches, and ministries in need of being equipped for the ministry."

Reaching across borders

Knowing the extent of her work, we asked Lyuda how the ministry developed from there.

She replied, "From the beginning, we realised the need was just so big and that four people could not reach all the children in Ukraine, let alone the other CIS countries. Therefore, we used a multiplication strategy by raising more and more tutors and mentors.

"During the first four courses in 1999, we trained 73 children's ministry workers. Thereafter, we followed-up the students and also translated and adapted the material, which the institute allowed us to use. Fortunately, from the start, we translated it into Russian, so it could be used in all the Russian-speaking countries.

"In 2000, we trained our first 28 Ukrainian tutors and started with the first 10-day courses that I was mentoring, while all the tutors facilitated the training. I noticed how some of them stood out and other tutors were looking up to them to learn from them. They then became the regional leaders.

"After four years, Bernard and I appointed the first two mentors and then with their help, we started training in two regions in Russia and then in Moldova. And so, as more tutors developed, more and more mentors were raised.

"In the first ten years, and in all the regions, we trained 75 tutors and almost 2 000 children's ministry workers, parents and Bible college students in different parts of Ukraine, Moldova, Russia, and Armenia. But for children's ministry workers to be effective, someone needs to take care of them – guide, encourage, and nurture them. Therefore, strong and trusting relationships from top to bottom of the ministry are very important."

We then asked her about the size of her current network as well as in how many countries she has done training.

She continued, "In 2017, we already worked in seven former USSR countries. Up to now, we have trained people in Ukraine, Russia, Moldova, Armenia, Latvia, Georgia, and started in other countries, with more possibilities in other Baltic countries.

"We now have self-sustained ministries without any support from outside, run by local people in their local language, in Ukraine, Russia and Armenia. That means there are national coordinators, local teams of mentors with their teams of tutors, some full-time, some volunteers – in total about 80 people – a number that grows annually. And I don't go to those countries anymore to train tutors as they now train their own tutors and children's workers."

Changing lives, culture and perceptions

"What difference does your work make in the lives of children?" we asked.

She replied, "We see that those we train, start practising what they learn first with their own kids. While presenting a course, there are many testimonies about their own families. Many moms come back saying they applied what they have learned with their children and then lead them to the Lord. We often hear that children were saved through this while their parents were trained."

Lyuda then told the following story: "At a conference in 2017, one of the pastors approached me and said, 'I was at your seminar and I agree with you, but can you tell me or show me the fruit of your ministry, that it really works?'

"I told him, 'Do you remember that young man on the stage this morning, who is so excited about Jesus and about evangelising young people and use creative ways to do it?'

"He said, 'I was very impressed with him.'

"I replied, 'Well, he grew up in a church where all the children's workers were trained in the first year we started. He attended children's ministry since he was six years old and as a teenager started to minister in our children's camps. He later felt the Lord has called

> *"In some ways, kids are like the guests in the parable of the banquet in Luke 14. They are invited last to the celebration, yet are the most available to attend and to respond to the generous gifts of the King."*
>
> Sylvia Foth

him to work full-time with young people in creative ministry, reaching out to non-believers at stadiums through bands and dramas.' The pastor was convinced!

"Obviously, it's not only we who influenced him – he has parents and other teachers, but we as children's workers create awareness that churches should be friendly and welcoming towards children. When this happens – *that* is what helps children to seek God and as such, we have our part in changing the culture towards children in the local church. But each one of us has his place in the faith and personality formation of every child that we touch."

"Do you notice any change in the culture of the church and society as a result of your ministry?" we asked.

She told us, "As said, we cannot claim all the changes happened because of us, but we see it in the churches where people are being trained for the past 15 to 20 years, as some churches are still working with us since the first year of children's ministry training.

"Those who were trained understand how to approach children, their needs, and age characteristics. This brings about a change in the way they deal with children, and this leads to a changing culture. When they reach out into schools, orphanages, camps or some social projects, people who are not believers see the difference in approach and have a better understanding of who Christians are and of Christian ministries. Little by little, this changes the attitude towards

Protestant churches and movements in Ukraine.

"Also the perception about and the importance of children changed in the Church, especially in Ukraine, Russia and Armenia, while in some of the other countries we are still working towards it."

With a sparkle in her eyes, she added, "Something special is happening in Ukraine with young people. We had to lower the age of admission for training to the age of 17, then to 16 and now we already train them at 14, because these children grew up in our churches and children's ministry in the Children Mission way. Therefore, it is very easy to train such teenagers, because they say, 'Oh, I know this game! I remember how it worked for me. Oh, that's why Aunty Lyuda or Aunty Natasha did it!'

> *"The needs and potential of this age group should inspire a purposeful response by those charged today with forming the world of tomorrow."*
>
> *Luis Bush*

"Nowadays, the churches are becoming more willing to support the training and the participation of their people. When we started in 1999, we paid everything with South African money, but later we charged for the material, coffee breaks, lunches and travelling expenses. They are not yet supporting the ministry itself, but the training sessions are self-sustained. Sometimes we receive extra money, which we then use for leader development."

Signposts for success and overcoming challenges

"What are the core elements guiding your ministry?" we asked.

"I think" she thoughtfully said, "it is most important to *perceive and obey God's will and guidance*, where He is leading us – for sometimes attractive ways and means are not God's way, while at times you have to obey and follow the less attractive. There may be only a few people for training, but you realise you need to invest your time and effort in them, as God is busy raising up something.

"Also *building relationships* and *working together as a team*, because it's not a ministry of some important individuals, but of all the different people.

"We are very strong on personal relationships and investing in people's lives – knowing them and supporting the different ministries and leadership staff in day-to-day life.

"And when we facilitate training, we're not only formally to-gether as leaders. All the time, we are *modelling* and building people up in ministry, developing skills, encouraging them and praying for them. Therefore, throughout the process, the building of relationships with the students and modelling of relationship-building continue, so that they can build relationships with children, know them personally, answer their individual questions and show God's love to each one of them.

"During training, we also involve them in training teams to present courses. In so doing we get to know their potential to become tutors and members of our team. And through strong relationships, we remain a team with the same dream and focus in our hearts – to have *many* adults trained. The more we train, the more children can be reached.

"Furthermore, we keep contact with their leaders and pastors to see what is happening in their lives, their churches, and families. That is how you build the next generation of leaders – and how it works!

"To keep people *united*, we help them being focused on our mission and vision, by having directional meetings for leaders.

> The ministry of Jesus was relational. Building relationships – that makes it work in any country in the world.

Every three, four years we try to have an international meeting of the country coordinators and mentors from the different countries."

"And how do you handle challenges – something all ministries are at some time confronted with?" we asked.

Lyuda explained, "By having good and trusting relationships among our country coordinators, it is easy for us to discuss and seek wisdom in how to deal with the issue, and we pray for each other. If we need extra advice, we call or keep Bernard informed and he as founder, main supporter and overseer of our ministry, gives some advice. And with some situations, we can even approach local pastors who are interested in children's ministry."

Look at the stars and see the fruit

"Thinking of the CIS context, what excites you about your ministry there?" we asked.

Immediately she responded: "I'm excited to see God raising up people in whose hearts He put the vision to reach children. It is not by my strength or my effort. I don't see my role as to ignite the fire, but to keep it going and make it grow stronger. I am not like Elisha, feeling I am the only prophet left. There are many other prophets – some just need extra encouragement and some extra equipping. God is already working in their hearts and they are called in their local context. My role is to help a little here and there to ensure the ministry and the children are blessed."

Reflecting on the past, we asked Lyuda how her role in this ministry influenced her personally.

She continued, "I see God's hand in all of this. He shows me his ways and I follow. I consult with Him and wait upon his guidance.

"Once, when I visited Petra Institute again, I was standing outside, looking at the stars. I felt God speaking to me, saying that even though I was not directly reaching children in so many countries, the people I was training, who in turn train others, were influencing children – children as many as the stars! I do not even know all the people who Children Mission is training nowadays and this picture of the stars encourages me more and more.

"At some point, I also realised why Jesus said, 'My food is to do the will of him who sent me and to finish his work' (John 4:34). It means if I am where God wants me, this becomes like everyday food for me – you receive this inner satisfaction because of what you are doing.

"Furthermore, when parents ask me, 'What should I do with my children now? Please, I need your advice', I can see it works for them and they can see this is something important, something upon which they can build their lives. And when I see lives changing as children grow up to become teenagers and young people who follow God, and now want to receive our training, I see the fruit of what we do.

"The foundations from God are the same and they continue to work and encourage people, as God is using it to change people's lives for eternity."

Expanding the territory!

"Any dreams and plans for the future of the ministry?" we asked.

"New countries, new people!" she responded immediately, full of enthusiasm.

"But here in Ukraine, even though we have much freedom, it remains very difficult to introduce spiritual values into the official education system.

"Fortunately, there are ways to get around it. I completed a post-graduate programme, whereby programmes with Christian ethical or moral values can be presented to teachers as further training at any official educational institution. I am now writing a doctoral paper on this topic. It is also a kind of inner fight, since being in the ministry for so many years, I know how to influence believers, but I believe God is now leading me into how to influence non-believers for the sake of influencing society and education in general. It will also bring me into contact with some other believers and professionals."

She concluded, "Even though I am very new in this and have to find my way in new territory, I believe God is leading me, so I try to be obedient and not to fear or be scared."

Website: www.childrenmission.net

Chapter 14

Growing from poverty to serve marginalised children

...whoever welcomes one such child in my name welcomes me.

Matthew 18:5

When we started our interview with Frank and Minky Mashego, directors of SizaBantwana, a remarkable story started to unfold.

Frank & Minky Mashego

Both grew up in poor workers' class families in the Mpumalanga province of South Africa. Frank grew up on a farm, together with friends, some whom later joined politics because of the earlier situation in South Africa, and are now still in politics and government. Minky's parents divorced when she was 12 years old, which caused her to move with her mother to Bushbuckridge where she matriculated.

Getting out of the whirlpool

"How did you become involved with children? Was there something that made an impact on you and led you to it?" we asked.

Frank explained: "In my earlier years, and because of the situation in our country, politics were driving us. Also, the places where I worked and some incidents caused me to change inside, unfortunately to the harder side. But since my mother brought me up with the Word of God, I later experienced God was talking to me and eventually brought me to a place in my life where God focused me on his will for me. Simultaneously, my heart was touched with the current situation of so many children and it was as if God pushed me towards becoming involved with them, to guide them out of such a whirlpool.

"As we were a very poor family, I know the hardship and suffering of children who have nothing. So from that background, I saw the need and experienced a growing burden to provide care, support and empowerment holistically to orphaned and vulnerable children, who, because of the HIV/AIDS pandemic and other socio-economic barriers, are deprived of so much. I then started reaching out to children of the nearby community in the Masoyi region where I lived, an outstretched area between White River and Hazyview."

Small beginnings

"How did you find and identify the children in need of ministry and what have you done to get them interested in what you were trying to do?" we asked.

Frank replied, "I actually didn't go and look for children. I also did not give them anything physically; I was only welcoming them by playing with them and listening to them, as sometimes they were not welcomed at home. The children came to me because they trusted me. Some adults saw my passion and potential and brought children to me, saying, 'Hey, the children are suffering. Please come and help us.'

"It grew from there and eventually I started the ministry called SizaBantwana (IsiZulu and SiSwati for 'Help the Children')."

He explained: "We want to ensure there is a bright future waiting for these children. Furthermore, we believe children need a positive environment to reach their full potential and it is our objective to create this environment for them."

"Frank, apart from the founding of SizaBantwana, you also became involved with Petra Institute. What was the connection and why did you become a staff member?" we asked.

He explained: "At some point in my life I experienced an inner urge to study theology – a desire that stayed with me. Then one day, a friend of mine was in a conversation about children's ministry with the then principal of the institute, Dr. Johannes Malherbe, and told him about me. Eventually, Johannes came to me, saw what I was doing in the Masoyi and invited me to come and see what they were doing – and it started from there.

"After only knowing some theory, I learned much more during my training there about how to work in relationships with children, which influenced me a lot in helping them. But in the beginning, and while I was completing my studies, we cared for only a small number of orphans. So, after graduation, I was able to give my full attention to the project."

Frank also started to recruit volunteers and within weeks their number had grown to 10, and with them, the number of children under their care grew to more than 80, with new children added frequently.

Children need a positive environment to reach their full potential and it is our objective to create this for them.

"How did you find and persuaded volunteers?" we asked.

He replied: "I prefer to involve people from the church. Whenever there was a big church gathering or conference, I asked for an opportunity to share about the need for children's ministry and the project that was thriving, but also the need for more volunteers."

"And did they react readily?" we asked.

"Not really. Only a few," he said and continued, "Then I decided – *let me look for people who have the heart for children, who love children and have a clean record*. Because in a poor community it is hard for people to work as volunteers, as they want some income for what they do. So they came little by little."

Meanwhile, Minky worked at another mission station focusing on the whole community. She continued, "Initially I preferred working with adults. However, I learned to love what a colleague was doing with children – the interaction, activities, and the way of sharing the Word.

"After attending Bible College, I had the opportunity to study at the institute and interacted with international students which broadened my view by what they were doing."

(The simultaneous involvement of both Frank and Minky at Petra Institute eventually led to their joining of hands, literally in work and in matrimony when they got married in 2005.)

The tribal community got involved

Their work was growing and they gained the trust of the people. So we asked them what they did to attain greater involvement in the communities.

Frank continued: "When we met the volunteers – the people caring for children – they didn't have any knowledge and structure, and we had to bring that in."

"So, it was their *trust* as well as *advocacy* and *marketing* at the churches, and also *structure*?" we said.

"Yes, one has to respect all the structures within the community," he said, and added, "You need the consent of the traditional leaders."

"And were they receptive?" we asked.

"Yes, very receptive, for they realised the need, but didn't know what to do."

"And do they support you?"

"It's not actually by supporting. They said, 'Just do it. *Do it*.'"

> *Trust, advocacy and marketing together with structure set the basis for involvement in the community.*

"How was the community influenced? Did it change their perception in any way about children, to see greater value in children? Was there a change in the community in the way they treated children?" we asked.

Minky answered: "We saw it in the caregivers working with the children. Before, they were treating people without emotion – shouting at the children, without comforting them, which made the children cry and we realised how important it is *to look at children through the eyes of Jesus* (according to Matthew 18). But they've changed since we have set the example and gave them some training. Even now in our absence, they are treating the children with love."

This reminds of a poem which Darrow Miller from Food for the Hungry International wrote:

> When we work among children who are poor, how do we see them? Do you see them as mouths to be fed? They are hungry and they do need to be fed.
>
> But if that's all you see, you don't see with God's eyes.
>
> Do you see the child who has a song that's just waiting to be sung? Can you see the child who has a poem he's just waiting to write? Can you see the child who has a dance in her legs just waiting to be performed, but no one's there to encourage her?
>
> Maybe that young leader before you is the next president of the country. Can you see that? Maybe that poor child in the slum will become the doctor who will discover a cure for cancer.
>
> Can we see with God's eyes?

So we asked: "And the kids' response to the caregivers who have changed?"

Minky responded: "Yes, before, when they treated the children harshly, the kids were rebellious. But after the caregivers have changed, the kids also started to respond positively."

Their territory enlarged

Eventually, their ministry developed much faster and further when, in 2005, members of the local churches of Hazyview became aware of the dismal situation and needs in their surrounding communities.

While the Mashegos were at this stage already involved in evangelisation among farmworkers and their children in the Hazyview area, and among children in the Masoyi area, the church, in pursuit to address this need, became aware of the relationships of trust that developed between them and the larger Christian community. Together, the churches and business persons of Hazyview joined hands with Frank and Minky and officially formed the SizaBantwana Children Benefit Organisation and registered it as a non-profit organisation in 2007.

We continued, "After the community got involved, you successfully handed over the project in the Masoyi region to another organisation, the Masoyi Homebased Care, now part of Hands at Work."

Frank replied, "Because there are so many projects being run in the Masoyi area, we moved further in 2008 to the poor area of Marite within the greater Bushbuckridge district, where there is 'nothing' and crime is rife."

(The Bushbuckridge area is known for its poverty where more than half of the people who could be economically active are unemployed and the crime rate in the Marite community is of the highest in the country. Service delivery is very poor and less than a third of the residents have access to running water in their houses. People also have to travel far for employment opportunities, with the result those parents and caregivers are often absent. HIV/AIDS-related sicknesses and deaths are a huge problem and it is tragic to see young children heading many households.)

Care, support and empowering

Local homeowners and benefactors made garages and outside buildings available to provide safe communal facilities, and so they established two 'drop-in' centres in the Marite community where children receive afternoon care – Amukelani ("Welcome") and Siyakhula ("We are growing").

SizaBantwana themselves equipped these properties with very basic kitchens, playgrounds, fences and other necessary facilities. However, the Mashegos dream of eventually setting up neat centres that will meet all the needs for both projects and have already obtained a small piece of land.

But here at SizaBantwana's Care Centres, nearly 800 orphaned and vulnerable children receive care, support and empowerment as SizaBantwana is shaping their future. Also, for five afternoons per week, 159 (and becoming more) children of all ages and different schools in the area gather at these two centres.

Frank and Minky continuously recruit volunteer caregivers to support the children's primary needs and development. Daily, some of the volunteers cook meals planned by a dietician, so that each child receives at least one healthy balanced meal per day. During school holidays they receive two meals, making up for the meal they normally get at school. Many members of the community and farmers from the Hazyview and adjacent Kiepersol districts donate food and avocados, mangos, bananas and other sub-tropical fruits regularly, while the local churches and members of the community have open hearts and hands for the needs of SizaBantwana and the children they serve and care for. They also received a light delivery van and petrol to visit the projects.

The volunteers also have daily gatherings with the children, engaging them in activities such as sport, homework supervision, and other life skills programmes, giving them hope for a brighter future.

Besides, SizaBantwana runs a computer centre for children from all grades at Moduping Combined School where they use programmes to strengthen the children's English language and reading skills. Minky tells about the reading centre with their own library where children can borrow books to read at home. "We encourage the caregivers and parents to read together with the children. Children also learn to return the books in time and good condition. We even have media-prefects!"

Furthermore, they organise different projects, excursions and camps regularly for the children to prepare and empower them as best as possible for life.

Frank explained, "Some of the children get frequent opportunities to attend weekend-camps together with the staff. During these camps we focus on their spiritual growth and development. We also address the larger issues in the community and put much emphasis on life orientation and other constructive and edifying activities, including team building. And yes, because of the high level of ignorance about HIV/AIDS, we educate them about it during these camps. But as a whole, not everything we present at these camps is serious stuff. Local business friends, also serving on the board of SizaBantwana, entertain the children with adventurous fun, something they thoroughly enjoy every time."

Open hearts and hands for the needs... spiritual growth and development and life skills programmes give hope for a brighter future.

Homebased care of orphans

Frank continued, "Because of HIV/AIDS and other factors, many children in the area are orphans and grow up on their own without an adult caregiver. These kids are so vulnerable and can easily fall prey to people who exploit them or get into dangerous situations. To address this, we provide home-based care in partnership with an organisation called Isibindi, who contributes partly to the running costs, such as the salaries of the workers."

Both Frank and Minky emphasise that the children not only need a place of security and a meal, but also love, and understanding for their circumstances. "So the volunteers receive specialised training to assist the children in this way. Twenty-four children and youth care workers have so far been trained by the National Association of Child and Youth Care Workers, Department of Social Development, and can visit and care for more than 600 children at home every month."

"Perhaps the most devastating effects of poverty are those on the inside of a child. With severe poverty a child feels devalued, worthless and powerless, often leading to hopelessness that is hard to repair."

Sylvia Foth

Minky further mentioned, "At a ratio of ± 40 orphans per caregiver, they build relationships with all the kids in their care, deliver food parcels provided by SizaBantwana and train the children at the drop-in centres to prepare the food. They also help them with homework, give them love and further support and guidance to take care of themselves, getting into a routine of housekeeping, going to school, and so on. Medical care is given, and where necessary they help to apply for ID documents and governmental allowances for the kids. Sometimes we can disengage some children when they become adopted and can be taken care of."

The Dutch Reformed Church of Hazyview supported them in implementing the Accelerated Christian Education (ACE) programme for 20 learners. Thereafter, they expanded the programme to help more children. Frank mentioned, "We are trying to help, as in the rural areas education is neglected."

Since these projects are now running for several years, we asked them, "Are there some stories of children who went through the programmes and are now adults?"

Minky replied, "Yes, many of them already matriculated and are studying. Others, for example, were trained as chefs in Cape Town or graduated in computer studies. We make sure that a child in our care has opportunities to develop further. We can now also help them apply for a job. Some even start supporting SizaBantwana."

"One can only think what would have happened to them if they were not embraced by your care programmes," we commented.

Meaning for life

Focusing on their personal fulfilment, we asked, "What does your role mean for you?"

Minky responded: "It gives *so* much meaning to my life to work in SizaBantwana and my passion for our communities grew. While being with another mission before, through whom I've reached out to other countries, I became more aware of our need here and am excited to be involved with community development among our people. It's not about people expecting help from far away. We are here among them, understand the culture and can motivate others to face the challenges and take up responsibilities. And thereby we can help them with planning and strategizing."

"You expand people's understanding of the problem and help them think differently, see it in perspective and take ownership and responsibility for their communities, and you enable them to do something," we said.

Minky added, "I don't like it when people say there are no jobs, for there is a lot of work. Maybe there's not money, but I cannot find myself in my community seeing the children and youth and do nothing. I always feel compelled to get people involved with the needs in their communities."

"But for me", Frank said, "it is the fulfilment of what God has called me to do in this life, because hearing, 'I was naked and hungry' – God will ask me, 'What have you done; *being saved, what have you done?*' I'm fulfilling my calling of 'saving' the little ones and the poor. I've been serving my purpose and am still doing so."

Minky continued, "Here, we are so much more determined to work with the children, for to transform

> We are here among them and we can also motivate others to face the challenges and take up responsibilities... I cannot find myself in my community seeing the children and youth and do nothing. I feel I always have something to do to get the people moving.

the community of Bushbuckridge, it is not only about feeding the kids. If they grow up without *knowing* God, and we didn't build biblical values into their lives that can also work through to the others, we are just raising future criminals."

"You started to touch on it – what is it that excites you in ministry and provides you with the greatest fulfilment and satisfaction?" we asked.

Frank answered, "You know, children are 'empty', they want to hear anything and it is my opportunity to bring them good things – the Good News. They are very open and have many questions about it, and it makes me excited to have the opportunity and see them develop."

Minky added, "I think it is seeing their hearts changing and I look forward to ten, twenty years from now to see the change I helped bringing forward in communities through children."

"And late at night, what ministry matters keep you awake before you fall asleep? What would you like to see still happening in your ministry?" we asked.

Frank replied, "If a child comes to me and says that he or she doesn't have any shoes and needs it, I'll look everywhere to see where I can get those shoes. And when I find it and give it to the child – the excitement on the face of the child and the excitement when they show it at school to their little friends – make me *very happy*."

Minky continued, "For me, it's all about implementing the theories that I have learnt, especially in management. I'm busy with further studies in social work and community development – about making people aware that *they* can do something about developing their communities. It is to get key community leaders and childcare workers together and discuss with them what they dream about and what they want to achieve. It is also to do monitoring and evaluation to do better, and so on."

Then we asked, "What is your toughest duty or responsibility?"

Frank replied, "I can summarise it by saying, to see that this programme runs. To run this organisation is tough, really, even to take care of the caregivers. They have to take leave, or some of them become sick and they need to be replaced."

Minky added, "I always say that when you work in the community with orphaned and vulnerable children, you also get orphaned and vulnerable caregivers. It's trying to get the people motivated – the responsibility of caring for the care workers, as they are a very important link in the whole system."

"Were there some experiences that produced great disappointment, and how did you counter it?" we asked.

Frank answered: "For me, it was with people whom we hired at a time when it seemed as if the ship was sinking. They left the two of us suffering, having to do almost everything."

Minky added, "Sometimes, it's also bribery… Organisations like this will sometimes hire people and then find out that their hearts are not in what they are doing. But one thing I like – then we can teach our community and the children that in such times *they* must *do* something. Sometimes people become upset when things don't materialise and it demotivates them, but then we can help them see the right perspective."

Future goals

"What goals do you have? What's next?" we asked.

Minky answered: "There are still villages that we've not reached in this vast area, and we would like to have satellite care centres spread out with care workers there as well, and to see the change in the lives of those far away children. But it includes the challenge of finances – I wish we can have a 4WD vehicle to reach them and eventually also train some people at the village where I once worked in Mozambique and its surrounding area."

"The last question – currently, what is your biggest need?"

Frank concluded for both of them: "My biggest ambition, my biggest future – we have to duplicate the Franks and the Minkys. Succession! If I can do that, I can rest."

Website: www.sizabantwana.org

Chapter 15

Nurse impacting society in Mozambique

Speak up for people who cannot speak for themselves.
Protect the rights of all who are helpless.
Speak for them and be a righteous judge.
Protect the rights of the poor and needy.

- Proverbs 31:8, 9

Sybil Baloyi, the director of Hlauleka Mumpswa, an NGO she started in Chokwe, Mozambique, is a woman of determination – what she sets her mind to, she does.

Sybil Baloyi

Growing up in rural Malamulele in the Limpopo Province of South Africa, she finished school and trained as a staff nurse. "I was very serious about education and was planning on being trained as a tutor for nurses," she recounted.

However, a trip with some friends to Mozambique to visit a missionary doctor became the turning point in her life. She told us how.

"Mozambique came to my mind after I took a trip with hospital workers from South Africa to visit Maputo. It was a fun trip as we had passports and the finances to visit a former colleague, Dr. Pieter Ernst, who works for World Relief in Chokwe.

"When I was in Mozambique, I saw the street kids begging. I spoke to them about the Bible, but they had no Bible knowledge. At that stage I was in the process of attending a Bible College – I was a very serious person and just wanted to win adult souls for Christ.

"While still there, the Lord spoke to me one evening about 'I was hungry and you fed me, thirsty and you gave me a drink...' I felt, yes, I saw hungry children begging for bread just to survive the day. I also saw sick children who had terrible scabies (a skin condition), and some had burn wounds and other wounds because of fighting on the streets. One day, I also saw children who received clothes. They took off their dirty clothes right there and put on those they received – they had nothing else to wear.

"This touched me intensely, but I had my reasons for not getting involved. I thought of myself and said to the Lord, 'This will not work with me. My goals are very different.'

"Another reason was that I am the firstborn at home and I was helping my parents financially. They sacrificed much to send me to school and afterwards to be trained as a nurse. I felt I had a responsibility towards them. I could rather pray for missionaries in Mozambique and support my parents financially."

Submitting to God's call

"But when I came back, I found that it started to haunt me, and I made another visit to Mozambique. Back home and being tired of carrying this burden, I prayed, saying to the Lord if it is Him calling me and He opens the way, I am willing to go. I then surrendered my future to Him after which I experienced peace and started telling people God was calling me to Mozambique."

Sybil then set her heart to change the plight of children in Mozambique, believing them to be "diamonds in the dust."

"It was very difficult – only a few people supported me, but the rest were opposed to the idea. They said people were fleeing from Mozambique and would remind me of all the atrocities of the war and poverty. In spite of them, not understanding, I still wanted to go.

"The worst, however, was with my parents. They did not want me to go and for almost a year, I stayed on, waiting for them to come to another decision. I still remember my mother saying, 'Are you mad! What do you think? If you stop working, you are going to suffer in life. But now you are working and have so many opportunities.' This was very hard for me and I was struggling.

"Then after some time, I sat down and wrote them a letter, saying, 'You are my parents, I am not married. If I had a husband, you would accept his permission if he said I could go. You would not say anything. But now I am not married, Mom and Dad. The One who is calling me is the Lord Jesus – He is far more faithful than a husband. You are concerned because I am your child and about my future, but He is faithful. I want to promise you today, if you hand me over into his hands, I will never come home hungry, I will never come back without clothes, and I will never come back begging. If He calls me, He will go with me to Mozambique for the rest of my life.' Then my father said, 'If you explain it like this, I cannot hold you back.'

"I resigned from the hospital and went to Mozambique."

It was... *hard*!

Giving up many of her personal dreams, she started dreaming and working on behalf of the many orphaned and neglected children in post-war Mozambique.

"Was it difficult to adapt to your new life in Mozambique?" we asked.

She said, "The peace treaty was signed in 1992 and I went there in 1994. Coming from South Africa, quite well developed compared to Mozambique, which has been ravaged by a 16-year long civil war, was not easy. But what kept me going, was having peace that this is where God wanted me to be."

Sybil laughingly added, "Another adjustment was from working for a salary to working without a salary! After staying with other missionaries, my first house was a single-room mud house – a little bit more than three meters by three meters, with a very small window, about 30 cm square, which was closed with a piece of rusted corrugated iron. All I had inside the room were two sponge mattresses, one for myself and one in case I would receive a visitor; a box with kitchen utensils, and my suitcase. There was a little open-air kitchen outside made of grass, and a toilet – a hole dug in the ground – near the house."

"How difficult was it for you to stay there?" we asked.

Again, she laughed. "It was... *hard*! No electricity, sleeping on the ground, and it was pitch black at night. But I adapted. I was living next door to a pastor who had no electricity at his house, so I decided I better join them, living the way they live as

> "That consuming, selfless desire to give to God is the essence and the heart of worship. It begins with the giving first of ourselves, and then of our attitudes, and then of our possessions – until worship is a way of life."
>
> John MacArthur

if I knew nothing else but that type of life. That helped me.

"To start working with those children was also an adjustment. There were many children, no order, and people were confused. Whenever I would start calling children to come and play, they would come in tons, with no discipline, *nothing* – they wore me out! I thought the crash courses I had on children's ministry would help, but it didn't. After working in Mozambique for just a month, I was so exhausted!"

Getting equipped, influencing culture

"Fortunately, someone left the contact details of Petra Institute for Children's Ministry when they heard that I was going to do children's ministry in Chokwe. As the children knew nothing about the Gospel, I decided to apply to be better equipped for the task, so I would know where to start with them. Perhaps I would also learn how to handle the discipline, as there were so many children! Even the members of the church did not have much knowledge of the Bible. So I did a three months' course in 1995.

"When I went back to Mozambique, I was so structured – making plans for the children's clubs and knowing where and how to start training people. I had courage and was no longer afraid."

"And was there something that God did in your past that better prepared you for what you are now doing?" we asked.

She said, "I am thankful for having been trained as a nurse. My first choice was teaching – but I ended up in nursing, which I enjoyed while doing it, but realised that teaching was what I enjoyed the most.

"Looking back, I could see why God made me go through it, because most of the time, I work independently, not having a boss. In nursing, you have to keep record of every second and report everything you do. This helped me when I started working here in Mozambique. In the beginning, I did not even have an office – I worked from home and decided I should have a set routine: wake up, have quiet time with God, and at 07:00, I should know what I am doing until the end of the day.

"When I trained people, I would have them in my house. After the training sessions, I would go to the children's club, and work until the end of the day. Then I would write a report on all I was doing – even though there was no one to read it! I had no overseer and was not responsible to anybody apart from God, but I had files with all the reports on the activities of the month, and planning for the way ahead. I worked that way as a nurse by reporting what I did and being accountable. Up to now, I work independently, but I must make sure things are going properly and I have to be accountable before the Lord."

"So how was your disciplined lifestyle and approach to work received by the local community?" we asked.

Sybil replied, "Culturally, it was difficult, since I came here as a sister in the Lord, and if they see you do not have an office to work from, people tend to think this is something to take leisurely. They grew up in war conditions in which they were not used to a fixed routine and focused more on survival than on time management. So some would come late, with all kinds of excuses, but I told them, 'No, this is not how we do it.'

"Therefore, one of the first things I told the people was, 'This is work and we have to be on time and get used to the routine. We do not make excuses. No matter what happens, we adjust and make the necessary precautions to be on time.' They were shocked! It was hard for them, but gradually they've changed. Those who now work at the school got used to a time schedule and disciplined routine."

Changing perceptions led to ownership

When we continued, asking her about changing perceptions and her strategy to establish and expand her ministry – finding the right people to be trained and to take ownership – she replied:

"First of all, I started doing children's ministry in the community myself, not just training people and expecting them to work with the children. Initially, I would take a ball and start playing with kids and people would wonder why I was playing with them. When we were busy teaching the children, the adults would come to listen as well, in spite of us telling them it is for children. In time, they would start wondering if they could do something like that themselves. So they saw what I was doing, and when I invited people to come to the training, they were ready and wanting to be trained.

"The next phase of the strategy was to work with the church, as the people are already there and the pastors are part of the community leadership. If something is being organised for the community by the government, the pastor has a seat in the meeting. Thus, when I started working in Mozambique, I told the people that I am part of the church."

The pastor's 'hard porridge', my 'soft porridge'

Sybil went on, explaining her role in the church by using a beautiful analogy.

"I told them the pastor 'cooks hard pap' (stiff porridge) at home, I 'cook soft pap' for the kids. The pastor 'cooks' for the whole church, I 'cook' for the children of that church – I give them 'soft porridge' bit by bit, and playfully until the child finishes. Children sit in church, not being able to eat the 'hard porridge', and in the end they are 'dying malnourished' while being in church.

"In other words, I am assisting the church, taking care of the little ones, bringing the Word of God to them on their level of understanding until they are grown up and then I give them to the pastor. Then they, as young adults, in turn, stand up and also 'cook soft porridge' for the little ones. So when I introduced the programme in a community, they would ask the pastors to choose the people who could work with children, to be trained.

"In implementing the training, many of those who helped me with the children were eventually chosen. After their training, they would start children's clubs in their communities and those belonging to the churches would start Sunday schools for their churches. It also became community-based programmes where everyone was responsible, especially the community leaders.

"After two years, I started separating the children and started teenager clubs, realising that these teenagers could be helpful in their churches and communities by teaching the smaller children in their clubs. So I chose those from ten to twelve years old whom I saw were spiritually mature, trained them and gave them certain responsibilities with the younger children. By the end of the year, I would give them small incentives such as a little cloth or a T-shirt to say they have taught the little ones well. In this way, they grow up wanting to continue teaching children younger than themselves and sharing what they know with the younger ones.

"With the youth programmes also in place, we now have many young people coming to our clubs. Many of the small children who initially were in the clubs when I started have developed into strong leaders in their churches.

"So through teaching and training the children from a young age, they were moulded as future leaders and it is easy for them to take ownership of the programme, even as teenagers and young adults. They are also involved in their churches, most of them being Sunday school teachers, youth leaders and some are volunteers in our programme. Now, they own the programme, and the 41 people who work for me, see the programme as their responsibility. About ten of them were growing up in the clubs."

Different roles reaching wide

Knowing that Sybil's work extended over a large part of Mozambique, we asked her about the different roles she fulfilled thus far.

She told us, "When I first came here, I founded a Christian NGO, *Hlauleka Mumpswa*, which means *'Be ye holy young person'*, derived from Leviticus 19:1-2. So I initially started with children's ministry – training children's workers and holding clubs for children.

"After a while, I started to work for World Relief where I was the director of all the children's programmes as well as the youth programme. The programmes were funded by US Aid, and we worked from Maputo, Inhambane, Gaza, and Beira. Because it was well funded, we had 72 workers who had to target 10 000 children each year, reaching out every week. After four years, we exceeded it since by then we were reaching more than 80 000 children. But I later resigned from World Relief as I felt I wanted to be more directly involved with children.

"The following year, I started a pre-school in Chokwe, where I am still based. After three to four years, we started a primary school. Currently, I am the director of Hlauleka, having a pre-school director, school director, and a clubs director. We have 41 staff members at the moment – pre-school and primary school teachers, drivers, children's workers and club teachers. In the clubs in Chokwe and several villages, we are covering about 3 000 children."

Impacting society

"Sybil, your ministry have touched the lives of many children and through that also the community. You see yourself as part of the church, working alongside the church. In which way has your ministry benefited the church and society?" we asked.

She explained: "The church is benefiting, as most of the Sunday school teachers in the churches in Chokwe have been trained by Hlauleka. It helps the church to have properly trained Sunday school teachers. Previously, children would only sing or act dramas in Sunday school. The church is also benefiting since children coming from non-Christian families come to the clubs and accept Christ. We advised them to join a church, and as they do so, churches are growing. So today, many children are in churches because of Hlauleka.

"Through Hlauleka, the town of Chokwe is being influenced and lately the government is taking notice of Hlauleka's fruit – they realise that the lives of the children who have gone through the programme, have changed, and even when they leave the town to go and study, most of them remain in the Lord. These children grow up to become responsible citizens with sound work ethics, and they help to build the country and build into the lives of a younger generation."

She continued, "When I started here in Mozambique, education was not important at all to the children. It was a rarity for children to complete grade 7 or 8. However, by following a holistic approach and not only teaching the Bible but also life-skills, health, and whatever else children need in life, I encouraged them to look differently at education and to work hard to educate themselves better. And now many of the children are attending universities. Others were trained as nurses, teachers, or other professions. They are the future leaders. In fact, many of them are already leaders in their churches or the workplace.

"Also Christian organisations in Chokwe, Maputo and other places sometimes call me in connection with applications they have received. When they hear that those who have applied for positions attended my clubs, they know that they are *I strongly believed these children were 'diamonds in the dust.'* level-headed, mature Christians who can be trusted. I have seen how the children who grew up in the clubs have changed.

"Initially, children would get married as early as 15 or 16 years. Nowadays young people marry in their late 20's or early 30's, putting in place proper education, a career and a good income to provide for a family. And so we now have fewer weddings and more graduation ceremonies! Gone are the days when the girls said, 'You will marry me and buy everything for me. I will stay at home and work in the field and cook for you.' No! Most of our kids are now at university

– we even have a very intelligent boy who received a scholarship to study in Russia. We see how the children's level of education has been positively influenced.

"I would like to share the story of a boy who grew up in the clubs. He said that one day I was talking to them about making a difference in your own life, and said there are things that you can change and some you cannot, and as a young person, you should know the difference. The things you can change, work hard to change it. Those you cannot, forget about them and go on.

"He said that day was the breakthrough for him in his life. His mother died giving birth to him. His father then married her sister. During the war, when he was 10 years old, his second mother was killed. This made him bitter as he felt he was not worth having a mother – he had two mothers and both died. When he was alone, he would cry. But on that day, when he realised it depends on him how he would handle what life brings to him, he decided to change how he thought about his mothers' deaths, accept it and go on to make a success of his life.

"Today he is a smart young man – he completed his degree at university and is now working at our school. He is married, with two beautiful children. He also has taken into his family an orphaned boy, saying Mozambicans should not wait for foreigners to adopt Mozambican children, but take responsibility of vulnerable children themselves. On top of this, he also heads up one of the churches!"

Children become change-agents

The norms of society have changed for the good. Children become change-agents in society themselves. Sybil shared stories of children who stood up against ill practices in society, in spite of having to pay a price for that.

The children growing up attending the Bible clubs are learning to live according to biblical standards and principles – like being honest and that God does not approve of wrongdoing. When confronted with situations where their biblical principles are challenged, they stand their ground and say that no matter what it takes, they will not compromise their Christian principles in spite of being discriminated against. This started a process of opening the eyes of the community.

In Chokwe, there are many orphans and Sybil and her team are involved with them as well. They provide free schooling, food, clothes and accommodate them when necessary.

She explained, "Many of these orphans live with grandmothers or aunts. Some lost one parent, others both. I challenged the teenagers who grew up in our clubs to adopt an orphan and become that child's big sister or brother. They visit their adopted brother or sister once a week. During these visits, they listen to their stories, ask about their health, help them with schoolwork and pray for them. They are role models for the orphans and the community is surprised by the involvement and commitment of these teenagers. Even the caretakers are surprised. These teenagers are setting a new standard, a new way of treating orphans with respect. The broader community is curious why they do it as it is new to them

> *"Children are change-agents. Jesus saw them as such, and present reality proofs that."*
>
> Amy Barstad

and they talk about it. Things are changing in our community and people start treating orphans with respect."

Taking care of vulnerable children

Sybil also adopted children and we asked her about it.

She replied, "God gave me four daughters and a son, all from different families with different stories that led me to take them to be mine. I would like to tell you about one of the girls.

"One of the women in the community became interested in what we are doing and thought she would like to become involved. Soon after she joined us, she told us that she was expecting a baby. When the baby was born, the mother was disappointed that she again had a girl, as this was her third daughter and she wished to have a boy.

"For quite a time, the baby was without a name, so I asked her if I could give her a name, and the mother agreed. Then I called her Tlangi, which means, 'Praise God'. I told her one should praise God in whatever He gives you – there is a reason why God is giving her girls. When Tlangi was about four years old, she started coming to my house – she was in and out of the house, and I realised she was a bright little girl, so I started giving her more attention and teaching her. Unfortunately, the mother passed away, so she remained at my house and she is still with me."

Growing up with an adopted mother like Sybil resulted in Tlangi getting involved in children's ministry from a young age. As she grew up, she started ministering to children herself, having her own children's club and later also received training in children's ministry.

Sybil also took in a baby boy, named Tom.

"One day, someone came to my house, saying there is a house where the mother died and nobody knows where the father is. The children, two girls – one eight and the other five years old, as well as a baby boy, not even a year old, were left by themselves. I went to the house and found that Tom was extremely ill. He was skin and bones, but his stomach was swollen and he had yellowish hair. I took him to the hospital where he was diagnosed with severe kwashiorkor, marasmus, oedema, and anaemia. He was in such a bad state that his skin started coming off. I told people about the baby I admitted to hospital under my name, asking them to pray that he will make it. When he was discharged, I started feeding him. By then, he was more than one year old, but still could not walk – he would just sit. I made sure his diet was sufficient, and one day, he started crawling! I was so excited! After that, I started training him to walk.

"Today, Tom is eleven years old, a strong and healthy boy, and very smart – it is God's miracle. Children with severe malnutrition can be mentally impaired, but he is not at all! He is fluent in English, Portuguese and Tsonga; he reads books from cover to cover – in all three languages!"

Pondering on her ministry

Aware of the fruition on her work, we asked Sybil what excites her most about the ministry, to which she responded:

"Seeing an opportunity to mould and helping unfold someone when still young – to be involved in the first years of someone's life, because I know that lasts for the rest of that person's life. I have been blessed to be able to do that. Our preschool is reaching children from the age of three years.

"And what gives me the greatest fulfilment, is to search and study the Word of God when I have to speak to the children, the youth, teachers or whatever group I have to address. This helped me over the years to discover many things and I would see my shortcomings and where God wanted me to change. I have learned that in life a person never stops learning. So, even if the children have grown up, I can continue teaching them, and I can continue to learn. I keep on asking myself what else I can do, or what else can I learn."

"What guidelines have you implemented in your work?" we asked.

She said, *"I will never stop sharing the Word of God with them, and fasting and praying together for the work.* Every Friday we come together as staff, sharing the Word and studying the Bible together. But first, *prayer.* Every second month we have a day of praying and fasting – everyone, all the workers, are fasting – and at the end of the day we have dinner together. During holidays, when we are not too busy, we will take three days, fasting and praying together for the work."

"What does your role mean to you and how do you see meaningfulness?" we asked.

"I have a very strong sense of accountability, for my life must speak of what I am teaching others," Sybil responded. "But I thank God for what He has taken me through, taking me out of nursing and bringing me into this ministry. I feel I have shared my life with many more children of Mozambique than I would have shared in nursing elsewhere. And God is still giving me the courage to carry on.

"I am greatly encouraged by the story of the starfish – the person that kept throwing them back into the sea, one at a time, saying, 'For this one, it made a difference.' So, for as long as God wants me here in Mozambique, even if I can make a difference for one more child's soul to be a child of God – it will be worthwhile."

She paused shortly and continued, "I know that in our African culture being a woman and doing something like this, is not seen as normal. But I often tell myself that in the eyes of God, being a man or a woman does not make a difference – all that matters is that it is through Him that I am doing what I am doing. I am encouraged that God can use anybody, a woman or a man. He is the One who sent me, and He will use me and I keep on encouraging myself with it.

"And what else keeps me going, is the support from friends – I would never have been able to do this alone without their encouragement through letters, SMS's, calling me – always thinking about me. It is mostly fellow Christians outside the country. And I want to mention Petra Institute that helped me a lot by opening my eyes to children's ministry and many of the staff who shared the vision with me and helped me a lot."

"So what are you dreaming about and what ministry outcomes do you still want to see?" we asked her.

Laughingly, she said, "Of course it is to know that everyone whose life I've touched will reach heaven one day!

"I'm also thinking of the school we now have and am dreaming of a secondary school as well as a technical college, but a Christian college. We also have a programme where we work with the orphans; they also need to be educated."

She continued thoughtfully, "I think, seeing Mozambicans doing what I do on a much bigger scale – them taking over from me, mentoring others and duplicating their lives.

"The Lord did that with twelve men, and look what the result was!"

Website: http://www.sybilskids.org
Blog: https://hlauleka.wordpress.com

Chapter 16

Transformation creating
heaven on earth

Vision for ministry is a clear mental image
of a preferable future imparted by God
to His chosen servants
and is based upon an accurate understanding
of God, self and circumstances.

- George Barna

Cassie Carstens is one of those dynamic leaders with whom it seems as if all happens so easily – the apparent (easy) success story – sports, academics, leadership, starting as early as primary school through high school and university, into ministry – born with the proverbial silver spoon in his mouth and making things to happen. But behind the many things he and his wife Jenny do, there are many deep lessons to learn.

At the beginning of our conversation, Cassie responded: "We sometimes give too little recognition of where we come from – the daily

Cassie & Jenny Carstens

prayers of Grandma on my father's side for all grandchildren, by name. Grandpa on my mother's side, that very strong and stable figure – the big tree in which many people could find refuge. Those roots were laid very strongly."

Added to this was his good relationship with his parents – "Dad, the pastor and good preacher with a passion for evangelisation, who founded two ministries that are still standing; Mom's influence as the real leader – where Dad was the positional leader, she taught me of the importance of your effective second position. I would learn that in most cases it is your most effective position – to keep the crown on the heads of positional leaders and to determine the dynamics by your contact with them.

"And then I came to know the Lord in a very close relationship with Him since an early age, with my faith integrated with everyday life, seasoned with a passion for evangelisation and sports.

"But in the things I experienced, I saw dualism, including a dualism in the church – I could never understand that the church is only church on a Sunday and has so little influence from Monday to Saturday. *That* laid the foundation for all I am and what I am doing – also as a pastor. I did not become a pastor because I had a need for a specific position – my main concern was that I had seen the ineffectiveness of the church. I also strongly believe that in our evaluation of the church, we shouldn't look at membership numbers, rather look at its environment – *that* tells you about the state of the church.

"As a result, I wanted to leave the denomination, when still a teenager, but my father's remark – 'If you leave, who's going to change the church?' – stayed with me until I said to the Lord I will 'sign up' for a church that will be an active transformation agent in society. That's why I also founded sports ministry movements, because they are 7-day-a-week ministries and effective as a tool in community transformation. That's also why I started *The World Needs A Father* [1], because if the church cannot change the family, then it doesn't change much. Fortunately, through this, the Lord gives me the opportunity to work with church leaders worldwide, and I trust that I do contribute there. I'm still on that journey; not done yet."

Calling – God, context and myself

In response to our question about life purpose and calling, Cassie replied, "I believe the biggest misconception people have about calling is that they start with *their* qualities and interests. They think, 'What is *my* calling?' But life is about God. We are not on

---

[1]   https://www.theworldneedsafather.com/videos-twnaf/https://www.youtube.com/wa tch?v=QHGYrGGOxS4

our mission. God is on his mission, and in the Bible history, many people received their calling in spite of their weaknesses.

"So you should not think, 'What is *my* calling?' You have to think, 'What is *God's* calling? What does God want in a certain context and situation, right now?' *That* determines your calling – 'Where and how do I fit into his plan? How does He want to use me?'

"And your calling can be different in different contexts. My calling in South Africa with 4 million orphans is quite different from what it would have been in London, England. Therefore, context and time and such things determine our calling, but it's all about what's on God's agenda."

Cassie explained it well by saying, *"Passion is created between crisis and vision.* In other words, you must see the crisis, and that crisis must speak to your heart. And the vision isn't *your* vision. Therefore, one must be careful with concepts such as goals, because it sounds so much like self-made plans. But with vision – as in the Promised Land – you have to see what God wants to do, as his Word tells us what heaven looks like. And we know what it looks like – because He came to live heaven here on earth. We saw it happening in Jesus. He told us about what heaven should be on earth.

> What does God want in a certain time, context and situation, right now? That determines your calling. Where and how do I fit into his plan? How does He want to use me?

"So, we see the vision. We know what the perfect world should be like, and then we should live and work towards it. And *that* is passion – in that way, *calling* must be fulfilled through *passion.*"

He explained further: "I took time out and for three months I travelled the world with my family. Our visit to Mother Teresa's place in Kolkata, India, had an indelible impact on our lives and our calling. All my children now work with people in need. My daughter works among the prostitutes. My son goes to the Syrian refugee camps in Jordan, and my black adopted daughter is a social worker. My other daughter is a teacher in a less privileged school because of the struggle they have there. Those events in Kolkata told us: *Do not seek opportunities for your talents, but seek where God wants you to work and go to work there with Him, with your talents and your weaknesses.* It is not about our talents; it is about Kingdom opportunities that we should utilise – that's the core of my understanding about calling."

Radical interventions

"At the time you experienced these things, could you foresee all the later developments?" we asked.

"No, not in the least," he replied and continued, "The wonder of growing older brings a much better understanding of life, much clearer than earlier when you became involved. However, I can say with honesty, if the Lord did not stop me in my tracks, in some places, I do not know where I would have finished. The Lord had to intervene very radically in my life, even though I followed Him. He also had to do it with his disciple, Peter.

"In our case, the most important experiences that had touched and affected my life – even more than Kolkata – was the deaths of our first two children, because it coloured everything we did from there. *That* was the turning point.

"In short, my life up to that point – growing up, sports, studies and so on – was very successful. I was primary school and high school head prefect, rugby captain, and played provincial rugby and so on – leadership opportunities that I had from the beginning. I was very successful in everything and it could not be better. But then the danger is that you think you can be successful by yourself.

"The highlight was when we got married, loving each other very much; Jenny became pregnant and the first child was born on my birthday – who could wish for more? However, a week later we thought the baby had an allergy and we took her to a doctor, who, with the surgeon, told us that she was born with a heart defect – she is going to die, having only a few weeks to live.

"That time, with very long hours – hour after hour – talking to the Lord, with the baby in our hands, brought the first radical change in my life. There God showed me how precious life is – that every day and every hour is important. *That* put my life at a pace nothing else could have done, because there I said I would not waste one day in my life.

"Something else also happened there. The Lord has always been Number One in my life, but at that stage, I realised there is a very big difference between Number One and *Everything*. Then I understood what it means to leave everything and follow Him – in other words – wife, children, to travel and fly when you do not like driving and flying, just because God asks it and since everything is about God and his kingdom. At her little grave, I promised the Lord He would not only be the first in my life; He will be everything in my life. So that was the big turning point where I realised one is absolutely dependent on the Lord. *That*, and what I will tell you now, was the biggest conversions in my life.

"Then my wife became pregnant again, and twice a day I prayed to the Lord, saying, 'Lord, please give us a healthy child.' About a month before birth, we went to our doctor for a routine check-up and he said, 'Your child is dead – Jenny must give birth to the dead baby...'

"*There* I went into a crisis of faith. I could not understand that if you ask the Lord so sincerely, and your life is completely sold out to the Lord, He does not hear you! Nothing I learned at university and seminary for seven years, made sense – nothing. Nevertheless, with the grace of the Lord my faith crisis was not for long, about three months, but very intense. I walked on the verge of eternal glory or eternal perdition.

"When we sat at the small grave and put the second box on the first, it was very traumatic for us, as we did not have money – we had to dig the grave out ourselves; we only sat there all alone... Then the Lord said, 'You are worried about *your* pain, but tell Me, how worried are you about *my* pain? Your whole world now exists out of your pain, but what about mine?' Then the Lord said, 'Until you do not understand my pain, you will not understand your pain.'

"Together with this, something very interesting, but not spectacular at all, happened. While I stood at the elevator in Tygerberg Hospital, the Lord said to me, 'I do not give you the answers you're looking for. I am asking you just one question – who is the one who has to ask questions – Me or you? If I take away fifty of your children, will you still follow Me?' There, at that elevator I told the Lord, 'You may take away fifty. I will follow You as a dog behind his master, even though he does not get food; whether sunshine or rain, it will make no difference, because I do not know about another true God and I cannot be my own god. So, I take the risk that you are God and therefore I will follow You.' And for the first time in my life, Hebrews 11 verse 1 made sense to me.

"It was a radical event in my life, and from that day on I no longer ask questions, whether I like it or not. That was the major turning point in our lives. The relationship between Jenny and me became more intimate and we praise the Lord – it was a very special experience for us."

After a short pause, Cassie continued, "Strangely, the fact that I married Jenny had a huge impact on my life, because she is English and my grandfather fought in the Anglo-Boer War against her grandfather. I believe the Lord used the process so that I had to learn to understand her culture and could adapt to other cultures – to gain the ability to listen to others, hearing what the other wants to say – because I work on average with forty cultures each year."

Defining moments

"What contributed to your decision to change from a pastor leading a congregation to also being the founder and leader of various ministries? What did you experience?" we asked.

Cassie responded, "The amazing defining moments in my life – right from the start. One of them was when a friend and member of the congregation came to me, saying, 'Close your church. It's useless.' Then he shared about his work as an attorney and that the church did nothing for him as it does not speak about labour ethics, how to handle staff and so on. So, from 8 am. to 4 pm., the church means nothing to him. When he comes home, the church does not mean anything to him, for he learned nothing about how to be a father, how to participate in sports, and so on. He said the only aspect in which the church means something for him is for the 30 minutes he does Bible study per day. Apart from that, it is useless to society, and will never change it. *Those* were radical words, but also corresponded with my initial thoughts about the church and led me to preach on relevant issues.

"Another defining moment developed still in the apartheid era, when 500 meters down the street from my previous congregation was a congregation of the Uniting Reformed Church. We had many relevant and straightforward discussions about the church's role in politics and society, which led me to interracial cooperation and joint worship services with other churches.

"An invitation by the Haggai Institute in Singapore gave me a worldview. When I did my presentation, as the only white person among 45 other leaders from 19 countries, they did something they have not done before another speaker's turn, by saying, 'Brothers, let us take hands and pray for the Apartheid Church, because the Apartheid Church can change the world.' It took me by surprise because I didn't think that we were significant at all. Looking back, I believe that if the Dutch Reformed Church had resisted apartheid at that time, for decades now, it would have been the strongest prophetic church in the world. Then the world would have changed. Therefore, that participation in Singapore helped me to think globally in all strategies."

Cassie remained silent for a few seconds. Then, with noticeable seriousness in his voice, he continued, "I'm going to tell you something more, outside of my theological framework, that was one of many defining moments.

"I was 36 years old, and for the last few days of January 1996, we went camping with 200 young people from the Service Year for Christ movement.[2] We took them to a flat mountaintop for an experiential learning session. All of them were spread out for a night of solitude – they were not allowed to see each other and talk to one another. The rule was that one should only use a flashlight in case of an emergency.

"And so I lay there with the stars all around – a fantastic experience in the presence of the Lord. Later, I fell asleep. Suddenly a light woke me up. I thought it was someone who had a problem. When I put my glasses on, I saw the moon, and I wondered why I woke up from the moon. Therefore, I started talking to the Lord. The next moment I got the fright of my life, because when I looked up again, I saw that the only clouds in the sky were in the form of a word, 'JESUS', in large capital letters. Then, of course, I made very sure that I was not dreaming. It was significant to me, because that particular year, I started to place much more emphasis on the centrality of Jesus in everything.

"However, the last 's' of the name was not clear and I mentioned to the Lord that I could never tell this to anybody if that letter does not become clear. The letter moved into a perfect position – and I became worried that people may think I am a dreamer.

"I said to the Lord that between Him and me it is fine; I appreciate that I saw his Name written in the sky and promised He will always be central in all of my life. But then the clouds started moving again, spelling in Afrikaans, the words for 'JESUS shall give you (in the Afrikaans singular form)...' I then realised the Lord was speaking directly to me and He was busy spelling out a promise. Thereafter it formed a ball with a clear silhouette of Africa, followed by a few

---

[2] See: http://syc.vcsv.co.za/

dots. But the last 'e' of the Afrikaans word 'gee' (give) was not clear. It rather looked like a 'c'.

"I realised I had to obtain specific clarity from the Lord, because first of all, if no one else saw the first word, I would not be able to tell anyone else. Secondly, if the word 'give' is not clear, I will never be able to tell the second part as it's a promise and it seems too self-centred.

"The next morning as we descended from the mountain, one of my staff members came to me, saying, 'Cassie, I have to talk to you – I'm not mad, but I saw words written in the sky last night.' I asked him, 'What did you see?' He said, 'It was a word, five or six letters, but I didn't have my glasses on.' I said, 'Five.' He said, 'What was it!?' I told him that I will not tell him immediately – I needed more confirmation.

"Back at the camp, we had a debriefing session. I asked the young people what they have heard from the Lord during the night. The first person who raised his hand said, 'Uncle, it's very strange, but I've seen letters in the sky.' Immediately, I instructed them not to talk to each other, for we had to verify something. 'Who of you have seen letters in the sky?' I asked. Seven raised their hands. I then arranged to see them separately, where none of them could talk to the other.

"As I was alone with them, I gave each a piece of paper and asked them to write what they have seen. One of them then said to me, 'Sorry Uncle, they were big capital letters, but I could not figure out what I saw.' I asked them, 'Who of you could figure out what you've seen?' Only two. 'Do you know exactly what it was?' I asked. Both of them said, 'Yes, I do.' Then I asked them to write it down, and both of them wrote, 'JESUS.'

"So, then I could go back to the group and tell them, 'Jesus himself wrote his name in the sky, and Jesus is central.' But then I could not tell anyone about the last part because someone still had to confirm that the last word is 'gee'". (In the Afrikaans construction the verb comes last).

"At the end of the third day, one of them came to me, saying, 'Uncle, I'm struggling, for I believe the Lord told me to say something to you, but it's strange, it does not make any sense. But I have to say it now, as the Lord does not want to let go of me. I must tell you that the last word is 'give'. You could knock me out with a feather.'"

To Africa and beyond

"At that time I have not yet been working in Africa, outside South Africa, and for almost two years I walked with this awareness in my heart, asking questions to the Lord about my relevance as a white South African in Africa.

"Then I received an invitation to be a speaker at the Youth Conference of the Reformed Church of Zambia, and that is where my connection with Africa began. One month later, we were in Kolkata, India, and the next month I was at a meeting of the International Sports Coalition in Thailand, because of my role as chaplain of the Springbok Rugby team in 1995, after which they voted me on the executive committee. The same month they decided there should be a leadership school and that I had to present it in South Africa. We started the school with 22 people from 12 countries, and in its third year, I told Jenny, 'Can you believe we already have had 50 people at school now?' She said, 'But that's exactly what the Lord said to you on the mountain!'

"What I initially did not understand, started to make sense. Currently, we already had people from 140 countries and I can now understand that the Lord gave me an instruction, without my intervention, and that He had assembled the blocks, one after the other. It was neither my strategy nor my dream, because I did not think of becoming involved in the rest of Africa and even beyond.

"Then things started happening in rapid succession. First was the International Sports Leadership School (ISLS), that, to date, has trained leaders in more than 100 countries, who are training more than 10 000 leaders each year in this network.

"As a speaker at a day of prayer, called 'Transformation Africa', I experienced the Lord saying to me, as I descended from the stage, 'Never again use the word 'transformation' unless you become involved with a project in Kayamandi (a slum suburb of Stellenbosch, South Africa), for it's nice using the word if you do not take the pain also.' In response, we started an NGO there, *Kuyasa Horizon Empowerment*, focusing on multidimensional services required by vulnerable children. Its mission is to empower children and youth of previously disadvantaged communities to become independent while embracing Christian values. The dream is that they will lead and empower others to follow the same set of values." (*Kuyasa*, means 'The Rising Sun'.)

The following year (2002), another major defining moment occurred when Cassie was asked to facilitate leadership training at the Nyarugusu refugee camp in Tanzania. Having asked some of the leaders then living in the refugee camp to share their experiences with him, he heard the most horrific stories of how people were not only maimed but literally slaughtered, cut up in pieces – small children, pregnant women, the babies – same kind of stories, just different villages.

Cassie continued, "I never knew that the story of the first person would change my life forever. He was the pastor of a small village, with a story too horrendous to tell here about the brutal killings of a little boy and then a woman and her unborn baby. What impacted me most, was when he bent forward and looked me into the eyes, and literally looking into my soul, saying, 'That wasn't an unnamed boy – *those* were my grandson and my daughter and grandchild to be born...' I was dumbstruck. That statement ripped everything apart inside of me... Generally speaking, I'm a phlegmatic person, but that just shattered every emotion I ever had.

"When they all have left the room, I sat back and I cried out to God – 'God, what is the problem with Africa, and how are we going to solve this problem!?'

"And then the clear soft voice of the Holy Spirit led me to look out of the little window, and outside this mud hut where I was sitting, there were around 300 boys, about six years old, with soccer balls. Every 30th boy would have a soccer ball under his arm, made of plastic bags. Then I sensed God saying to me, 'The problem of Africa is not poverty. The main problem in Africa is not even HIV/AIDS. The main problem in Africa is *fatherlessness*. And *unless* you address *that* problem, *none* of the other problems will be solved. Fatherlessness is the biggest problem in Africa...' And then the clear instruction: 'You change the youth into the future fathers and you do this through soccer – you train coaches how to become fathers for the children who are fatherless.'"

With a smile, Cassie said – "And therefore I had to get involved in soccer. I never knew anything about soccer. So, I said to God, 'Why me? I know nothing about soccer! I'm a white guy and Africa is black. I'm old – talk to the young people, Lord.' I will never forget, it was as if He grabbed me by my chest and as if He hit my chest, saying, 'Do you want to change Africa on your agenda or my agenda...?'

"I had to surrender – give up all my plans, ideas, all my thinking about the future in Africa and what I would do in Africa. I had to adopt God's plan and obey his instructions – which I did. We created a programme for soccer coaches, called *Ubabalo eAfrica* – 'the grace of God for Africa' – that equips coaches to speak into the lives of athletes as a father figure and mentor.

"We did this for several years and then, in one of the trainings I did for master trainers of Ubabalo, God showed me the depth of the problem – how fatherlessness is the game of Satan and how he has captured the fathers of the world. It is the strongest game he plays and the biggest flaw in society, and if we ever would shatter Satan under our feet, we would have to address the issue of fatherlessness by training fathers how to be fathers.

> *"Virtually every major social pathology has been linked to fatherlessness."*
>
> *Stephen Baskerville*

"I went to the Bible and discovered that God is very sincere on this issue. The very last verse in the Old Testament says, *'He will turn the hearts of the fathers to their children, and the hearts of the children to their fathers; or else I will come and strike the land with a curse.'* That same instruction was given to John the Baptist, and that's why we read in Luke, chapter 1 verse 17 – two things that John the Baptist had to do to prepare the way for Jesus: Firstly, he had to bring the fathers back to the children. Secondly, he had to bring the unrighteous back to the wisdom of the righteous – that is bringing good moral values – and those two things would prepare the way for Jesus."

With a serious tone in his voice, Cassie continued, "How sincere are we to deal with this problem? We need people that will persevere and will be determined to change a fatherless world into a world that has adopted the principles of God the Father for a restored society.

"I truly invite people to join us on this journey – go to where the crisis is; to where boys do not have fathers; to the prisons and see the horrendous impact of fatherlessness in society, and you will be inspired to intervene.

"On the other hand of the inspiration, with the tension between the crisis and the vision, you have to ask God to create in you a vision of the future life, a vision of the Promised Land. We have to dream again about the world where there are stable families, a father and mother in close harmony and where the children indeed grow up to reach their full potential because of this environment.

Together with other ministries that are also working on this issue of fatherlessness, we will have a collective move across this world, changing this into what God intended it to be."

Discovering Father God

With sincerity and compassion in his voice, he continued:

"Adding to my experience in Tanzania, a further defining moment came from my wife's involvement in the *Kuyasa* project in Kayamandi, where she worked with young orphans. Amongst them was a specific girl that she really liked, who didn't have a home. Her name is Abongile Kwaza, and she brought her home. Abongile would just be in our house, live with us and observe my three biological children. At night she would see how my children come and would hug and kiss me goodnight and go to bed. Abongile would stand at a distance, waving and saying 'Goodnight', and then disappear to her room.

"But one night, a few weeks later, I was busy with something, and the next moment I saw Abongile next to me. She just opened her arms, and with her big eyes, looked into my eyes and said, 'Goodnight, Daddy.' I knew at that moment I was the very first person she ever called 'Daddy' in her life... And the next few seconds would define, not only her life, but would define my own life – because, would I say to her 'Goodnight, Abongile,' or would I say to her 'Goodnight, my daughter'? – *That* would define everything. I embraced her; I thought for a moment, I weighed my options and I whispered into her ear, 'Goodnight, my daughter.'

"As she turned around, I could see she was different. I didn't know that I would be different the next morning, for I cried the whole night like a baby – because that night I discovered that I knew Jesus and I knew the Holy Spirit, but I wasn't sure if I knew the Father – Father God. Other than my children, Abongile is astonished every day of her life by the opportunity she has – every day of her life – and I am not astonished by God, every day of my life. That night changed my life. God used Abongile to change my life.

"I went on a journey to rediscover who God is and asked Him to reveal Himself and his Father-heart to me and to show me what it is to be a father like God, the Father. I took the Bible and read every single verse about 'Father God' and thoroughly studied it. I searched for an answer, and the answer was: How did God father

Jesus? Because if I know how God fathered his Son, then maybe I would know how I can father my children. And I discovered very pertinent things in the Bible on this, and Abongile Kwaza became part of our family and she remains part of our family."

With subtle wittiness in his voice, Cassie said, "I can say this to you – fathers across this world are not trained, and unless they are trained, they will do the same as they saw their fathers do, and not all of us have great examples from our own fathers. So we have to renew the minds of fathers on their biblical responsibilities as fathers. They have to understand exactly what they have to do every year of the life of a child. Therefore, our movement is mainly a training movement – training trainers so that they can train the people of all the different cultures.

"On top of training fathers and mothers, we also empower the church to be a fatherhood training hub that recruits mentor-families for single-parent families and recruit families to adopt orphans. Secondly, we empower single mothers to embrace the significance of a father-figure for the sake of the holistic development of the children, and we educate the children and youth so that they can become future fathers and mothers. And God wants us to turn orphans into proficient future parents, not only proficient future adults."[3]

From calling to starting a ministry

"To become practical – you have founded a number of ministries that are still running fruitfully – how did you move from clarity of vision to starting a ministry, and how do you approach people for whom it will be new and help them to take ownership?" we asked.

Cassie explained: "First, for the courage and energy, you must be hundred per cent sure it comes from the Lord. It is of utmost importance that it is not something from your own thoughts, and in this process, your faith communities around you are very important, something that is often undervalued. My two biggest decisions about callings, I didn't take on my own – the Lord led me through other people in exactly the opposite of what I wanted to do. I obeyed and experienced wonderful blessed results.

---

[3] For 'Main responsibilities of fathers' etc., see this video: https://www.youtube.com/watch?v=wSUINyAC55k and other videos on https://www.theworldneedsafather.com/videos-twnaf/

"With *Service Year for Christ*, three people called me in one week, saying they believe there should be such a ministry and that I must start it – and they did not know each other. Therefore, I heard it as an instruction from the Lord and when I started it, it was accepted since it was already birthed in the hearts of many people and it came at the right time.

"Secondly, if I do not have someone to validate and endorse it – if there is no confirmation – I do nothing on my own. I strongly believe the Holy Spirit speaks to more than one person when the Lord wants something done. I am convinced that when God writes, He writes at the same time in the hearts of many people.

"So, the moment the Lord tells me something, I am looking for the people with the hearts in which God already wrote it, since it's not my idea – it's his plan and He will definitely speak to many other people too, for I cannot do it alone. Then I seek the best people and equip them.

"This I do in everything I undertake – the sports school for example: When I talked about it at the meeting, I immediately realised that God had put it in the hearts of many people, but nobody had the courage to do it. Then it was easy to ask them, 'Do you believe this is important to the Lord?' 'Yes!' said everyone. 'Are you part of this?' 'Yes!' Then it was just my simple task to connect them in this vision and mobilise them.

"But thirdly, in mobilising those people, it is very important to get the right leadership who accepted it in their hearts, not only for their own benefit but also for the sake of the bigger picture. Many times, I have to talk a person out of his own story when he has discovered it and just wants to use it for his own benefit.

"It is also important to realise that the proper leadership for a specific task is not necessarily the people in high positions. Sometimes, leaders of ministries approach church leaders and at times I also end up with them – there are countries and places where it works, where the Lord gives goodwill – but that's the exception. I do not seek positional people; I am looking for the right leadership for a specific task – someone in whose heart the Lord has written it and who can influence others. Then I only have to guide him or her about what should be done, as he or she will not do it for me, but for the Lord. However, it is essential to have the right leadership – someone who can mobilise other people.

"And this was my key to everything I initiated, like a catalyst. I am very aware of my weaknesses and limitations. Therefore, I cannot say that *I* did it, as many people worked together, and I was only part of it. I believe the Lord gave me the role of a pioneer with a plan, but I prefer not to coordinate things, even though I can do it – remember the 'effective second position' my mother taught me. Consequently, I could be effective with the vision and mobilisation so that someone else can coordinate it. I'm not a manager – for everything I start and do, there is a manager – and I always pray and search until I get one.

"So, know your limitations and get the right people with the calling, vision and skills to do it with you – you alone are not significant. You never see a leader in a person. You see it in his followers. That's a very essential principle in what I do. Therefore, if you ask about vision, *I don't see it as my vision – it is God's command.* I have always asked the Lord for a listening heart so that I can hear what matters to Him for a specific time, and secondly, to give me firm obedience."

Raising financial support for the ministry

When we asked Cassie how he raises financial support for his ministry, his answer corresponded much with his strategy to find co-workers for a particular ministry.

He responded, "Firstly, you have to discover those people in whose hearts God has written his vision for this course, who have the same passion as you have, with the only difference that they are not called to serve in the field themselves. Then you actually become an extension of them. With the right heart and in a sound relationship, in which you spend time with them, they later may get so much confidence in you that they support you without questions, even when they see God leads you to work broader than the initial vision.

"But I report on everything I do and also provide them with an annual report at the end of the year. Every time I do something, I ask for prayer from the intercession group of which they are also part. When I return, I write my report on the plane and send it to them as well. In the annual report, I also give an overview of all the work as well as a forecast for the next year. They need to be assured that you are committed to the kingdom of God, for that is where they invest their money. Secondly, you need to be very conservative with money.

"Nevertheless, at times I had to take risks. I think the Lord often tests us. People hear a call, they know it's from the Lord and they should do it, but then look around and say, 'But I don't have money.' I do not think it works like this. I think if the Lord tells you something, you sometimes have to jump, and the first way of jumping is sometimes to your detriment. The Lord wants to know how selfless you are in this calling He gave, as it is his calling; it's not yours.

"That was my experience with everything I did. At times the Lord thoroughly tested me whether I was convinced of what had to happen, to such an extent that I would be willing to make sacrifices.

"When I started SCAS – Sport for Christ Action South Africa[4] – there was no money and I told my wife, 'The only thing we have – an apartment – is at stake now; is that OK, because God told us to launch the ministry? And she said, 'Yes, we can put it on stake.' Then we started with a loan from the bank.

"When I started Service Year for Christ, we were 18 people who had to eat every day, from the first day of training, and I did not have a cent – and we still had to buy vehicles. For the first three days, I bought food from my own pocket, with the prospect that I would have to take care for these 18 people for the whole year, which I would not be able to do. Then I went into debt and on the third day I received R6 000 from a friend and from there it came in for the whole year, ending the year with R6 000 in the bank – an absolute miracle.

"It was the same when I started ALICT – African Leadership Institute for Community Transformation[5]. I could not find another group, nowhere in the world, who did something like what we planned. Therefore, I had to do it, but I had no money. On a certain weekend I asked a prayer group to pray for it and that the Lord would lay the right people on my heart, as I had only three hours to get R140 000. The first three people I phoned gave the total amount – and that was just to launch the ministry. Then I knew if I do not receive further donations, I would have to sell my house – as simple as that – as the calling is much more important than what we have as security.

"Yes, I did such things – we took risks. We needed R7 million a

---

[4] https://scas.co.za/
[5] www.itl.org.za/

year for the various ministries. Other people might think the risks were too big. I don't see it like that. The Lord instructed us and He provided. Of course, if something has to happen, you must take risks. Everything I had to do was not done by anybody before me, but a pioneer is more comfortable with risks than other people are. Uncertainty is no threat to me. It is a stimulus to listen carefully to the Lord and for creative thinking. For

> "What if a successful risk would bring great benefit to many people, and its failure would bring harm only to yourself?
> It may not be loving to choose comfort or security when something great may be achieved for the cause of Christ and for the good of others."
>
> John Piper

others it may be a risk, but for me, it's an adventure," he said with a smile.

Kingdom DNA is nice

"What are the most important guidelines, values and principles that you use in your ministries?" we asked.

Cassie answered by saying, "It's about *Kingdom DNA*, in other words – what culture do you need to create?

"The Calvary Road" by Roy Hession made a tremendous impact on my life, and the principle of *'selfless sacrificial life is the key to having heaven on earth'*, is of utmost importance in discipleship and leadership schools, in *The World Needs A Father*, and all I do. It is the key principle in a house, because if you live like that – not for yourself, but for others – then you have heaven, the most selfless place that exists.

"That is what we teach everyone – the pivotal value to understand 'Kingdomness'. We believe it is what Jesus had come to demonstrate: It is the core principle of everything – if you do not start from a selfless sacrificial life, and do not stay connected to it, you always struggle.

"The second key theme in all our ministries, in our offices and the house, is *the concept of 'heaven on earth'*. You need to create an atmosphere in which people experience heaven on earth – the whole concept of God's kingdom.

"Also, there are of course several core values of which the key is – *God is central, Jesus is present and the Holy Spirit leads* – the presence of God must be the foundation.

"But what is also of extreme importance to me, and I am so glad that the neuroscience confirms these things, in plain language – *it should be nice* – the 'happy hormone factory' you have to create. You have to create it in the church, in your house, in the office, everywhere. We work very hard, but it is nice when you enter your house and feel – this is where I want to be.

"So, the ethos of how you do things is extremely important – as *the ethos along with the values create culture*. Therefore, it is very important to me what culture I create, as culture quickly swallows up strategy. You can have a brilliant strategy, but if people do not feel comfortable, they will not do well. The culture you create everywhere must be a Kingdom culture."

Saturating transformation

Then we asked Cassie, "Evaluating the ministries you are running, what transformation do you see in the communities where you work?"

He replied, "It reminds me of training we have given in Sri Lanka, where a man came to me and said, 'I just want to tell you what the impact of your training was since two years ago. I was divorced from my wife and after the training, I returned to her; we were reconciled and soon married again. Now after two years there is still great joy in our marriage.'

"We experience a lot of this, with the greatest transformation of course within the household. Almost everyone testifies that where he or she adheres to the principles of our training, transformation takes place at home, and – everyone is talking about the 'heaven at home.'

"Sri Lanka is an example of one of the countries where most of the leaders of all the churches are involved in our programmes, and therefore we have a fairly large movement there. We hope to train all Christian homes – 60 000 homes – within five years, and we are well on track with this. We also involve their education system by meeting with many of the school principals. Besides, we also do this with their sports system.

"We dream that every church will live the Kingdom DNA – to be like Christ on earth. Therefore, we believe each congregation should train all the families and have monthly small group sessions where they revise the principles. Helping people acquire the Kingdom DNA is a lifelong process, and you have to acquire a Christ-centred attitude and commitment and constantly practise it."

On our question about how different cultures experience this, Cassie replied, "It obviously conflicts with many cultures, because they are not essentially Christian cultures – rather Christians who live in secular homes whose values for life differ greatly from the values they believe. Therefore, these principles confront almost everyone, simply because so many have not yet learned how to translate their faith into daily life.

"So, the important question and challenge is: Who has the courage 'to enter the Promised Land'? You must have the courage to kill the enemy, but many people are not prepared to do this, and nowhere it is easy." With a smile, he said, "It's like the majority report of the spies returning from Canaan – 'It looks fantastic, but the people are too big.'"

To see optimisation

Reflecting on his life – the roles he has fulfilled thus far, and experiences in his ministry that give him the greatest fulfilment or satisfaction, Cassie responded: "My greatest joy is to see someone who I have empowered, doing better than I can – to see how they optimise. In other words, if I could unlock something and see it bears fruit."

On asking one of our standard questions about dreams for the ministries that excite him, Cassie told us: "The things I mentioned excite me – the transformation of people, church and society, and such as *The World Needs A Father*, because I realise it is the Lord's movement.

"Therefore, I'm still working hard, but do not feel under pressure – I enjoy just listening to the Lord and float on the wings of the Holy Spirit.

"A request I keep asking the Lord with a yearning in my heart, is that we would like to train 100 000 men in a hundred countries every year. It is not really a goal, but that is what we would like to achieve. If culture is to change, you must have a critical mass, and therefore you need certain numbers. We are not chasing numbers, but transformation. This needs a certain mass. Whether it will happen while I'm still alive or after that – this is our hope."

Then he told us, "But what is indeed like a favourite child, is the discipleship movement we started. We intensively minister to

29 friends and it may sound strange to call them my disciples –
in fact, it took me seven years before I managed to call them my
disciples, because actually they are Jesus' disciples. But I find a
big difference in saying they are my disciples, for then you take
responsibility for their growth. Of course, thousands of others are
affected by our work, but we can call these 29 'faith children' for
whom I take responsibility, pray, see all of them even twice a month,
and for whom Jenny and I are pouring out our lives.

"They also meet monthly in three groups and I hope it will
become an irreversible movement. We learn a lot from this and
everything you believe from the Scriptures is tested in practice.
What makes it so different from the congregation in which I am a
minister, is accountability – something that is not always attainable
in a congregation. We have been busy for about four years now, and
those who hold on to it experience a total transformation in their
lives.

"Now *that* is heaven on earth! It keeps me awake as it is almost
a kind of laboratory that has the potential to be of great value to the
Church."

The Mother Design

We enjoyed listening to Cassie's energetic enthusiasm while he
spoke, and then the conversation again moved to Jenny's role alongside Cassie, on which he responded:

"She moved with me in facilitating the training, and then the
men asked, 'But what about our wives? Who will help them to see
the light?' Then she felt the Lord led her to write the curriculum, *The
Mother Design*. The Lord abundantly blesses it and it is beautiful to
see how the two groups harmonise together. It is now hosted in 30
countries, and we hope will soon expand to 100 countries. In each
country we train trainers who train others, using all our equipment.
Jenny has just finished writing a curriculum for single mothers, as
this too is a big need."

With a smile, Cassie said that we cannot write about him if we
do not write about Jenny, because nowadays when he is talking, he
does not really know who the people hear – him or his wife – as there
is already as much of her in him, blending and shaping each other.

"A major influence on her, which also had a very big influence
in our household, is the 13 years she worked in Kayamandi. More

than anything else, this experience was the school of our lives for us as a family – the struggles, pain and joy, that purified and shaped our lives. The fruit in our family was immense."

Surely, heavenly fruit on earth...

Website: https://www.theworldneedsafather.com

Chapter 17

What would be your Kingdom legacy?

Most men are not satisfied
with the permanent output of their lives.
Nothing can wholly satisfy
the life of Christ within his followers
except the adoption of Christ's purpose
toward the world He came to redeem.

- J. Campbell White

Would you be content with a life of mediocrity, or rather live a purposeful life and leave behind a legacy, being like the image and effect of the water described in Ezekiel 47:1-12?

Remember, you are reconciled and adopted into the royal family of God. As part of this family, what will be your Kingdom project? Let the Lord renew your mind. Then think like a royal representative under his authority and mandate (Matthew 28:18-20; 1 Corinthians 3:9; 4:1).

God believes in you and trusts you with what He has placed in your hand – your gifts, skills, position and relationships in the workplace and society – for his plan and purpose. And so He used Joseph, Esther, David, Paul and others in biblical history.

As an ambassador of Christ the King, search for situations and opportunities to represent Him and create awareness of his presence and sovereignty in fulfilling his purpose. You can ask for wisdom and guidance "to understand the times" – situations, challenges and opportunities – like the sons of Issachar, and decide on the best course to take (1 Chronicles 12:32).

Therefore, God gives you the potential and creates opportunities for *your* specific role for such a time as this.

To each according to ability

Just two days before the Easter, followed by his death, resurrection and ascension, Jesus tells his followers how it will be in the Kingdom thereafter (Matthew 24 and 25). Thus, before He leaves them, He teaches them what to expect and how they should work in his Kingdom until his Second Coming.

Within this context, He tells of a man who went on a journey for a long time and entrusted his possessions to his servants, to manage and make the most of it. He does not expect the impossible and give *"to each according to his ability"* (Matthew 25:15) – not above what they can handle – so everyone can do something!

God works through ordinary people. He knows our fears, how small and weak, young or old we are in our own sight. He called Abram in his old age and a young Jeremiah. The history of God's people throughout the Bible, the church and her global mission shows that He calls people from many backgrounds, cultures, personalities and qualifications.

The apostle James wrote about Elijah, who performed great tasks for God: *"Elijah was a man just like us"* (James 5:17). God does not always call those who seem best equipped for a task. He knows the potential of everyone, equips and guides those whom He calls for the task and will add others to support them, as with Moses who said he's not eloquent (Exodus 4:10-17). He sent his angel to Gideon, who doubted his ability because he came from the weakest clan and was the least of his father's house, to say, *"The LORD is with you, mighty warrior... Go in the strength you have and save Israel out of Midian's hand. Am I not sending you?"* (Judges 6:11-16). And about David, He said to Samuel, *"The LORD does not look at the things man looks at... the LORD looks at the heart... and from that day on the Spirit of the LORD came upon David in power"* (1 Samuel 16:7,13). Think about Moses, Peter, Paul and many others – God, in his wisdom, also grants second chances!

You have potential beyond expectations

So, don't think you need to be a theologian or a pastor or highly qualified to be an effective servant of the Lord. With God's help, every person has the potential to do much-needed work for Him whose grace spans the whole world with all its situations, faces, challenges and opportunities.

There is a unique purpose for everybody – for you too. Some are needed to serve in and through the local church into surrounding communities, others in the marketplace, and others through missions elsewhere. And for each missionary working far afield, a group of supporting staff is needed to keep him or her there.

Churches and mission organisations have a crucial need for staff in a wide variety of roles such as administration, finance, technology, technical and medical services, pilots, cooks, artists, artisans and more. They are as much needed and valuable as those who do evangelism. Somewhere, there are people who need what God can do through *you*.

And do not underestimate yourself – God often uses people of lesser esteem and qualifications in the structures of organisations, to utilise crucial opportunities that ultimately lead to results beyond expectations.

When the Holy Spirit gives you a concern for God's kingdom, He equips you and counts *you* worthy to engage in a specific role in the greatest movement in the world, to bring salvation and transformation for the blessing of people and to the glory of God.

"God always uses imperfect people in imperfect situations to accomplish His will."

Rick Warren

We need to have perspective on *Who* is calling us, and on his master plan we follow – whose dynamic wisdom and power is behind "the secret of the kingdom of God" (Mark 4:11), as exemplified in the DNA of the small mustard seed (Matthew 13:31-32).

A.M. Hunter put it this way about the parable of the Sower:

> Jesus is saying, 'the farmer reaps a splendid crop. In spite of all frustrations and failures, God's rule advances, and his harvest exceeds expectation.' What we have to keep in view is the harvest, and not the failures... It is then we must learn from Christ that, however gloomy the outlook for the church may seem to be, God's kingdom 'stands and grows for ever', that God's Spirit, like a great wind, is invisibly but unceasingly at work in the affairs of men, that the 'little flock' (Luke 12:32) which the Good Shepherd gathered in Galilee is now the greatest society on earth... It is therefore also a parable about hearing the gospel – about the need for a hearing which issues in decision and action. If it says, 'Have faith in God', it says also, God depends on you.[1]

[1] A.M. Hunter, *The Parables Then and Now*. London, SCM Press Ltd, 1979, 36-37.

Take courage, prepare and do

When Christ is central in your life, as Lord and King on earth, He will reveal your Kingdom purpose and meaningfulness within a specific context for something He wants *you* to do.

Since God equips people He calls, a calling may challenge you beyond your ability and comfort zone. Sometimes you will have to take risks and be willing to let go of your dreams, preferences and plans. It may ask of you to reach out to where circumstances are miserable. This can only be done with the help of God by allowing Him to mould you into the person He wants for that specific purpose. In so doing – living and serving *there* – might seem strange in the eyes of many, but will be a testimony of new life to a 'valley of dry bones', heavenly treasures where the loving power of God is reshaping 'flawed clay pots' (Jeremiah 18:6).

George Verwer, the founder of Operation Mobilisation and one of the most experienced leaders and practitioners in missions, said, *"We have a great and sovereign God who specialises in working in the midst of a mess."*[2] That shifts the focus away from yourself and your own abilities to where the results will spring forth from his love, authority and power – causing transformation, turning a mess into a blessing, for others, and for you.

It is about *obedience* and *availability*. God called his people to the Promised Land, described to them the 'big picture' and gave them instructions and advice. Joshua and Caleb had the spirit and determination not to delay, but to execute God's commands. They were convinced: *"We should go up and take possession of the land, for we can certainly do it"* (Numbers 13:30 – 14:9). Then, in response, Israel had to act in obedience, prepare themselves, trust in his plan (his vision for them), take courage and step out in faith through the Jordan. But the defiance of the other spies and their influence on the people were detrimental to their future.

So, how we respond to God's call may either limit or allow his blessing on what He wants to do for and through us.

In Deuteronomy 1:6-8, we read how Moses reminded the Israelites of what God said to them at Horeb: *"You have stayed long enough at this mountain. Break camp and advance into the hill country of the Amorites; go to all the neighbouring peoples... See, I*

---

[2] George Verwer, *Out of the Comfort Zone*, OM Books, Secunderabad, A.P., India, First Indian Edition, 2000, 13.

have given you this land. Go in and take possession of the land that the LORD swore he would give to your fathers... and to their descendants after them." In verse 30, Moses reminded them of his earlier words, *"The LORD your God, who is going before you, will fight for you..."*

God planned, announced that He has given them the land and promised that He will go before them and fight for them. However, in verses 26, 27 and 32 we read how they distrusted God, rebelled and grumbled against his command. Ironically, verses 2 and 3 make an

> *"To miss out on the mission He gives is to spend our entire lives trying to win the wrong game."*
> John Ortberg

astute remark: *"It takes eleven days to go from Horeb to Kadesh Barnea... In the fortieth year..."* they have not reached the land of Canaan!

A spectator sport or we all together?

Likewise, in modern times, we tend to neglect God's commands about our promised Kingdom heritage, opportunities and potential. Many of us are leaving our responsibilities to someone else 'over there'. George Miley wrote, "We made missions a spectator sport. Most of us are sitting in the stands watching the players (missionaries) do their thing down on the field...[3] Mission is not something somebody else does who is far away and whom we hardly know. Mission is something we do – we all do – together."[4]

After numerous big mission consultations and much awareness during the 1990s, we currently see only flickers of mission awareness and action here and there. Missions should not only be seen as something 'over there'. Indeed, it ought to be missional church-in-action awareness every day. It is about *doing* church and not abusing it as a mere 'spiritual culture club' where we only go for spiritual entertainment and feeding. The practice of *being* church must be seen in multiple specialised ministries into all spheres of society, locally and globally. And that's where you *can* fit in.

The challenge for us as mandated people, sent by our King, Jesus Christ, has been described so well by Dutch theologian Abraham

---

[3] George Miley, *Loving the Church... Blessing the Nations.* Gabriel Publishing, Waynesboro, Georgia, 2003, 185.
[4] Ibid., 192.

Kuyper: *"There is not a square inch in the whole domain of our human existence, over which Christ, who is Sovereign over all, does not cry, Mine!"*[5]

Every Christian is called to engage and deliver crucial service in God's global enterprise of church and world missions, whether you remain in the local church or whether you go. Every 'square inch' should be in our sight as assigned people with our gifts and skills of grace, to win it back for his glory.

If you have peace about being called to stay, your Kingdom purpose should be found in and through your local church, serving through 'marketplace ministry' in the local community or where and how God shows you to be involved. Then you, as part of the Body of Christ, from your local basis, are also co-responsible as a calculated supportive extension to the mission field. John Piper explains, "You are free to stay or free to go. Many of you must stay. Your staying is crucial for God's purposes where you are, and it is crucial for his purposes where you are not, but where others may go. There is no need for guilt or resentment. There is great need for joyful partnership."[6]

Those being sent and supported by the local church are actually the bearers of the 'export goods of mercy' birthed through local faith and ministry. As part of the 'home base,' you can serve as a partner by praying, supporting in practical ways or as a steward investor (donor) and co-worker with those in the field[7] – ensuring priceless rewards (Revelation 7:9-10).

Take the step!

Whether you are called to go or stay, take the step! Realise your potential in God's hands to help transform the world into a Kingdom society. *You* might be the catalyst to influence the influencers and set them moving to transform latent potential into action, which will get a Kingdom movement going and growing.

---

[5] From his 1880 Inaugural Lecture at the Free University of Amsterdam, quoted in James D. Bratt, Abraham Kuyper: *A Centennial Reader*, Eerdmans, Grand Rapids, Michigan, 1998, 488.

[6] John Piper, *Don't Waste Your Life* (Group Study Edition), Crossway, Wheaton, Illinois, Text updated 2009, 164.

[7] In this regard, you can read Neal Pirolo's book, *Serving as Senders*, Emmaus Road International, San Diego, California, 1991.

Read about missionaries and various ministries – how they received and responded to God's call, and their ministry stories. Attend mission consultations. Go to a mission event. Some congregations, even universities and colleges, have annual mission weeks or weekends with missionaries as speakers of whom you can learn much. Learn about missions and Christian organisations, their focuses, needs and how you can fit in.

Join a short-term mission or ministry outreach team. You can support and pray with so much more insight if you have experienced first-hand the context and culture of missionaries and ministries. You will be able to understand their needs, the problems, the threats and restrictions they daily face and how to go about it. Go with a teachable spirit and not with a preconceived 'whole answer' or quick-fix ideas and an attitude to rule. Don't be a burden to the people in need of your help and don't waste money on unnecessary things that they don't really need (T-shirts, etc.), while that money could be used in much-needed projects in which you can serve and assist them. Be there, see and feel the need as well as the change that *your* participation helps to bring about.

The key element for your venture ahead

Gratitude and passion for God and his reconciling plan for the world is the source and driving force for the church and missions. This you can only attain when you are really *with* Him and He could imprint his vision upon your heart and mind – for a world that needs restoration towards Kingdom life.

Take time *with* God. The crucial element in this relationship and our service in God's kingdom is *prayer* – to understand the plan within the big picture that will indicate the direction of church action and missions for each one called. George Verwer said, "Prayer is at the heart of the action and a worldwide prayer movement must run parallel with any kind of worldwide mission movement... Mission mobilisation, in a sense, starts on our knees."[8]

Pay close attention to what God is doing in your community and the world today. And in anticipation, ask his Spirit to reveal to you his desire on how and where you should engage with Him to bring his plans to fulfilment. Because of *being* with Jesus, the disciples were changed into change-agents.

---

[8] George Verwer, *Out of the Comfort Zone*, 74.

By faithfully acting upon your calling and fulfilling your purpose, you are worshipping God. He will be present where He wants to use you and with his guidance will empower your calling and develop your potential to fulfil your assignment. You will grow in your role and be more effective. Then, as with a small mustard seed, dough, salt and light, this will have a powerful transformative effect where and when it was planned for – on something

> *"Faith is deliberate confidence in the character of God whose ways you may not understand at the time."*
>
> Oswald Chambers

much bigger and more comprehensive, with God-sized results – much bigger and more than we can pray or think. Think Psalm 67!

See in your mind's eye how the effect of your obedience to God will grow ever wider and deeper as it will live on and multiply in the lives of many, and in many communities – how He will activate the mustard seed effect in you and let the mystery of his kingdom unfold in unanticipated fruition (Matthew 13:31-32).

Your send-off

So, we want to send you off on your road ahead with the words of Isaiah 58:11-12, followed by the words of Christ the King, sending his disciples out to serve (John 20:21):

[11]The Lord will guide you always;
   he will satisfy your needs in a sun-scorched land
   and will strengthen your frame.
You will be like a well-watered garden,
   like a spring whose waters never fail.
[12]Your people will rebuild the ancient ruins
   and will raise up the age-old foundations;
you will be called Repairer of Broken Walls,
   Restorer of Streets with Dwellings (Isaiah 58:11-12).

"Peace be with you! As the Father has sent me, I am sending you (John 20:21)."

Is something holding you back? Don't let your current affairs be your end goal and a distraction from his vision for you. Jesus said to someone who hesitated, *"No one who puts a hand to the plow and looks back is fit for service in the kingdom of God"* (Luke 9:62).

What price compares to God's love-offering on the cross of Christ on Calvary (Philippians 2:6-11)?

Remember, *"I have the strength to face all conditions by the power that Christ gives me"* (Philippians 4:13 – Good News Bible).

"The man who beats the drum, doesn't know how far the sound goes." (African Proverb)

Trust God and take the step!

Acknowledgements

No words would ever be able to accurately describe and give enough expression of our true gratitude, appreciation and respect for the following precious people:

The 'characters' in this book – these remarkable friends who were willing to share their personal walk of faith and servanthood in ministry, the sufferings and victories gained and whose stories shall encourage others to obey our King's calling and purpose for their lives.

Our respective families and supporters – who have enabled us over the past three decades to continue with our ministry and for their encouragement to write this book.

The leadership of Petra Institute – who allowed us time and space to work on this project. Thank you for your enthusiastic encouragement. What a wealth and journey to serve alongside you with whom we experienced so much of God's wonders in the work He does through obedient people in his kingdom!

Chris Richter – for your gentle advice, guidance and encouragement as retired publisher.

Christian Literature Fund – We have so much appreciation for the partnership and the way we could work together with CLF as publisher.

The donors alongside CLF – for your unselfishness and even excitement with your generous participation in enabling the message of this book to reach out.

And God – who we believe designed this book.

www.ingramcontent.com/pod-product-compliance
Lightning Source LLC
Chambersburg PA
CBHW070329090426
42733CB00012B/2411